The Complete Idiot's Ref

D1191829

Hexagram Identification

TRIGRAMS UPPER ▶ / LOWER ▼	QIAN	DUI	LI	ZHEN	XUN	KAN	GEN	KUN
QIAN	1	43	14	34	9	5	26	11
DUI	10	58	38	54	61	60	41	19
LI	13	49	30	55	37	63	22	36
ZHEN	25	17	21	51	42	3	27	24
XUN	44	28	50	32	57	48	18	46
KAN	6	47	64	40	59	29	4	7
GEN	33	31	56	62	53	39	52	15
KUN	12	45	35	16	20	8	23	2

ALPHA

tear here

The Coin-Toss Technique

To perform the coin-toss technique, follow these steps:

1. Gather three like coins.
2. Find a quiet place. Clear your mind and write your question on a clean sheet of paper. Remember, ask "what," "why," or "how" questions. Do not ask yes or no questions beginning with "is," "will," or "should."
3. While you hold the question in your mind, cup your hands around the coins and shake. Cast them on the table. Refer to the following chart to determine what kind of yin or yang line your first toss (line 1 of your hexagram) correlates to.

Coin Combination	Number	Line (Yao)	Name
3 Heads	9	▬▬O▬▬	Old Yang
2 Heads, 1 Tail	8	▬▬ ▬▬	Young Yin
2 Tails, 1 Head	7	▬▬▬▬	Young Yang
3 Tails	6	▬▬X▬▬	Old Yin

4. Toss the coins five more times (for a total of six), building your hexagram from the bottom line up.
5. Refer to the Hexagram Identification Key on the front side of this card to determine your present hexagram representing your current situation.
6. Create your future hexagram by transforming any changing lines (represented by the numbers 6 and 9) into their young opposites. Refer to the Hexagram Identification Key on the front side of this card to determine the future hexagram's number.
7. First, read the hexagram statement corresponding to your present hexagram. Then, read the changing line text (if any) followed by the hexagram statement corresponding to your future hexagram.

For a detailed explanation about how to use the coin-toss and yarrow stalk methods, please consult Chapter 6, "How to Cast the *Yijing*." For a detailed explanation of how to interpret your hexagram reading, please consult Chapter 7, "How to Interpret Your *Yijing* Reading."

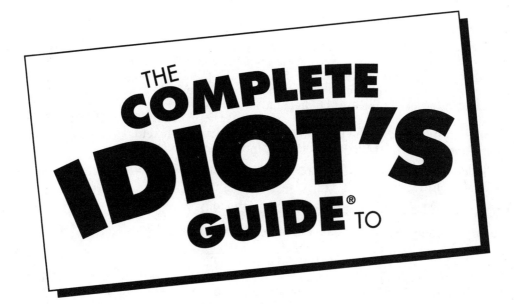

THE COMPLETE IDIOT'S GUIDE® TO

The *I Ching*

by Elizabeth Moran and Master Joseph Yu

ALPHA

A Pearson Education Company

THE COMPLETE IDIOT'S GUIDE TO and Design are registered trademarks of Pearson Education, Inc.

International Standard Book Number: 0-02-863979-0

Library of Congress Catalog Card Number: 2001091093

04   03   02   8   7   6   5   4   3   2   1

Interpretation of the printing code: The rightmost number of the first series of numbers is the year of the book's printing; the rightmost number of the second series of numbers is the number of the book's printing. For example, a printing code of 02-1 shows that the first printing occurred in 2002.

Printed in the United States of America

Publisher
Marie Butler-Knight

Product Manager
Phil Kitchel

Managing Editor
Jennifer Chisholm

Senior Acquisitions Editor
Randy Ladenheim-Gil

Development Editor
Lynn Northrup

Production Editor
Billy Fields

Copy Editor
Susan Aufheimer

Illustrator
Tim Neil

Cartoonist
Jody P. Schaeffer

Cover Designers
Mike Freeland
Kevin Spear

Book Designers
Scott Cook and Amy Adams of DesignLab

Indexer
Lisa Wilson

Layout/Proofreading
Angela Calvert
John Etchison

Contents at a Glance

Contents

Part 7: Understanding and Applying the Ancient Tradition of Feng Shui   271

13   Increasing Your Health, Wealth, and Relationships with Feng Shui   273

14   Learning Yigua Feng Shui   283

Appendixes

Foreword

Change is a powerful thing. In fact, there's no escaping it. We're all subjected to changing forces. Physically, our shape changes with time. Mentally, our beliefs and perceptions change over the course of our lives. Our goals and objectives change. Our financial situations change. We change jobs, locations, and even spouses!

The word "change" surfaces in a number of common expressions: "I need a change of scenery"; "The times are changing"; and "You can't change someone." With regard to human nature, the last expression particularly rings true. For you can't change unless *you* want to change! Which raises the question, why not move with change instead of resisting it?

So, what does change have to do with the *I Ching?* In English, the *I Ching* (or *Yijing*) is called the *Book of Changes*. Stated simply, it's a book that helps you see the invisible forces of change in your life. It foretells *your* change.

You use the *I Ching* to help you change, progress, alter, or transform the course of your destiny. When you are indecisive or need guidance about something that can greatly affect your livelihood, well-being, or a relationship, you consult the *I Ching*. You get a second opinion, so to speak.

But how does the *I Ching* work? This is not an easy question to answer. The Chinese believe their ancestors aid them. However, there are other explanations. Some people believe you draw information from your inner spirit. Some believe the answers to your questions are divine, coming from God or a higher power. Then there are those who believe we obtain guidance from the collective consciousness—an all-knowing universe. Despite your opinion, the *I Ching* strikes a cord of truth. The answers resonate with—or are in sync with—your situation, providing you with the foresight, wisdom, and confidence to see clearly the path ahead.

If you're looking for an indispensable and thoroughly researched guide to understanding what the *I Ching* is and how you can use the ancient Chinese oracle to better yourself, read *The Complete Idiot's Guide to the* I Ching. Elizabeth Moran and Master Joseph Yu have done a masterful job presenting a very complex subject that originated with eleventh-century B.C.E. ruler King Wen of Zhou and his son, the Duke of Zhou.

—Val Biktashev

Val Biktashev is a Siberian-born master of feng shui and founder of the American Healing Arts, Incorporated, based in Beverly Hills, California. Val travels worldwide providing feng shui assessments and I Ching *readings for individuals and businesses. He has had several articles written about his work in nationally distributed newspapers. Val has made numerous television appearances and was featured on* CBS Sunday Morning. *Val is the co-author of* The Complete Idiot's Guide to Feng Shui *(Alpha Books, 1999).*

Introduction

You're faced with an overwhelming problem that must be resolved. You must make a decision that could alter your life's path. You wish to seek guidance devoid of bias. You go to the bookstore and purchase a translation and interpretation of the *I Ching: Book of Changes,* hoping for an answer, direction, and clarity. Anything that can help bring into focus a vision of truth.

Armed with your oracle, you follow the directions to obtain your answer, your personal hexagram—a six-tiered figure composed of solid and broken lines. Whether you use the coin-toss method or the more difficult yarrow stalk procedure, line by line, bottom to top, you diligently build your hexagram. For example, the resulting configuration may yield Hexagram 63, Ji Ji ䷾.

With great anticipation and mounting excitement, you read your answer from one famous interpretation: "The woman loses the curtain of her carriage. Do not run after it; on the seventh day you will get it .... The neighbor in the east who slaughters an ox does not attain as much real happiness as the neighbor in the west with his small offering."

Huh? What does this mean? How do these ancient and esoteric statements solve my problem? Frustrated and disappointed, you have more questions. What is the *I Ching,* anyway? Who wrote it? How does it work? Why am I consulting an age-old oracle written at the end of the second millennium B.C.E.? How is it relevant to the modern world?

The book in your hands addresses all of these questions and many more. Here, you'll learn that this revered work is not just a silly book of fortune-telling, a superstitious relic catering to the gullible and vulnerable. Rather, you'll come to understand the *I Ching* is a profound work grounded in science and mathematics. That somehow, magically and mysteriously, it connects us to the universe (or what you may choose to call the great unknown, the sea of consciousness, the spirit world, God) to provide a meaningful answer that speaks to our situation.

More important, our book offers a clear and concise, easy-to-understand interpretation that won't leave you scratching your head, confused. Our book will change the way you view the world and yourself. It's a user-friendly guide you will use and cherish time and again.

What You'll Learn in This Book

This book is divided into seven parts sure to help you understand the oldest book of divination in continuous use in the history of humankind.

Part 1, "Introducing the *I Ching* and Ancient China," introduces you to the *I Ching.* We explain what it is and how it works. Also, you'll learn about ancient China and how divinatory methods evolved to form the basis of the *I Ching.*

Part 2, "The Historical and Mythical Origins of the *Yijing*," traces just that—the historical and mythical origins of the *Yijing.*

Part 3, "Learning to Use the *Yijing*," shows you how to use and interpret your *Yijing* reading.

Part 4, "The 64 Hexagrams: A New Interpretation for the Twenty-first Century," offers a new interpretation, one written for the Western reader.

Part 5, "Understanding the Principles of the Chinese Cosmos," informs you about the fundamental concepts of qi and yin and yang.

Part 6, "Modern Science and the Ancient Oracle," discusses the *Yijing*'s relevance to modern physics, chaos theory, and binary mathematics.

Part 7, "Understanding and Applying the Ancient Tradition of Feng Shui," teaches you about feng shui, an art and science of improving your health, wealth, and relationships. Feng shui is derived from an ancient mathematical model of the universe that we will discuss in Part 3.

Extras

In addition to the thought-provoking text, you'll find four kinds of information boxes scattered throughout the book. These boxes will explain unfamiliar terms, provide useful information relevant to the discussion at hand, and give you insightful quotes that will advance your study of the ancient Chinese oracle.

Yi Edicts

These boxes give you fascinating facts related to the subject at hand.

Master Class

These boxes offer supporting information of key points about the topic under discussion.

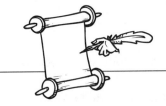

Wise Words

These boxes define new words that help you make sense of it all.

Notable Quotable

In these boxes, the noted are quoted.

Acknowledgments

We are deeply grateful to many people who have helped to make *The Complete Idiot's Guide to the* I Ching possible. We wish to acknowledge the following individuals:

Andree Abecassis and Lettie Lee: Our literary agents who have gone *way* beyond the call of duty. Susan Aufheimer: Our meticulous copy editor. Bill Clement: Elizabeth's researcher, counselor, and friend. Ron Fontenot: Elizabeth's long-time and life-long friend and head tweaker. Randy Ladenheim-Gil: Our executive editor, who took on this project. Billy Fields: Our production editor; and the production department: Thank you for turning this manuscript into a printed book. Mom and Dad Moran: Thank you for tolerating Elizabeth's fascination with all things Chinese even though she majored in television production. Tim Neil: Our fabulous "art slave"! Lynn Northrup: The most patient and diplomatic development editor on this planet. Samantha: The long walks were appreciated. Scott Ransom: Who knows more about chaos theory than he wants to. Dr. Dina Ralt: For the interesting discussions about qi. Jonathan Seiter: Thanks for the math instruction. Dr. Yakov Treyzon: Our number-one supporter! Viktor Yudkin: Elizabeth and Val's good friend and business advisor.

The authors especially wish to acknowledge Dr. Stephen Field, whose writings on early China and whose personal assistance in putting the I Ching into its mythical, historical, and philosophical context were indispensable to the authors in preparing this work.

Trademarks

All terms mentioned in this book that are known to be or are suspected of being trademarks or service marks have been appropriately capitalized. Alpha Books and Pearson Education cannot attest to the accuracy of this information. Use of a term in this book should not be regarded as affecting the validity of any trademark or service mark.

Permissions

Chapter 1

Information about Fibonacci numbers is taken from *Fascinating Fibonaccis: Mystery and Magic in Numbers,* by Trudi Hammel Garland. © 1987 by Dale Seymour Publications. Used with permission of Pearson Education, Inc.

Quotation by Joseph-Marie de Maistre taken from *The Concise Columbia Dictionary of Quotations*, by Robert Andrews. © 1992 by Columbia University Press. Reprinted with permission of the publisher.

Chapter 2

Excerpt from *The Cambridge History of Ancient China from the Origins of Civilization to 221 B.C.*, edited by Michael Loewe and Edward L. Shaughnessy, is used with permission of Cambridge University Press. © 1999.

Chapter 3

Photographs of turtle shell divinatory fragments are used with permission of Associate Professor Hung-hsiang Chou of the University of California, Los Angeles.

Part 1

Introducing the *I Ching* and Ancient China

Part 1 introduces you to the I Ching, *the ancient Chinese book of divination formulated at the end of the second millennium* B.C.E. *In this part, you'll learn fundamental information that will set you on your journey. First, you'll learn about the two different systems of spelling Chinese sounds—Wade-Giles and Pinyin. The latter is recognized as the international standard. It's the system we use in this book. So, from the first chapter forward, we will refer to the book of divination as the* Yijing. *Next, you'll learn what the* Yijing *is and what a hexagram is.*

Part 1 also takes you to ancient China. You'll meet members of the Shang and Zhou dynasties whose lives are the subject of the Yijing *line texts. Gaining an insight into these historical figures will help to enrich your understanding of the oracle and your own prognostication. Finally, we'll talk about divination. Specifically, two methods used by the ancient Chinese: divination by heating the scapulas of animals and the plastrons of turtles and reading the resulting cracks, and divination by casting stalks of yarrow. The latter technique is used to cast the* Yijing.

Chapter 1

Just what IS the I Ching?

Ground Zero: Understanding the Basics About the *I Ching*, *Book of Changes*

In This Chapter

➤ How much do you know about the *I Ching?* Take the *I Ching* challenge!

➤ *I Ching* vs. *Yijing:* the spelling of Chinese words

➤ What is the *Yijing?*

➤ How does the *Yijing* work?

➤ Numbers, science, and the *Yijing*

This chapter will help to clarify and define your basic questions about the *I Ching:* What is it? How does it work? How can it help me? Armed with this rudimentary understanding, successive chapters will help you to build on this knowledge.

Will I be able to grasp such an ancient and profound work, you ask? Absolutely! Don't let the size of this book overwhelm or intimidate you. Don't worry that your limited exposure to Chinese culture may inhibit learning. You need not speak Chinese or even like their food to divine insight from the oracle. All you need is patience, integrity, and an open mind.

Take the *I Ching* Challenge!

Before you begin your journey, take a few moments to take the *I Ching* challenge. Just circle the answer that you feel is correct. Upon completion of the book, take this short quiz again. While you may be unable to answer each question now, we believe you'll pass with flying colors later on.

1. What is the *I Ching?*
   - **a.** A book of divination
   - **b.** A book of etiquette
   - **c.** A book of poetry

2. Who is purported to have authored the *I Ching?*
   - **a.** Confucius
   - **b.** King Wen and his son, the Duke of Zhou
   - **c.** Fuxi

3. Qi and yin and yang are fundamental concepts underlying the original *I Ching*, assembled in the late Shang/early Zhou dynasty (c. 1045 B.C.E.).
   - **a.** True
   - **b.** False

4. Sometime during the Warring States Period (475–221 B.C.E.), the *I Ching* transformed from …
   - **a.** A book of divination into a book of philosophy.
   - **b.** A book of philosophy into a book of divination.
   - **c.** A book of etiquette into a book of philosophy.

5. What type of divination was common to the ancient Chinese?
   - **a.** Reading tea leaves
   - **b.** Interpreting the entrails of animals
   - **c.** Heating turtle shells and the shoulder blades of mammals and interpreting the resulting cracks

6. Numbers play an important role in the *I Ching*.
   - **a.** True
   - **b.** False

7. Feng shui, the art and science of harmonizing your environment, is derived from the numerology of the *I Ching*.
   - **a.** True
   - **b.** False

8. What is needed to consult the *I Ching?*
   - **a.** Three like coins and a positive attitude
   - **b.** Fifty stalks of yarrow and a positive attitude
   - **c.** Both of the above

9. The *I Ching* can foretell your ...

    a. Present situation.

    b. Future prospects.

    c. Both of the above.

10. The *I Ching* can help you ...

    a. Gain insight into yourself.

    b. Solve a problem.

    c. Become more centered.

    d. All of the above.

How did you do? The correct answers are 1. a, 2. b, 3. b, 4. a, 5. c, 6. a, 7. a, 8. c, 9. c, and 10. d. Don't worry if you didn't get many right! While these questions represent only a smattering of the topics you'll find in this book, we hope we've piqued your interest. Let's move on.

You Say *I Ching,* We Say *Yijing*

What we call *The Book of Changes* in English is known as the *I Ching* in Chinese. This rendering of the Chinese name uses the Wade-Giles system of spelling phonetically Chinese words. Developed by British sinologist (a person who studies Chinese language, culture, literature, and history) and Cambridge University's first professor of Chinese, Sir Thomas Francis Wade (1818–1895), he introduced the system in his 1859 book *Peking Syllabary.* Some 30 years later in 1892, Herbert Allen Giles (1845–1935) helped to popularize Wade's *romanization* scheme in his *Chinese-English Dictionary.* Although the Wade-Giles spelling system is still used in the Western world today, it is not recognized as the international standard. The system called Hanyu Pinyin Wenzi (the alphabet of Chinese phonetic combinations) holds this claim.

Developed by the Chinese, Pinyin is based on the pronunciation of the Peking dialect of Mandarin Chinese, considered one of the three major dialects in modern China (Cantonese and Wu comprise the other two dialects). Although script modification commenced in 1913, it wasn't until the advent of

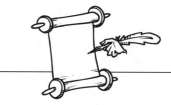

Wise Words

The *I Ching* is considered the oldest book of fortune-telling in continuous use since it was assembled during the eleventh century B.C.E. by King Wen and his son, the Duke of Zhou. The *I Ching* is used to help you gain clarity about a problem, concern, or dilemma.

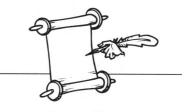

Wise Words

To **romanize** Chinese means to use the Roman (Latin) alphabet to spell its words. English, Spanish, French, German, Portuguese, and Italian (among others) use the Latin alphabet.

Yi Edicts

Not only is China bursting with a population of over one billion, there are more dialects of Chinese than any other language in the world. In fact, Mandarin Chinese is one of the five official languages of the United Nations. The other four are English, French, Spanish, and Arabic.

communism in 1949 that serious progress was made toward creating a romanized system. In 1956, after several proposals were offered and rejected, the Committee on Language Reform chose the Pinyin system. In 1979, it became the international standard and is used in dictionaries, newspapers, television, Braille for the seeing impaired, and finger spelling for the hearing impaired. Eventually, it will fully replace the accepted Wade-Giles system in Western publications.

Where does all this information lead? From here on, we will use the Pinyin spelling system. Therefore, *I Ching* (Wade-Giles) becomes *Yijing* (Pinyin). Despite which transliteration system you may use, both words are pronounced the same. *I* or *Yi* is pronounced "ee," as in the word "feet." *Ching* or *Jing* is pronounced "jing," as in the word "jingle." Both *I Ching* and *Yijing* are pronounced "eejing."

Life Is Change: The Fundamental Basis of the *Yijing*

The words comprising the word *Yijing* contain its meaning. While the "jing" part is usually defined as a book, by no means is it an ordinary book! A more appropriate word for jing is canon, a literary work held in high esteem. Admired and honored, it is a book (or canon) that withstands the test of time. It is ageless and wise. It is sacred. For example, the Chinese translation of the *Bible* is *Shengjing*—Holy (Sheng) Book/Canon (Jing).

Yi Edicts

The first use of the word "jing" appears in the *Si Shu Wu Jing* (four books and five canons), an assemblage of important Chinese books. The four books (*Si Shu*) are a compilation of sayings by Confucius (551–479 B.C.E.) and his greatest follower, Mencius (371–289 B.C.E.). They are the *Lunyu* (Analects), *Daxue* (Great Learning), *Zhongyong* (Way of the Mean), and *Mencius* (Book of Mencius). The five canons (*Wu Jing*) or books are literary works that existed before the time of Confucius. They are the *Yijing* (Book of Changes), *Shujing* (Book of History), *Shijing* (Book of Poetry), *Liji* (Book of Rites), and *Yuejing* (Book of Music).

The "yi" of *Yijing* means to change, hence the English rendering, *The Book (or Canon) of Changes*. Composed of two characters, yi also means sun and moon, their relationship representing the dynamic of change. Day (sun) changes into night (moon). Spring changes into summer. Everything and everyone changes, transforms, and evolves into another state of being. Everything and everyone moves through the eternal cycle of birth, growth, decay, and death. Everything has a beginning, middle, and end: your life, the stock market, a novel, war. Undeniably, your beliefs, emotions, attitude, and perspective change over the ebb and flow of your life.

Master Class

The Chinese concept of yin and yang, the two forces of the universe that propel us through ceaseless cycles of birth, growth, decay, and death, was perhaps understood, but not fully developed, when the original *Yijing* (called the *Zhouyi* or *The Changes of Zhou*) was composed about 3,000 year ago. Only in the Warring States period (403–221 B.C.E.) when commentaries called the *Ten Wings* were attached to the divinatory text, did the concept of yin and yang (and qi) become closely associated with the *Yijing*. We'll tell you more about yin, yang, and qi in Chapters 8, "The Mystery of Qi," and 9, "Can You Spare Some Change? The Unchanging Truth About Yin and Yang."

Indeed, life is in a constant state of flux. By avoiding change, you miss opportunities to develop an in-depth understanding of yourself and the world in which you live. By resisting change, you're going against the flow of nature. You're swimming against the current, climbing the descending escalator, spinning your wheels. Why be stuck, stagnant, and stubborn when you can be dazzled by revelations and experiences that can propel you forward? Let your insights and clarity raise you to new levels. Let change be meaningful. Be in sync, at one with the harmony of nature.

A Model World

The ancient Chinese made astute observations about the tides of nature and of the heavens. In fact, they believed humankind is a small replica, a microcosm, of the cosmos (the macrocosm). Mentally and physically, we mirror its cycles. Life, situations, relationships, and history cycle and repeat in perpetuity, creating a veritable kaleidoscope of change. Round and round we go, spiraling forward. Each ending marks a new beginning; each beginning signals completion. This notion gives new meaning to the oft-used phrase, "What goes around, comes around."

Based on this idea, a model of the cosmos embodying every possible manifestation of change was constructed. This model is the *Yijing,* a collection of 64 six-lined symbols composed of solid ▬▬▬ and broken ▬▬ ▬▬ lines called *hexagrams.* For example, this is Hexagram 3: ䷂. (You'll find a complete illustration of all 64 hexagrams on side 1 of the tearcard at the front of this book.)

Emulating life's cyclic nature and the assumption that history repeats itself over cycles of time, many scholars believe the arrangement of the 64 hexagrams models the decline (decay) and end (death) of the Shang dynasty and the rise (birth) and expansion (growth) of the Zhou dynasty. Using these historical events as a model, we can project our situation into it and seek intelligent solutions. In other words, because a situation and its outcome have occurred before (or are similar to another situation), using the *Yijing* we can divine an answer, a resolution, from an all-knowing universe. The *Yijing* (the model), therefore, becomes an oracle capable of foretelling our present and future changes or prospects.

Wise Words

A **hexagram** is a six-lined (hexa means six) graph or message (gram) composed of a combination of solid and broken lines. In total, the *Yijing* comprises 64 hexagrams arranged in a certain sequence that many believe models the history of the Shang and Zhou dynasties.

The Spirits Speak!

The ancient Chinese believed a pantheon of ancestors provided the link between the question and the answer (the hexagram). These spirits were thought to guide the diviner to the best solution to the situation in question. They sought to set you on the highest possible path, one grounded in virtuous behavior. One that accorded with nature's flow, or rather *human* nature's positive progression toward a harmonious and content existence.

How did these wise spirits communicate their answer? They spoke using numbers, the language of the gods. You see, your hexagram is obtained by performing one of two different divinatory procedures: the coin toss or yarrow stalk methods. Regardless of which method you choose, both yield a set of six numbers that correlate to either a solid ▬▬▬ or broken ▬▬ ▬▬ line, the configuration comprising a certain hexagram. This hexagram is your primary answer, representing your present situation. For reasons that we will explain later on, your primary hexagram then changes into a second one, representing your future outlook. If this seems confusing, don't fret. How to divine and interpret your reading will be fully explained in Chapters 6, "How to Cast the *Yijing,*" and 7, "How to Interpret Your *Yijing* Reading."

The Number of Life

Yet, you may believe your answer is divined from somewhere else. Perhaps you believe your inner spirit or subconscious mind guides you to the appropriate answer. Some people believe we mine knowledge from the collective, or sea of, consciousness. Others believe God bestows information, direction, and insight. Whatever your personal conviction, know that the ancient Chinese understood that numbers provide the connective link between the Great Unknown and human development. While the Chinese equated these integers to the language of the gods, modern science has proven that numbers provide the language of the universe.

Unfortunately, for many people, numbers and mathematics invoke not-so-pleasant memories of grammar school arithmetic drills. In high school, math meant learning to perform abstract calculations of algebra, calculus, and trigonometry— complex computations that had little to do with our relationship to the world. However, this contrived notion is far from true. Mathematics is about finding hidden order and patterns in things that are not detectable to the naked eye. A diverse lot such as special-effects artists, physicists, oceanographers, geneticists, and musicians use mathematics to plumb the mysteries of their field. While math may be technical, it undeniably yields profundities about life.

Notable Quotable

"The concept of number is the obvious distinction between man and beast. Thanks to number, the cry becomes song, noise acquires rhythm, the spring is transformed into a dance, force becomes dynamic, and outlines figures."

—Joseph-Marie de Maistre (1753–1821), French author

Fascinating Fibonacci and the Magic of Numbers

Numbers speaks to us and through us. In fact, we conform to mathematical laws of the universe. For example, take the *Fibonacci sequence,* a pattern of numbers discovered by thirteenth-century mathematician Leonardo de Pisa, also known as Fibonacci. Referring to the following diagram, the sequence begins with the number 1. Each number that follows is the sum of the previous two numbers: $0 + 1 = 1$; $1 + 1 = 2$; $1 + 2 = 3$; $2 + 3 = 5$, and so on to infinity.

| 1, 1, 2, 3, 5, 8, 13, 21, 34, 55, 89, 144, 233, . . . |

The Fibonacci sequence.

If you divide each number in the series by the one preceding it, the answer produces a ratio that stabilizes at 1.618034. For example, $2 \div 1 = 2$, $3 \div 2 = 1.5$, and the results continue to change until we get to $1597 \div 987 = 1.618034$, $4181 \div 2584 = 1.618034$, and so on to infinity. This figure is called the *Golden Ratio.*

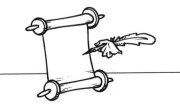

Wise Words

The **Fibonacci sequence** is a sequence of numbers "discovered" by a thirteenth-century mathematician named Leonard of Pisa (also known as Fibonacci). Each number in the series is the sum of the two previous numbers. The **Golden Ratio** is related to the Fibonacci sequence. By dividing each number in the series by the one that precedes it, the result produces a ratio that stabilizes at 1.61834.

While these "divine proportions" may not seem awe-inspiring on the surface, the Fibonacci numbers and ratios appear repeatedly in a remarkable range of fields. Taken mostly from Trudi Hammel Garland's fun-filled book, *Fascinating Fibonaccis: Mystery and Magic in Numbers* (Dale Seymour Publications, 1987), here are a few examples to ponder and marvel at:

➤ **Natural phenomena.** The head of a giant sunflower reveals two distinct spirals of seeds, 55 rows spiraling counterclockwise and 89 rows spiraling clockwise. The ratios of galaxies, ocean waves, seashells, flowers and leaves, and beehives, among other things, conform to this wondrous number series.

➤ **Human proportions.** Psychology research in Canada concluded that people positively or negatively rate others consistent with golden proportions. Positive characteristics are attached 62 percent of the time and negative characteristics about 38 percent of the time. Our fingers conform to Fibonacci numbers. We have 2 hands, each of which has 5 fingers broken up into 3 parts by 2 knuckles.

➤ **Art and architecture.** Artists Leonardo da Vinci (1452–1519), Albrecht Dürer (1471–1528), Albert Fitch Bellows (1829–1883), and Piet Mondrian (1872–1944) have consciously incorporated the Golden Ratio into their works. Many scholars believe the Great Pyramid of Giza was built to an original height of 5,813 inches (5, 8, and 13 are Fibonacci numbers).

➤ **Music and poetry.** The octave on a piano keyboard is comprised of 13 keys of 8 white keys and 5 black keys, which are situated in groups of 2 and 3. Poetic limericks are composed of 13 beats of 5 lines, which are grouped into 2 and 3 beats.

➤ **Science and technology.** Astronomers have discovered that Fibonacci numbers appear in a formula used to calculate the "distances of the moons of Jupiter, Saturn, and Uranus from their respective planets." Computer science uses the Fibonacci sequence to sort and search for data.

The Fibonacci sequence and the Golden Ratio represent just one example of number series made manifest in life. Other transcendental mathematic principles you may wish to research on your own include Pi, the exponential e, and the esoteric practices of gematria and numerology. Certainly, these dynamic correlations inspire many to seek the origin of life. While we won't dwell on this mystery, understand that somehow numbers guide our development. Unquestionably, it is the fabric of nature connecting everyone and everything.

The Yijing, Science, and Mathematics ... Oh My!

In later chapters, you'll learn about the striking similarities between the *Yijing* and chaos theory, theoretical physics, and psychology. What do these sciences have in common with the oracle? Why, numbers, of course!

In the next chapter, we'll take you on a tour of ancient China, where you'll meet the Shang and Zhou leaders who are featured in the 64 hexagrams.

The Least You Need to Know

➤ This book uses the Chinese international standard of transliteration called Pinyin. Therefore, the book many know as the *I Ching* becomes *Yijing*.

➤ The word "jing" means book or canon. The word "yi" means to change. Hence, the English rendering, *The Book of Changes*.

➤ The *Yijing* models universal changes of birth, growth, decay, and death. Based on the repetitious principle of nature (and human nature), you can project your situation into the model to foretell your present and future prospects.

➤ A hexagram is a six-lined graph composed of a configuration of solid and broken lines. It is derived by casting yarrow stalks or tossing coins.

➤ The ancient Chinese believed the spirit world guided the diviner toward the best possible solution to his or her problem.

➤ To the ancient Chinese, numbers are the language of the gods. To modern science, numbers (and mathematics) are the language of the universe. Somehow, we conform to nature's mathematical laws.

A Short History of the Ancient Chinese

To present any history in one chapter is a daunting task. That said, we don't mean to offer here a history of the ancient Chinese as much as a historical overview with respect to the development of the *Yijing*. In this chapter, we'll focus on the end of the second millennium B.C.E., the time when the *Yijing* was first assembled by King Wen of Zhou and his son, the Duke of Zhou. Besides learning about them, you'll meet other Zhou and Shang leaders. You'll learn how they lived, how they governed, and whom they worshipped.

Why is this important? Well, the story of the decline of the Shang dynasty and the rise of the Zhou dynasty is captured in the 386-line texts of the *Yijing* that we'll present in Part 4, "The 64 Hexagrams: A New Interpretation for the 21st Century." By understanding Shang and Zhou history, you will gain insight into your own personal history. Your present prospects and future outlook (the answers to your questions) will have more meaning.

In the Beginning: The Prehistoric Chinese

Prehistoric means just that—before "his"story. While we won't go into the political correctness of the word history, know that the prehistoric is based on items taken from excavation projects. Pottery pieces, bone fragments, structural foundations, and burial sites all reveal valuable information that is linked together to form a probable explanation of the peoples in question. For instance, we know the earliest Chinese were nomads, hunters and gatherers associated with the *Paleolithic* period. Primarily, these primitive peoples roamed the regions in and around north China's Yellow River Valley. In fact, this area is known as the "cradle of Chinese civilization." Take a moment now to survey the following map to become familiar with the many places that we'll speak about in this chapter.

The Paleolithic Chinese possessed an elementary understanding of the world. They were heavily influenced by nature. Their feelings, beliefs, and actions were dependent on natural events (earthquakes, thunderstorms, and eclipses, for example) interpreted by tribe members called shamans, a word originating with the Tungus peoples of Siberia. Shamans communicated with natural spirits and with spirits of the dead and demons to gain knowledge and to heal. Consequently, they were listened to and respected. In relation to Chinese history, the shaman was the forerunner of the court diviner, the religious specialist who divined knowledge from a hierarchy of gods and royal ancestors in Heaven.

Wise Words

Also called the Old Stone Age, the **Paleolithic** era refers to the first stage of human development, the hunting and gathering period that began about two million years ago and ended about 15,000 years ago.

A map of early China. Note: The cities Beijing, Shanghai, and Xi'an did not exist at the time of the Shang and Zhou. We include them here only as a point of reference.

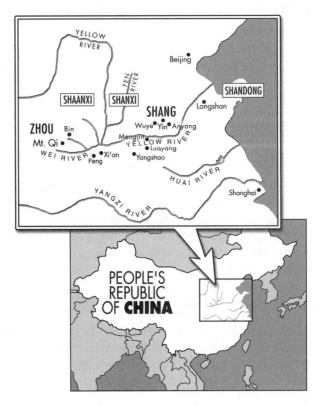

14

The Yangshao Culture

Each time a new archeological site is excavated and new artifacts are unearthed, our understanding of the prehistoric changes. One incredible find occurred in 1920 with the discovery of pottery shards near the Henan village of Yangshao. Dating to before 5000 B.C.E., this find revealed a variety of things:

➤ **Permanent settlements.** The fertile river valley area allowed for agricultural development (primarily millet) and a gradual end to the nomad existence. Villages sprang up around the cultivation of crops.

➤ **Shamanistic beliefs and practices.** The Yangshao revered their forebears and worshipped and sacrificed to them. Essentially, they believed the deceased could affect—either positively or negatively—the well-being of the living. For instance, if their ancestors were satisfactorily honored, they would send fair weather to increase crop yield. However, if the deceased were not revered, they would send floods and disease.

➤ **Pottery.** The production of pottery for storage of food bolstered the notion of permanent settlements. Also, the pottery featured geometric designs and depictions of animals, which points to an attempt to record information and to convey written meaning.

The Yangshao discovery was so important that the people and how they lived in China during the *Neolithic* period are now referred to as the *Yangshao* culture.

The Longshan Culture

The *Longshan* culture dates to 3000 B.C.E. It is called that because of another major archeological discovery, this time in the early 1930s in Chengziyai, Shandong province, an area formerly known as

Wise Words

Also called the New Stone Age, the **Neolithic** era represents the final stage of human development beginning some 15,000 year ago. It is characterized by the use of polished stone tools, crop cultivation, and permanent settlements. The ancient Chinese of this period are known as the **Yangshao** culture or the Painted Pottery culture, the latter name being derived from the abundant archeological finds made in 1920 near Yangshao village in Henan province.

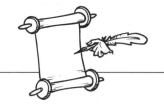

Wise Words

The **Longshan** or Black Pottery culture dates to 3000 B.C.E. It is named for a major archeological find in Shandong province in the early 1930s. The finer grade of ceramic ware found here is symbolic of the progress made since the Yangshao.

Longshan district. The pottery found here was more sophisticated. Because the pieces were burnished, thin, and black, the Longshan culture came to be known as the Black Pottery culture. Stemming from the Yangshao and migrating east to the coast, the Longshan provides us with a link between the prehistoric and what is considered the beginning of traditional Chinese history: the Three Dynasties (which we will soon address). Longshan's importance also can be seen in several other factors:

➤ **The beginning of China.** Longshan confirmed the idea that the area known as the cradle of civilization became the foundation on which modern Chinese culture is derived. It became the site where Chinese historical events with their celebrated figures began to unfold.

➤ **Villages and gravesites.** The layout of the Longshan towns, ceremonial objects, and valuables found in gravesites suggest a distinct stratification of society along class lines. Wealth was spread among a small group of people. Their settlements (composed of walls and floors of rammed earth) were fortified, larger, and more complicated than those of the majority, and their burial sites were more elaborate than the small, plain graves of ordinary citizens.

➤ **Development.** Agriculture saw much progress. The southern practice of cultivating rice spread north. Fertilization and irrigation enabled settlements to expand and grow larger. Ancestor worship proceeded apace with the use of a form of divination called scapulimancy (the heating of animal bones and the interpretation of the resulting cracks). We'll discuss scapulimancy and other forms of divination in Chapter 3, "Divination Chinese Style."

In addition, the later Longshan era occurred during the wan guo (10,000 states), the Chinese term referring to the establishment of people into distinct communities.

The Xia Dynasty

The Three Dynasties of China—the Xia (pronounced shya), the Shang, and the Zhou (pronounced joe)—developed from the Longshan. With improvements in warfare gear (bronze spearheads, battleaxes, and the use of horse-drawn chariots), the growth and reliance on ancestor worship, and the use of a matured system of writing, these dynasties defeated and absorbed many of the wan guo.

The Xia dynasty is problematic. Historians and archeologists disagree on its importance, with some even questioning its existence. While we can be sure Xia was one of the wan guo that became powerful enough to subdue its neighbors, little archeological evidence supports its dynastic claims. Written records do not exist either, unlike for the Shang and the Zhou. But what has survived are tales of Xia heroes (perhaps history, perhaps mythology).

The first king of Xia was Qi, son of Yu. Yu was a true hero who succeeded in helping his people overcome a flood problem devastating their settlements. While earlier people fought the water's flow with dikes and dams, Yu engineered a series of channels to guide the water out to sea. When this worked, the people were so thankful that when he died they named his son, Qi, king. This succession was the first time that rule was based on familial connection, hence the birth of a dynasty.

While Xia's place in Chinese history may be somewhat unclear, the same cannot be said of Shang, the first great Chinese dynasty.

The Shang Dynasty

The Shang dynasty (1600–1045 B.C.E.) is the first Chinese civilization to have supplied written documentation. Although records mainly consist of inscriptions on oracle bones and ceremonial bronze vessels, enough of these exist to provide sinologists with a plausible understanding of the Shang culture.

Developed from the Longshan group of Henan, the Shang prospered in the areas comprising the Yellow River Valley. The Shang capitals (which moved several times, the last being Yin near present-day Anyang) were situated here. This optimum location provided rich sediment carried by the waterways, and close proximity to the metal-laden highlands. Indeed, the Shang made good use of the metal deposits. Large-scale mining produced a host of bronze items: tools, containers, mirrors, jewelry, ritual objects, and armament. In fact, one royal tomb unearthed in Anyang contained more than 3,520 pounds of bronzework! It's no wonder that the Shang are affiliated with the bronze age of China.

Every Picture Tells a Story

Hands down, the Shang's most important contribution to the development of China is the invention of writing.

Although most Shang records have disappeared—having been written on bamboo, not a lasting substance—inscriptions carved on oracle bones, bronze artifacts, and even jade pieces survive. These inscriptions are uniquely Chinese, the form of writing a complex logographic system. Words originated as pictures or pictographs. For example, this graph ☉ is a drawing of the sun; this graph ☽ depicts the moon; and this one ￡, an ox.

Written texts—be they written on bamboo, oracle bones, or bronze vessels—were used for divination and record keeping. In fact, primitive libraries existed to store the data.

Yi Edicts

While 56,000 characters exist in the Chinese language, well-educated Chinese usually have the command of some 6,000 to 8,000 of these. If you wanted to read a Chinese newspaper, you would need to know about 2,500 characters.

The Politics of Shang

The Shang dynasty lasted for some 600 years and featured 30 kings, the last (Zhou Wang) of whom is the subject of many of the *Yijing's* line texts. A large-scale bureaucracy existed (usually composed of relatives of the king) to help administer the state. The governmental and religious center of the enclosed city featured a complex of above-ground (the structures were built on earthen platforms) temples and palaces housing the king and his entourage. Around this center lived farmers and craftsmen. Adjoining these were suburbs (of below-ground shelters) where the peasantry, the vast majority of the populace, lived.

Clearly, the king and other palatial inhabitants enjoyed a privileged existence. Exquisite palaces, abundant furnishings, sumptuous banquets, significant wealth, and artistic treasures were all within easy reach. The royal court featured a wide variety of positions, some of which included diviners, scribes, generals, guards, field officers, dog officers, and hunting guides. People occupying these elite positions grew increasingly comfortable in their higher status such that the common citizens were suppressed into inferior positions. Consequently, the Shang era is known as the start in China of the far-reaching exploitation and domination of its subjects by a central authority. But the average person still maintained some pride in that they shared with the royals and elite a belief in Shang Di.

Wise Words

Shang Di was the high god of the Shang. The shang of Shang Di should not be confused with the shang of the Shang dynasty. Although spelled the same, the two words are written with different characters and are pronounced differently. The difference is the tone or pitch used to convey the different meanings. Shang of Shang dynasty uses a high and flat tone; shang of Shang Di, a falling tone.

Shang Di, Lord Above

Shang Di was the supreme deity, the high god of the ancient Chinese. Considered the First Ancestor, Shang Di ruled a hierarchy of other gods, as well as the spirits of the deceased. Yet, according to *The Cambridge History of Ancient China: From the Origins of Civilization to 221 B.C.* (Cambridge University Press, 1999), Shang Di's power and influence waned over time. "After the reign of [Shang king] Wu Ding, the kings no longer divined about [Shang] Di ordering the rain or thunder or about seeking his approval or assistance. Di's virtual disappearance from the record suggests either the increasing confidence with which the Shang kings relied on their ancestors, their indifference to Di's existence, or their increasing realization that Di's will was inscrutable." All things considered, it seems the Shang came to place more importance on their ancestral kings, a notion supported by the fact that the direct-line rulers were bestowed the title Di. For example, Shang king Wu Ding is also known as Di Ding.

The king served as a go-between, petitioning the gods and royal predecessors on behalf of his people. This supernatural bond afforded the king a certain measure of immortality as was exhibited by the grand burial sites of Shang kings. In fact, a significant number of dependents "went with the king" (by either committing suicide or being sacrificed) when he died, serving as assistants to help the king fulfill his duties as an ancestor who is worshipped and to whom appeals are made.

Every Ending Marks a New Beginning

The Shang and the Zhou (whom we'll soon discuss) led parallel existences. With the Zhou living due west (in the Wei River Valley) of Shang territory, the two tribes were, for the most part, amiable. Because the Shang were politically and economically stronger than their neighbors, they probably didn't view the Zhou as a threat. Thus, while the Shang continued to prosper, the Zhou quietly strengthened. Things changed, however, when the 30th Shang king, Zhou Wang (also known as Di Xin), a despot known for lasciviousness and cruelty, ascended the throne.

The Wicked Zhou Wang

Zhou Wang of Shang was a dedicated, bright, and fair-minded prince. However, once he became king, his power and influence went to his head! He turned to depravity, celebrated licentious behavior, and turned wickedly despotic. His wanton acts were legion, his cruelty renown. Some of his more outrageous crimes are these:

➤ He created an elaborate pleasure dome with lakes of wine, choice meats hanging from trees, and nude merrymakers frolicking among exotic birds and animals.

➤ He ordered a large hole dug and filled with venomous snakes. Any concubine who offended him was unceremoniously cast into the pit.

➤ Fond of the smell of burnt flesh, Zhou Wang punished his officials by having them tied to a large pipe-like device that when heated, seared the skin off the wrongdoers.

➤ When the daughter of the Lord of Gui was offered to Zhou Wang, she criticized his conduct, such audacity enraging Zhou Wang. As a result, both father and daughter were unmercifully slaughtered.

➤ The Grand Duke of the East fervently opposed such cruelty. He, in turn, was butchered—his remains providing a base for a delectable stew, which was then offered to Zhou Wang's forebears.

Ji Chang (who would later become King Wen of Zhou) learned of Zhou Wang's heinous acts and groaned. However, when the Marquis of Chong was told of the groans, he quickly relayed this information to Zhou Wang. Interpreting the groans as criticism, Zhou Wang had Chang placed under house arrest for seven years. Purportedly, it was during his confinement that Ji Chang composed the *Zhouyi,* the divinatory text that would later be renamed the *Yijing.* You can learn more about this in Chapter 4, "As the Story Goes: The Historical Origin of the *Yijing.*"

Once his family paid ransom, Chang was released.

The Virtuous Ji Chang

Following in his father's (Ji Li) footsteps, Ji Chang wed a Shang princess. Called Tai Si, she was Zhou Wang's aunt (her brother was Di Yi, the next-to-last Shang king). Chang and Tai Si had 10 sons (many sinologists believe that some of his children were given birth by Chang's concubine, Tai Si's younger sister). Though loved by his people for his humility and gentle demeanor, Chang was not a weak ruler. He was a forceful military leader, who governed with a sense of justice and honor.

Upon his release from captivity, Chang began to foment rebellion against the Shang. He formed alliances, conquering resistant states. Three years later, in revenge, he destroyed the citadel of Chong, whose noble had been responsible for his seven-year imprisonment. At this point, Chang took the title King Wen. He did not live long to enjoy his status, however. In 1050 B.C.E., King Wen died. He was succeeded by his son Fa, who became King Wu.

Yi Edicts

The Zhou descend from a woman called Jiang Yuan. Legend tells how she became pregnant by walking on the footprint of Shang Di, the chief Shang god. After giving birth to a son, Jiang Yuan feared Shang Di's wrath. She abandoned the boy (who would become known as Hou Ji (or Chief Millet) on the road. But, rather than trampling him, the oxen, sheep, and horses assisted and protected him. Jiang Yuan then left him in a forest, where woodcutters discovered him. Next, she placed him on a flow of ice, only to have birds shelter him. When the birds left, Hou Ji stepped into the world. Learning to cultivate plants, he bestowed his knowledge on his people, becoming the agricultural benefactor of the Zhou.

The Fall of the House of Shang

Resolving to complete his father's quest, King Wu continued the Zhou revolt against the Shang. He made pacts with other states and sought the advice of Heaven, the pantheon of Zhou ancestors. Approximately four years after the death of his father, Wu led his army (comprised of 45,000 warriors and 300 chariots) across the Yellow River to Muye, near the Zhou Wang's capital at Chao Ge (Ji Xian). The Zhou reigned victorious; the Shang were thoroughly defeated.

Zhou Wang, the wicked Shang king, fled to his private pavilion and set it on fire. However, before he perished in the flames, King Wu shot three arrows into the Shang king's heart. While many members of the Shang leaders were executed, others were spared and used to help administer the new Zhou state. By state here, we mean the Zhou dynastic state because a Zhou vassal state had existed for some time.

Sibling Rivalry in the House of Zhou

The conquest of the Shang completed, King Wu (King Wen's son) assigned his three brothers, Guan, Cai, and Huo, to monitor the Shang king's son, Wu Geng. They were known as the Three Monitors. Although suspicious of their loyalty, King Wu first set about conquering the 99 nations who would not pledge allegiance to the Zhou. The military campaign was successful; however, Wu's health was severely compromised. He died two years later.

Upon King Wu's death, Wu's adolescent son, Cheng Wang, became king, but he was too young to rule. His uncle Dan (better known as the Duke of Zhou) was assigned the role as regent, while another brother of King Wu named Shi (better known as the Duke of Zhao) was to administer the western part of the country. Dan, an expert diviner, reluctantly took his new post. In fact, he is said to have prayed to Shang Di asking that his own life be shortened so as to lengthen King Wu's life. His appeals unsuccessful, the Duke of Zhou set about assisting his nephew.

The Three Monitors were jealous of the Duke of Zhou. They spread rumors that he plotted to kill Cheng Wang and supplant him. This created suspicion and instability within the Zhou empire. Wu Geng, seizing the opportunity, started to rebel against the Zhou. He was assisted by his old allies in the east. In reply, the Duke of Zhou first affirmed to the Duke of Zhao his loyalty to Cheng Wang. Having gained Zhao's support, he led his army east. Victorious, the Duke of Zhou had Wu Geng killed. His own brothers, the Three Monitors, were similarly dispatched. Seven years later, Cheng Wang was crowned in his own right. He became the most successful emperor of the Zhou dynasty.

The Mandate of Heaven

The Zhou shared with the Shang the tradition of ancestor worship. While Shang Di remained the principle god, the Zhou worshipped a distinct group of illustrious forebears called Tian, or Heaven. The Zhou king, being a product of his ancestors, called himself *Tianzi*, Son of Heaven. He became the conduit between humankind and Heaven. Since all Chinese rulers were Sons of Heaven, the country itself was known as Tian Xia, literally All Under Heaven or the Celestial Empire.

Wise Words

The Zhou kings called themselves **Tianzi** or Sons of Heaven. The conquest of Shang was sanctioned by Tian (the Zhou ancestors, referred to as Heaven), and became known as the Mandate of Heaven (Tian Ming).

The Zhou ruler had received a "Mandate from Heaven" to supplant the Shang. In other words, the Zhou's victory was a divine right bestowed by Heaven. From then on, dynastic change was based on the Mandate of Heaven.

Reigning for some 800 years, the Zhou dynasty (1045–221 B.C.E.) lasted longer than any other dynasty. During its rule, China was transformed from a primitive, quasi-nomadic state into a sophisticated and dynamic one on par with the Egyptian, Roman, and Mayan civilizations. In fact, modern Chinese regard the Zhou as the fount of their civilization. Large-scale public works projects helped the empire prosper. Roads and canals were constructed, paving the way for the exchange of goods and services. A monetary system was instituted. Iron was introduced. Warfare techniques and weaponry were honed. Yet, despite these significant advancements, the Zhou are perhaps best remembered for the development of the great philosophical schools (Confucianism, Daoism, and Legalism) and the formulation of the *Yijing*.

The next chapter discusses turtle shell and yarrow stalk divination, two methods employed by the ancient Chinese.

The Least You Need to Know

➤ The Neolithic Chinese are known as the Yangshao culture or the Painted Pottery culture. The Longshan or Black Pottery culture followed.

➤ The Three Dynasties of China (Xia, Shang, and Zhou) are derived from the Longshan culture dating to 3000 B.C.E.

➤ The Shang dynasty ruled from 1600–1045 B.C.E. Its last king, Zhou Wang, was known for his cruel and licentious behavior.

➤ King Wen of Zhou overthrew the Shang. When King Wen died, his son King Wu took the helm. Two years later when Wu died, his young son, Cheng Wang became king with his uncle, the Duke of Zhou, as his assistant.

➤ The Zhou ruled from 1045–221 B.C.E.

Chapter 3

Divination Chinese Style

In This Chapter

➤ The turtle and Chinese cosmology

➤ Oracle bone divination

➤ Yarrow stalk (or milfoil) lot divination

➤ The numerical hexagram

Humankind has always attempted to divine knowledge from a source greater than it-self. In fact, the word "divine," which is derived from the Latin word *divinus,* means of or relating to God or a god-like force. Divination, therefore, is the practice of fore-telling human events with the aid of the divine. Divination helps us make wise choices by providing us a glimpse into the possible outcome of our actions. It helps us make the changes we face meaningful.

In this chapter, we'll focus on two types of divination used by the ancient Chinese: divination by heating turtle shells and interpreting the resulting cracks, and divina-tion by casting stalks of yarrow (a fernlike plant). Although the Shang and early Zhou kings used both methods, the yarrow stalk procedure is the means by which the con-figurations of six solid and broken lines comprising the 64 hexagrams of the *Yijing* were formed.

In Search of Dragon Bones

Roughly three thousand years ago, during the reign of the Shang (1600–1045 B.C.E.), oracle bone divination was at its height of sophistication. Formally called *scapulimancy* and *plastromancy,* these methods used the scapula or shoulder blades of deer, sheep, pigs, cattle, beaver, camel, porcupine, and seal (among others) and the plastron or bottom shell of turtles as divinatory tools. For the record, the anklebones and ribs of mammals were also used. Yet, the more popular methods of heating shoulder bones of animals and turtle shells is well documented in Chinese texts.

According to the article "Chinese Oracle Bones" (*Scientific American,* April, 1979), by Hung-hsiang Chou, it wasn't until 1899 when a sickly Chinese scholar named Wang was prescribed "dragon bones" by his physician that oracle bone divination received modern academic attention. Upon his discovery that the medicinal fragments of bones and shells were inscribed with writings by the ancient Shang, Wang snatched up the remaining artifacts. Eventually, this led to a 10-year excavation project of Shang sites (located in northern Henan province) between 1928 and 1937, the project yielding a collection of some 20,000 oracle bones ripe for serious study. Since then, private collectors and archeologists have amassed over 200,000 fragments.

Wise Words

Scapulimancy and **plastromancy** are the practices of heating and interpreting the cracks formed on the scapula or shoulder bones of mammals and the plastron or bottom shell of turtles.

Yi Edicts

Ironically, in modern Chinese society, turtles play a leading role in many derogatory and sarcastic expressions. For example, "turtle egg" or "grandson of a turtle" serves as an all-purpose expletive. If you're called a "turtle" it means you are cowardly, unwilling to stick your neck out. On the other hand, "May the turtle and crane extend your life" exemplifies a benevolent expression.

The Almighty Turtle!

By the end of Shang rule, the use of turtle shells had fully replaced shoulder blades and other mammal bones. For the most part, the scapula bones were difficult to prepare, the asymmetrical shape offering an awkward writing template. However, the same cannot be said of turtle plastrons. While they were easier to manipulate and required less preparation, the plastron's best feature was its symmetrical shape, which allowed for a more uniform surface on which to record data. Also, the turtle may have garnered more attention because of its divine status.

In Chinese cosmology, four creatures ruled the heavens. They are the constellations of the turtle, the tiger, and two fantastic creatures—the dragon and the antlered phoenix. Although page restrictions prevent us from offering a more detailed discussion here, you can learn more about the Chinese celestial map in Chapter 8 of *The Complete Idiot's Guide to Feng Shui* (Alpha Books, 1999). For our purposes, understand the turtle's body encapsulated the order of the cosmos. How so? The ancient Chinese envisioned Heaven as round or domed and earth as square or flat. Hence, the turtle's domed shell over its flat breastplate symbolized a connective link between Heaven and earth, the divine and the human. Moreover, the motion of the creature's four feet seemed to illustrate the four seasons (spring, summer, autumn, winter) in perpetual change. With a life span of several hundred years, the turtle was considered wise, possessing supernatural powers. In fact, its body is turned inside-out. The bone is on the outside and the flesh is on the inside. All things considered, the turtle was a godly creature capable of transmitting a person's fate from the pantheon of ancestors in Heaven to humankind on earth.

In fact, turtles were so revered that besides being used for divination purposes, their shells were also used as jewelry by the Hemudu culture (5000–3500 B.C.E.) in Jiangsu and northern Zhejiang, and as currency during the Warring States Period (475–221 B.C.E.). By the Tang dynasty (C.E. 618–907), many gravesites were fashioned in the shape of turtles. Today, in Taiwan, turtle cakes are offered to gods in exchange for protection and as displays of gratitude.

Turtle Shell Preparation 101

During the Shang and early Zhou eras, divination by turtle shell was primarily a royal function. It was used to determine a whole host of things like the most auspicious time to hunt, launch military attacks, and build. It was used to forecast the weather and the outcome of childbirth; to seek approval and assistance; and to interpret dreams. In fact, the Duke of Zhou (King Wen's son) shared the auspicious results of this method to gain political support for the Zhou's conquest of the Shang.

Unlike the Shang, who appealed to their chief deity, Shang Di, the Zhou divined knowledge from Heaven (see Chapter 2, "A Short History of the Ancient Chinese" for a review of these terms). The intermediary between Heaven and earth was the diviner, the hierarchy composed of the Grand Diviner (dabu) and the Diviner (zhanren or bujen). According to a Zhou text called the *Zhouli (Rites of Zhou)*, these official positions were administered by the Ministry of Rites, a government division that set standards for burial, marriage, music, and divination ceremonies (among other things).

Photograph A (left): The inner surface of a turtle shell fragment shows two pairs of chiseled pits. Photograph B (right): The outer surface shows two sets of cracks produced by applying heat to the hollowed pits on opposite side of the shell. Photographs used with permission of Professor Hung-hsiang Chou, the University of California at Los Angeles.

Undeniably, turtle shell divination was serious business and required careful preparation. First, a turtle was selected. Although it is unclear, scholars believe diviners used

25

female freshwater turtles because their plastrons were more uniform in thickness than those of males. After the shell was separated from the plastron, each side was planed to create a smooth surface. Next, several rows of paired pits (usually about 30 pairs) were chiseled into the inner surface of the shell. Referring to Photograph A, these hollows consisted of one circular and one vertical pit, the latter chiseled parallel to the long dimension of the shell.

The Turtle Speaks!

Once the shells had been properly prepared, the divination ceremony began. In the preamble to his book, *Sources of Shang History: The Oracle-Bone Inscription of Bronze Age China* (University of California Press, 1978), David Keightley offers a realistic reconstruction of a ceremony arranged to determine the culprit behind Shang King Wu Ding's (1324–1264 B.C.E.) toothache:

> "Five turtle shells lie on the rammed-earth alter …. Into one of the unburned hollows, on the right side of the shell, the diviner Chui is thrusting a brand of flaming thorn. As he does so, he cries aloud, "The sick tooth is not due to Father Jia [Wu Ding's uncle, a former king]!" Fanned by an assistant to keep the glowing tip intensely hot, the stick flames against the surface of the shell. Smoke rises. The seconds slowly pass. The stench of scorched bone mingles with the aroma of millet wine scattered in libation. And then, with a sharp, clear, *puk*-like sound, the turtle, most silent of creatures, speaks. A ┠ -shaped crack has formed in the hollow where the plastron was scorched. Once again the brand is thrust, now into a matching hollow on the left side of the shell: "[The sick tooth] is due to Father Jia!" More time passes … [and] another crack forms in response. He rams the brand into the hollows and cracks the second turtle shell, then the third, the fourth, and the fifth."

Yi Edicts

Meaning crack-making, the Chinese character bu ┠ is derived from the shape of the crack formed on the bone or shell after it had been heated. Once pronounced puk, the word bu is now pronounced "boo."

(Excerpt used with permission of The Regents of the University of California.)

After this process was repeated for each of the five turtles, the diviners studied the cracks and reached a conclusion—or more specifically, offered a prediction or forecast. In the example just provided, the shape of the crack led the diviners to believe the king's uncle did not cause the toothache. Generally, if the perpendicular crack was no more than 20 degrees more or 20 degrees less than 90 degrees, the divinatory response was deemed positive. If the perpendicular crack exceeded 90 degrees, by at least 20 degrees or greater, the response was negative. This idea is demonstrated in Photograph B of the previous figure, where the 90-degree shape of the crack positively affirmed the *charge*.

Upon completion of the crack-making ceremony, a scribe engraved the date, the diviner's name, the charges, and the prediction onto the shell or bone. Later, when the result was known, it too was recorded onto the oracular instrument. The shell or bone with its assorted questions and information was then archived.

Cast Your Lot

Although the Chinese continued to use scapulimancy and plastromancy as late as the Western Han dynasty (206 B.C.E.–C.E. 25), these time-consuming methods were eventually replaced by *sortilege,* divination by drawing lots. Before we discuss this method's significance to the *Yijing,* it's worth exploring how our modern vernacular has made good use of the Latin root *sort,* from which sortilege is partially derived.

Literally meaning lot (to divide into lots), the word "sort" refers to the ability to gather, classify, and characterize information. The common expressions, "sort it out," "that sort of person," and "sort of" are just a few examples. By extension, the word "lot" refers to an object used as a counter for deciding something or determining an answer by chance. Typically, lots are stones, straws, or sticks, which is where the expression, "you got the short end of the stick" originates. It's where the process of "drawing straws" is derived. Although modern lottery games don't use sticks or stones, the premise is the same.

Where does this information lead? Simply, sortilege is a divinatory method the Chinese use to decide their fate. Following a specific procedure, lots are sorted and classified into either a broken or solid line, the configuration yielding a hexagram containing the insight (or information) which then leads the diviner toward a certain conclusion to the problem in question.

Sortilege Chinese Style

To the Chinese, divination by casting lots is known as shi. This method uses small stalks of bamboo or stalks from the *Achillea* plant (also called the yarrow or milfoil plant) to divine knowledge from the spirit world. Although scholars cannot pinpoint

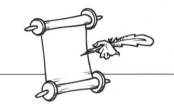

Wise Words

A **charge** represents a pair of antithetical (positive and negative) questions or statements. For example, take this actual pair of antithetical questions inscribed on an oracle bone: "On the 15th day diviner Cheng asks: Will it rain tomorrow, the 16th?" and "On the 15th day diviner Cheng asks: Will it not rain tomorrow, the 16th?" These paired charges were cracked and engraved on opposite sides of the shell.

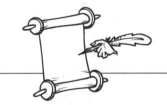

Wise Words

Sortilege is divination by drawing lots. The ancient Chinese used the stalk of the yarrow or milfoil plant in a procedure that randomly formed the six-lined hexagram graph.

when this type of divination began, archeological evidence suggests it was already widespread toward the end of the Shang dynasty. They know this because of inscriptions found on a pottery jar in a tomb unearthed in Pingyang county, a site on the periphery of Shang territory. The fact that the technique was used a great distance away from the Shang capital, together with the fact that the deceased was a person of low social rank, suggests the method, once reserved for the royals and elite, had sufficient time to spread to the border districts where it filtered down to the general populace.

Yi Edicts

Commonly called the yarrow or milfoil plant, its proper name is *Achillea millefolium*. A member of the sunflower family, Achillea refers to the Greek hero, Achilles, who understood the medicinal properties of the plant. The species name millefolium or "thousand leafed" refers to the flowering plant's numerous dissections of leaves, which are clustered at the base of the stalk. Yarrow can be found on all northern and central continents in open areas. It is used in ointments for wounds, in poultices for sore muscles, and as a tea to relieve depression, toothaches, colds, and fevers. Yarrow also has been found to ease hemorrhoids and urinary tract infections.

Regardless of when divination by yarrow stalk began, during the late Shang and early Zhou eras, this technique and divining by turtle shell were often performed together. Textual evidence of the dual use can be found in the *Zhozhuan*, purportedly written by an historian named Zuo Qiuming in 541 B.C.E. It records, "Before this, Duke Xian of Jin had wished to make Li Ji his wife. Divining about it by turtle shell, the result was inauspicious; divining by yarrow stalk, the result was auspicious." As the story goes, the Duke wished to follow the yarrow's prediction, but the diviner did not agree. The Duke prevailed and Li Ji was made a Duchess.

Super Sleuth Zheng Zhenglang

Unfortunately, because comprehensive records about yarrow divination are virtually nonexistent, the method that the Shang and early Zhou used to cast the stalks is not known. Nevertheless, scholars do know the procedure yielded a six-term numeric sequence composed of the numbers 1 through 8, a fact realized by Professor Zheng Zhenglang of the Chinese Academy of Social Sciences in Beijing.

In his article "An Interpretation of the Divinatory Inscriptions of Early Chou Bronzes" (*Early China*, Volume 6, 1980–81), Zheng conducted a statistical analysis of

32 artifacts yielding 168 numeric symbols. Referring to the following illustration depicting the ancient Chinese symbols for the numbers 1 through 8, he discovered that while initially all eight numbers were used in the casting procedure, ultimately, only a configuration of the numbers 1, 5, 6, 7, and 8 appeared in an oracular record. Specifically, the number 1 appeared 36 times; the number 5, 11 times; the number 6, 64 times; the number 7, 33 times; and the number 8, 24 times.

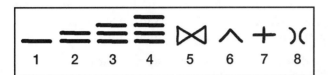

The ancient Chinese symbols for the numerals 1 through 8.

Interestingly, the numbers 2, 3, and 4 were not represented. Why the omission? Zheng believes these numbers were not used in a graph record because they could not be differentiated from each other in a vertical configuration. For instance, the number 3 could be a composite of the numbers 1 and 2 or 2 and 1. Because of the possible confusion, the even numbers 2 and 4 were classified under the number 6 and the odd numeral 3 was classified under the number 1. This left the numbers 1, 5, 6, 7, and 8. Says Zheng, "The fact that in the end only five [numbers] are a matter of record, shows that at the time … the main concern was yin and yang, and that the concrete numerals were altogether insignificant." In other words, Zheng discovered that even numbers came to represent yin and odd numbers came to represent yang.

Master Class

The casting procedure we use today was first introduced in the *Dazhuan,* one of the commentaries attached to the *Yijing* some 500 years after King Wen and the Duke of Zhou composed it. While you'll learn how to use this method in Chapter 6, "How to Cast the *Yijing,*" understand that the technique yields four numbers (6, 7, 8, and 9). Like the ancient method employed by the Shang and early Zhou, the even numbers symbolize yin (and a broken line); the odd numbers, yang (and a solid line).

Similar to the paired antithetical statements inscribed onto bones and shells, Zheng's discovery of the ancient Chinese categorizing numbers into two groups foreshadows the full flowering of the yin yang concept fundamental to many Chinese traditions.

Regarding the *Yijing,* Daoist and Confucian schools would use the interplay between yin and yang—the two dynamic forces that drives life through cycles of change—to interpret and analyze the hexagram symbols and the divinatory text.

What's Your Line?

Eventually, all odd numbers transformed into a solid line and all even numbers transformed into a broken line. Although it is not known who invented the familiar symbols or when this change was made, certainly by the Warring States Period (475–221 B.C.E.) of the Zhou dynasty, the line symbols replaced their numeric counterparts.

To be perfectly clear, the solid and broken images we are familiar with did not exist during King Wen's time. Until more archeological discoveries come forth and landmark theories are offered, we may never know the true meaning of the configuration of six numbers (from 1 to 8) used during the formative period of yarrow stalk divination. So, the mystery remains: How were number sequences correlated to human events? Yi scholars can only surmise that over time, the accumulation and analysis of oracular records produced a definitive text that linked a question with a numeric answer, and an answer with a probable result. For our purposes, this text is the *Yijing.*

In the next chapter, you'll learn who authored the *Yijing.* You'll learn about the order of the 64 hexagrams, a subject that has beguiled the most learned scholars. Finally, you'll understand how the *Yijing* went from being a sacred text to one espousing wisdom and philosophical teachings.

The Least You Need to Know

➤ Scapulimancy and plastromancy are two methods of divination the ancient Chinese used to seek knowledge from the spirit world.

➤ Scapulimancy is the practice of heating and interpreting the cracks formed on the scapula or shoulder bones of mammals. Plastromancy is the practice of heating and interpreting the cracks formed on the plastron or bottom shell of turtles.

➤ Divination by yarrow stalk eventually replaced scapulimancy and plastromancy. It involves sorting and characterizing stalks to yield a six-term numeric sequence.

➤ Yarrow stalk and turtle cracking divination were often performed together.

➤ In 1978, Professor Zheng Zhenglang discovered that the original hexagrams were not the six-line graphs composed of solid and broken lines, but were six-term numeric sequences made up of the numbers 1 through 8.

Part 2

The Historical and Mythical Origins of the *Yijing*

This part is devoted to helping you understand the Yijing's historical and mythical basis. While the historical version is grounded in archeological and textual evidence (scant though it is), the mythical account is imbued with legendary sage-kings and fantastic animals bearing inscriptions of cosmological maps that contain the secrets of the universe.

Part 2 also discusses how the Yijing changed from a sacred book of divination to a book of philosophy and wisdom. Here, you'll learn about a collection of commentaries appended to the Zhouyi. Known as the Ten Wings, these essays used cosmological, metaphysical, and moral ideas to explain the often archaic and mystical divinatory text. In fact, the esoteric concepts of qi and yin and yang are first mentioned in these essays.

Chapter 4

The I Ching according to King Wen

As the Story Goes: The Historical Origin of the *Yijing*

In This Chapter

➤ The meaning of *yi*

➤ Two other divinatory systems: the *Lianshanyi* and the *Guicangyi*

➤ The origin of the *Zhouyi*

➤ Understanding the *Ten Wings*

The *Yijing* is not the effort solely of one individual. Rather, it is an accumulative text compiled, interpreted, and analyzed by a body of people over a span of time. At each stage, the efforts of sages and scholars may seem to have been the definitive work. Yet, actually, a full understanding of the oracle will probably never be realized. As new archeological discoveries are unearthed and new textual evidence is discovered, the profundity of the *Yijing* becomes more apparent, further fascinating and beguiling the most learned authorities.

In this chapter, we'll introduce modern research on the origin of the *Yijing* and two other systems of yarrow stalk divination, the *Lianshanyi* and *Guicangyi*. Also, we'll discuss a collection of commentaries appended to the oracle some 500 to 700 years after King Wen and his son the Duke of Zhou initially assembled it. Called the *Ten Wings*, the seven commentaries (in 10 parts) sought to clarify and give meaning to the divinatory text and hexagram symbols.

The Sun, the Moon, and the Lizard

In Chapter 1, "Ground Zero: Understanding the Basics About the *I Ching, Book of Changes*," you learned that the yi of *Yijing* means to change. In ancient China, the pictograph for change 𝄞 is comprised of two elements: the sun ☉ and the moon ☽.

These entities represent the change from daytime into nighttime and, more broadly, the perpetual flux and change of nature made manifest by the birth, growth, decay, and death of life. Over time, the symbol for change evolved into the modern character: 易.

It's worth noting that many sinologists (like the venerable Richard Wilhelm) believe the word yi originally meant lizard, or more specifically, chameleon. This is a misunderstanding. It is the other way around. The chameleon is named for its ability to change color in response to certain environmental and emotional factors. In Chinese, the word chameleon 蜥蜴 is made up of two characters, each containing the radical (a character classifying the object in question) for reptile 虫. On the left side, 析 means to analyze (shi). On the right side, 易 means to change (yi). Together, shi yi means chameleon, a species capable of analyzing (and adapting to) change within its environment.

The Three Faces of Yi

At the time the *Zhouyi* (which was later renamed the *Yijing*) was composed by King Wen and the Duke of Zhou, two other systems of divination existed. Called the *Lianshanyi* and *Guicangyi,* very little is known about them. While they are mentioned in various ancient documents, artifactual evidence is scant. For example, in 1950, oracle bones were unearthed in Si Pan Mo Cun, a village in Henan province. Inscribed on one of the bones are three characters. In his article "An Interpretation of the Divinatory Inscriptions on Early Chou Bronzes" [*Journal of Archeology* (in Chinese), Vol. 4, 1980], Professor Zheng Zhenglang believes two of the characters (Kui) represent hexagram names taken from the *Lianshanyi.* This is because if the characters are linked together (Kui Kui), they represent the given name of the purported author of the system—Shennong. He is also known as Lieshan, a name that is phonetically similar to the word Lianshan. "Therefore, I suspect these two hexagrams [come from] the *Lianshanyi.*" Zheng suspects the graphs are a result of someone honing his carving skills while learning the yi system, and are "not the result of a divination process."

Despite the lack of textual or artifactual evidence, the *Lianshanyi* and *Guicangyi* have a few things in common with their famous cousin, the *Zhouyi* …

➤ Like the *Zhouyi,* the *Lianshanyi* and *Guicangyi* used stalks of yarrow to divine a hexagram, the answer to a question. Yet, the number of stalks the systems called for differed. The *Lianshanyi* used 36 stalks; the *Guicangyi* used 45 stalks; and the *Zhouyi* used 49 (out of 50) stalks. Unfortunately, the casting technique for the *Lianshanyi* and *Guicangyi* is not known.

➤ Like the *Zhouyi,* the *Lianshanyi* and *Guicangyi* used the 64 hexagrams and eight trigrams traditionally believed to be invented by Fuxi, China's first ruler. (You'll learn more about the significance of trigrams in the next chapter.) Although the names of the hexagrams are not fully known for the *Lianshanyi* and *Guicangyi,* we can surmise the three systems used different names; the hexagrams were arranged in a different order.

➤ Like the *Zhouyi*, the *Lianshanyi* and *Guicangyi* offered a prognostication or prediction. (In our interpretation in Part 4, "The 64 Hexagrams: A New Interpretation for the Twenty-first Century," the prognostication is called the hexagram statement.) While there is no concrete evidence to support this claim, it is a reasonable assumption because the characters adjacent to the various numeric hexagrams found on bone and shell fragments probably do represent a prognostication. However, the information is insufficient because an intelligible phrase or sentence cannot be constructed.

Wise Words

The **Zhouyi** (literally, the *Changes of Zhou*) is a system of yarrow stalk divination created by King Wen and his son, the Duke of Zhou. Later, the *Zhouyi* was renamed the *Yijing* when commentaries were attached to the divinatory text. The **Lianshanyi** (literally, *Linking Mountains*) is a system of yarrow stalk divination purportedly created by the legendary (and perhaps mythical) sage-king, Shennong. The **Guicangyi** (literally, *Restored to the Earth*) is a system of yarrow stalk divination said to be created by another celebrated (and perhaps mythical) king, Huang Di (the Yellow Emperor).

Another perplexing question has to do with origination. While modern scholars are confident the *Zhouyi* originated with King Wen and the Duke of Zhou, the origin of the *Lianshanyi* and *Guicangyi* is less clear. The purported creators of these systems, legendary figures who lived at the dawn of Chinese civilization, may not have even existed! In other words, they may be mythical figures. As we stated a little earlier, the sage-king Shennong (Lieshan) is credited with devising the *Lianshanyi* divinatory system. According to tradition, Huang Di, known as the Yellow Emperor, devised the *Guicangyi*. All things considered, we can assume one of the following:

1. The *Lianshanyi* and *Guicangyi* systems are much older than the *Zhouyi*. They were developed respectively by Shennong and Huang Di. Upon the advent of writing during the Shang dynasty, the oral traditions were documented on animal scapulas and turtle shells.

2. The *Lianshanyi* and *Guicangyi* systems predate the *Zhouyi*. When the oral traditions were written down, celebrated sage-kings were named as the creators.

Yi Edicts

The legendary (and perhaps mythical) sage-kings or tribal chiefs, Suiren, Fuxi, and Shennong (Lieshan) are collectively referred to as the Three Emperors. While Suiren is credited with inventing fire, and Fuxi with nets for fishing and the musical instrument called the zither (among other things), Shennong, the "divine farmer," is credited with instituting agricultural practices and recognizing the medicinal uses of plants. He is also credited with inventing a rudimentary form of record keeping by tying knots on ropes.

We simply can't be sure which scenario is correct. However, it does appear that a growing number of scholars are leaning toward the first notion—that Shennong and Huang Di *did* exist and that they probably *did* create methods of divination that were then passed down generationally. With the caveat that more discoveries are needed to bolster this opinion, for our purposes, we'll accept this view, which we will refer to as the traditional one.

The Lianshanyi

Many modern academics believe the *Lianshanyi* was handed down to the Xia by Shennong (Lieshan), who lived in the region where the Xia prospered. While some scholars believe the *Lianshanyi* is named after its author, there are other ideas. One hypothesis holds that the name Lianshan (literally, *Linking Mountains*) is derived from the place or the name of the mountain where the Xia lived. Others logically deduce that the name suggests the importance of mountain ranges. The fact that the hexagram Gen (mountain) is first in the *Lianshanyi* series of 64, is evidence. You see, the Xia (and their forebears) inhabited the area in today's Henan and Hebei provinces, regions prone to flooding. To survive the ravaging water, they sought shelter in the mountains. Hence, mountains became sacred; they were respected and revered. Therefore, it makes sense that the Xia (or perhaps even Shennong) would name the divinatory system after that which sheltered and protected them.

The Guicangyi

The *Guicangyi* was passed down to the Shang by Huang Di. In the *Guicangyi* (literally, *Restored to the Earth*), Kun (earth) is designated as Hexagram 1. Placing the earth hexagram first agrees with the Shang's reverence for the soil that provided means for crop cultivation and watercourses that irrigated the crops. Indeed, the north China plain was a fertile haven that allowed the Shang to prosper, grow, and expand.

The Zhouyi

The Zhou dynasty's divination system is the subject of this book. Called the *Zhouyi (The Changes of Zhou)*, sinologists disagree about the meaning of the word Zhou. Some scholars speculate that Zhou refers to the place where the Ji clan (King Wen's tribe) prospered. Others say Zhou refers to the Zhou dynasty. A third theory postulates that Zhou means cycle, and more broadly, that *Zhouyi* means cyclical (Zhou) changes (yi). While all of these presumptions are not without grounds, we will not detain ourselves with further discussion.

In the *Zhouyi*, Hexagram 1 is Qian. Meaning Heaven, the fact that this hexagram comes first indicates the Zhou's knowledge of the cosmos. It could also mean that Heaven, their pantheon of ancestors who manipulated the stalks of yarrow, is above earth, the realm of humankind.

Master Class

The earliest written record of the three yi can be found in the *Zhouli*, the *Rites of Zhou*. Referring to the Great Diviner Taibu, it says, "The Great Diviner ... uses the three yi. The first is called *Lianshan[yi]*, the second is called *Guicang[yi]*, and the third, *Zhouyi*. They each have eight trigrams and 64 hexagrams." Although the Duke of Zhou is credited with writing the *Zhouli*, many scholars believe it was written during the fifth and fourth centuries B.C.E., some 500 years after the Duke's death.

The King Wen Sequence of Hexagrams

The *Zhouyi's* arrangement of hexagrams is commonly called the "King Wen Sequence." It has perplexed the yi academic community since the late Spring and Autumn Period when Confucian and Daoist scholars first began to scrutinize the oracle. Like a secret code that cannot be cracked, the mystery of the oracle still escapes scholars' ability to produce a convincing explanation for the order of hexagrams. Nevertheless, scholars do agree that the arrangement has a purpose, and that it is meaningful, not random. While we won't concern ourselves with the myriad theories surrounding this complex issue, we will call your attention to a striking curiosity that causes the scholars to scratch their heads in utter puzzlement.

Master Class

Although King Wen probably wrote the hexagram statements, which give a general prediction about a person's situation, it is highly improbable that he arranged the hexagrams in the sequence that bears his name. We believe his son is responsible for the King Wen Sequence. This is because the hexagrams tell the story of the fall of the Shang dynasty and the rise of the Zhou dynasty. King Wen died before the Zhou came to power, and his son Fa (King Wu) completed the conquest. Therefore, it is impossible for King Wen to have created the sequence.

Disregarding Hexagrams 1 and 2, 27 and 28, and 29 and 30, which are opposing pairs, take a look at the following chart illustrating the King Wen Sequence of hexagrams. Beginning with Hexagrams 3 and 4, notice the similarity. Hexagram 4 is a right-side-up version of Hexagram 3. Stated another way, Hexagrams 3 and 4 (along with 5 and 6, 7 and 8, and on to Hexagrams 63 and 64) are a cyclical pair. Rotating each hexagram 180 degrees to the left or right results in its pair. This idea conforms to the cyclic nature of yi (changes). Where Hexagram 3 ends, Hexagram 4 begins. Death is recycled or reborn. Get it?

This arrangement raises many questions: Which is more important, the pattern of yin ▬ ▬ and yang ▬▬▬ lines made manifest within each hexagram or the relationship between the hexagrams? Should the focus be on the individual lines (called monograms) and their position in the hexagram, or should the hexagrams be studied as units of two lines (called bigrams) or units of three lines (called trigrams)? What about the correlation of the hexagram graph to the hexagram text? Moreover, let's not lose sight of the fact that hexagrams were initially numeric sequences. The solid and broken lines we are familiar with today did not exist during King Wen's time. Needless to say, we need to uncover more archeological evidence to resolve this monumental mindbender!

1	2	3	4	5	6	7	8
9	10	11	12	13	14	15	16
17	18	19	20	21	22	23	24
25	26	27	28	29	30	31	32
33	34	35	36	37	38	39	40
41	42	43	44	45	46	47	48
49	50	51	52	53	54	55	56
57	58	59	60	61	62	63	64

The King Wen Sequence of Hexagrams.

Two Halves of the Whole

When we refer to the *Zhouyi*, we are actually talking about two distinct parts written by different people at different times. The first part is called the *Jing* (literally, *Classic*). It consists of the 64 hexagram graphs, the hexagram statement *(guaci)*, and 386 line texts *(yaoci)*. Each hexagram contains six line texts (64 × 6 = 384). The exceptions are Hexagrams 1 and 2. They contain an additional line text each. (You'll learn more about the composition of a hexagram in Chapter 7, "How to Interpret Your *Yijing* Reading.")

Most scholars agree King Wen wrote the hexagram statements during his seven-year incarceration by the Shang king, Zhou Wang. Scholars also agree that King Wen's son Dan, better known as the Duke of Zhou, wrote the line texts. Because convincing evidence to the contrary does not exist, we will accept the traditional story. Yet there is controversy about who invented the hexagrams. While many yi scholars theorize that Fuxi, Shennong, or Yu (who engineered a system of levees and drainage channels to prevent flood waters from destroying the settlements) may have invented the hexagrams, the common theory maintains that King Wen invented them. As we discussed in Chapter 3, "Divination Chinese Style," archeological evidence dismisses this idea. Yarrow stalk divination with hexagrams was widespread long *before* King Wen created the *Zhouyi*. Keeping with the common theme of uncertainty in this chapter, we cannot hope to know the truth until more concrete evidence is unearthed.

The second part of the *Zhouyi* is called the *Zhuan* (literally, *Commentary*). Commonly called the *Ten Wings*, these are essays attached to the *Jing* part of the *Zhouyi*. During the Han dynasty (206 B.C.E.–C.E. 220), the compilation was renamed the *Yijing*. Before we delve into the *Ten Wings*, let's stay focused for a moment on the *Jing*, the divination part.

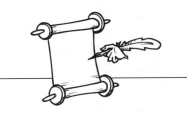

Wise Words

In Chinese, the hexagram statement or prediction is called the **guaci.** Each line text, which offers more information and advice about your concern, problem, or dilemma, is called the **yaoci.**

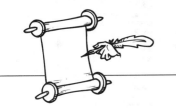

Wise Words

The *Zhouyi* is divided into two sections: the **Jing** (Classic) and the **Zhuan** (Commentary). The *Jing* consists of the original divinatory text and symbols; the *Zhuan* (known as the *Ten Wings* in English) is a collection of essays of unknown authorship appended to the text centuries after King Wen and the Duke of Zhou composed it. In the Han dynasty, the *Zhouyi* (the Changes of Zhou) was renamed the *Yijing* (the Classic of Change).

The Upper Classic and Lower Classic

The hexagrams tell the story of the decline and death of the Shang dynasty and the rise and growth of the Zhou dynasty. Hexagram 1 summarizes Hexagrams 3 through 30. Collectively called the Upper Classic (Shang Jing), these hexagrams describe the revolution against the Shang, the establishment of the Zhou dynasty, the conquest of the 99 rebel tribes still loyal to the Shang, and the suppression of Wu Geng's (the Shang king's son) attempted coup d'état. The historical tale ends with the succession of Cheng Wang, the young Zhou king who ascended the throne after his father's (King Wu) untimely death. While the Upper Classic is action oriented, the remaining hexagrams delve into the ruling philosophy of the Zhou. These hexagrams (31 through 64) are called the Lower Classic (Xia Jing) and are summarized by Hexagram 2.

The Ten Wings ...

When the *Ten Wings* (*Shi Yi*, in Chinese) were attached to the *Zhouyi*, the oracle transformed from being a religious artifact to a philosophical one. This is because the collection of commentaries used moral, metaphysical, and cosmological ideas to explain the often archaic and mystical divinatory text. Similar to people quoting from a holy book to accentuate a point, the Chinese began to use lines from the *Yijing* to bolster a position. Eventually, the original meaning of the oracular text was lost, overshadowed by the philosophical agenda. In a nutshell, the *Yijing* was reinvented. So, when a person divined the oracle, his or her ability to intuit the answer based on the original text was clouded by the subjective interpretations imposed by the commentaries.

Yi Edicts

Confucius (551–479 B.C.E.) was one of early China's great thinkers. Born in present-day Shandong province, Confucius witnessed the deterioration of the Zhou dynasty. The states warred; surprise attacks, raids, and mass executions were commonplace. Confucius wanted to return to the "Age of the Grand Harmony," the time of the early Zhou kings. His solution was to implement a code of ethics for all to follow. His philosophy became so influential that it was taught to schoolchildren until the end of the Imperial Period in C.E. 1911. In 130 B.C.E., his teachings became a guidebook for government officials, a mandate that continued until C.E. 1905. In the Han dynasty, Confucianism became China's official religion. When the Communist regime came to power in 1949, they wouldn't dare denounce Confucianism even though their Constitution recognizes only Marxism and Maoism! Indeed, the Confucian way of life has deeply impacted the Chinese.

But who wrote the *Ten Wings?* Like so many aspects of the *Yijing,* no one really knows. In fact, it is not even known when the essays were written. While modern scholars unanimously dismiss the notion that Confucius (551–479 B.C.E.) penned the *Ten Wings,* many agree that his disciples may have written the commentaries after their master's death. Others are convinced the collection of essays stem from the Warring States Period (475–221 B.C.E.), the age of the "hundred schools" of philosophy. We'll leave this debate to the yi scholars.

... That Help the Yijing Fly

When the commentaries were appended to the *Zhouyi,* it was said they would help carry the oracle far and wide—that the *Zhouyi* would fly on wings, becoming accessible to everyone. In fact, the Chinese character for wing means to assist and to guide. In total, there are seven commentaries. As you shall soon learn, some of them are divided into upper and lower parts. Here is a brief description of each wing:

➤ *Dazhuan (Great Commentary).* Also called the *Xicizhuan (Appended Words),* it is considered the most important of the seven commentaries. The *Dazhuan* offers a metaphysical analysis of change, the central theme of the *Zhouyi.* It says, "When the six lines move [change], it indicates the way of the three powers [Heaven, man, and earth]. An honorable man can live in peace when he follows the changes … In this way, he will be blessed by Heaven and there will be only fortune and no misfortune." The terms yin and yang originated here. The *Dazhuan* is divided into upper and lower sections called the *Xici Shangzhuan* and *Xici Xiazhuan.*

➤ *Shuoguazhuan (Explanation of the Trigrams).* This essay outlines the eight natural phenomena that are assigned to the eight trigrams, a three-term sequence of yin and yang lines. Besides being correlated with a meteorological aspect, each trigram is matched with a host of other things. Some of these are outlined in the following table.

While trigrams are not used for divination purposes, the configuration of two trigrams forms a hexagram. The *Shuoguazhuan* analyzes how the properties of each trigram can create an image, which, in turn, influences the interpretation of the divinatory text. This been the basis of *Yijing* divination since the end of the Spring and Autumn Period or the beginning of the Warring States Period. The term qi, the vital force at the heart and development of all things, is first used in the *Shuoguazhuan.* The concept of qi is the subject of Chapter 8, "The Mystery of Qi."

Trigram	ZHEN	XUN	LI	KUN	DUI	QIAN	KAN	GEN
Familial Relation	Eldest Son	Eldest Daughter	Middle Daughter	Mother	Youngest Daughter Concubine	Father	Middle Son	Youngest Son
Nature	Thunder	Wind	Fire Lightening	Earth	Marsh Lake	Heaven	Water	Mountain
Phase Element	Wood	Wood	Fire	Earth	Metal	Metal	Water	Earth
Time of Day	Morning	Late Morning	Noon	Afternoon	Evening	Late Evening	Midnight	Early Morning
Season	Spring	Late Spring Early Summer	Summer	Late Summer Early Autumn	Mid Autumn	Late Autumn	Mid Winter	Early Spring
Hou Tian Direction	E	SE	S	SW	W	NW	N	NE
Body Part	Feet	Thighs Buttocks	Eyes Large Belly(man)	Abdomen Stomach	Mouth Tongue	Head	Ears	Hands Fingers
Animal	Dragon	Chicken	Pheasant	Ox	Sheep	Horse	Pig	Dog, Rat Birds with powerful bills
Abstract	Movement	Penetrating	Brightness	Compliance	Pleasure Satisfaction	Strength	Hazardous	Arrest (stopping motion)

Trigram Correspondence Chart.

➤ *Xiangzhuan (Commentary on the Images).* This commentary divides the hexagram into the *Daxiang (Big Image)* and *Xiaoxiang (Small Image).* The *Daxiang* describes the image inherent in the hexagram, and the *Xiaoxiang* describes the image inherent in each of the six yao (broken or unbroken line). Also, the *Xiangzhuan* commentary divides the hexagram into its trigram parts. The idea is to understand the hexagram by examining the nature of each trigram. In other words, an image from nature (the macrocosm) is matched with an image from human nature (the microcosm). For example, take Hexagram 46 (Rising): ䷭. Here, the trigram for earth (Kun) ☷ is over the trigram for wind (Xun) ☴. The commentary for this hexagram's statement says, "Wood sprouts from the earth, the image conveying rising. The honorable man is cautious and virtuous. He allows it to accumulate; to become tall and great." The message given by nature is that a person will stand above the crowd if he or she acts with integrity, caution, and honesty. The *Xiangzhuan* is divided into upper and lower parts that are attached respectively to the Upper and Lower Classic.

➤ *Tuanzhuan (Commentary on the Hexagrams).* This essay deals with the auspice of the hexagrams, which can be determined by the proportion and arrangement of the yin (broken) and yang (solid) lines within the hexagram, and their relationship to the line text. The *Tuanzhuan* uses Confucian thought to explain each hexagram. For example, regarding Hexagram 31 ䷞ (Xian) it says, "Xian means influencing. The weak trigram (Dui ☱, young girl) is above the strong trigram (Gen ☶, young man). The two … respond to [and are influenced by] each other. There is joy …. Marriage brings great fortune." The *Tuanzhuan* is divided into upper and lower sections that are attached respectively to the Upper and Lower Classic.

➤ *Xuguazhuan (Sequence of the Hexagrams).* This text attempts to explain the sequence of hexagrams, interpreting the order in terms of the waxing and waning cycles of nature and human nature. For example, the *Xuguazhan* says that all things originate from Heaven (Hexagram 1) and earth (Hexagram 2). Tun (Hexagram 3) follows; it describes the birth of things. Upon birth, things are immature and unaware, and this idea is encapsulated in Meng (Hexagram 4). Xu (Hexagram 5) is next; it stresses the importance of fostering patience and perseverance, qualities that lead to a strengthened spirit. The description continues in this fashion, ending with Wei Ji (Hexagram 64). It warns that history may repeat itself, that the Zhou should avoid following in the footsteps of the tyrant Shang king, Zhou Wang.

➤ *Zaguazhuan (Parity of the Hexagrams).* It describes the relationship between the hexagram pairs. For example, Hexagram 42 ䷩ means increasing. It is a right-side-up version of Hexagram 41 ䷨, which means decreasing. Hexagram 64 ䷿ means not yet accomplished; it is a right-side-up version of Hexagram 63 ䷾, which means already accomplished. With the exception of Hexagrams 1 and 2;

27 and 28; and 29 and 30 (which are opposite pairs), all other pairs are inversions of each other.

➤ *Wenyanzhuan (Elaboration on Qian and Kun).* This commentary gives a detailed explanation of the meaning and significance of Hexagrams 1 (Qian, Heaven) and 2 (Kun, earth), which summarize Hexagrams 3 though 30, and 31 through 64 respectively. For example, take the first line text for Hexagram 2: "Tread on the frost. Gradually, it will become solid ice." The *Wenyanzhuan* explains it this way: "The family that accumulates good deeds is sure to have abundance of happiness. The family that accumulates evil deeds is sure to have abundance of misfortune." In other words, your accumulation of good or evil deeds will solidify into good or bad fortune.

Clipping the Wings

It is important to understand that we do not integrate the *Ten Wings* into our interpretation. We have restored the *Zhouyi* to its original form, the one used by the Duke of Zhou and his successors. Indeed, this is a daring venture as people have come to depend on the subjective philosophy to interpret their hexagram, the answer.

In the next chapter, we'll explain the mythical origins of the *Yijing*.

The Least You Need to Know

➤ Two other divinatory systems existed at the time of the *Zhouyi.* Now lost to history, they are the *Lianshanyi* and the *Guicangyi.*

➤ The *Zhouyi* originated with King Wen and the Duke of Zhou. The *Lianshanyi* is said to derive from the legendary sage-king, Shennong; The *Guicangyi* from another celebrated figure, Huang Di.

➤ The King Wen Sequence of hexagrams outlined in the *Zhouyi* is a mystery. Scholars agree the arrangement is not random, but ordered for a purpose.

➤ The *Zhouyi* is divided into two parts: The divination part is called the *Jing* and the philosophy part is called the *Zhuan.*

➤ The philosophy part of the *Zhouyi* is collectively called the *Ten Wings.* Comprised of seven essays in 10 parts, they were appended to the *Zhouyi* sometime between the late Spring and Autumn Period and the early Han dynasty. After the commentaries were appended to the *Zhouyi*, the compilation was renamed the *Yijing.*

Chapter 5

Once Upon a Time: The Mythical Origin of the *Yijing*

In this chapter, we'll examine the mythical origins of the *Yijing*. We'll specifically look at two cosmological diagrams called the Hetu and Luoshu. These numeric diagrams were gifts from Heaven given to China's ancient sage-kings. They contain the secrets of the universe. From them arise the eight fundamental trigrams (three-tiered configurations of solid and broken lines) that form the basis of *Yijing* divination and interpretation. Besides their significance to the *Yijing*, the trigrams are used extensively in other Chinese traditions like feng shui (which you'll learn about in Chapter 13, "Increasing Your Health, Wealth, and Relationships with Feng Shui," and Chapter 14, "Learning Yigua Feng Shui"), the martial arts, and Chinese medicine.

Fuxi? Who's He?

You learned in the previous chapter that Fuxi, Shennong, and Yu were China's earliest sage-kings, celebrated for inventing a host of things that advanced their civilization. What you didn't learn is that Fuxi is credited with inventing the eight fundamental trigrams that combine to form the 64 hexagrams of the *Yijing*. Of course, we cannot know for sure that the symbols are derived from him. While so much about the *Yijing*

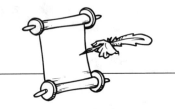

Wise Words

A **trigram** is a three-tiered symbol composed of a configuration of solid (yang) and broken (yin) lines. Each trigram represents an aspect of nature, familial relation, direction, and season, among other things. Collectively, the eight fundamental trigrams of the *Yijing* are called the **bagua**.

cannot be substantiated with concrete evidence, nevertheless, we'll accept the traditional account.

But what exactly are *trigrams?* Simply stated, they represent transitional stages of all possible cosmic and human conditions. The *Dazhuan (Great Commentary)* explains it best:

"In ancient times, when Baoxi [Fuxi] was the king of the world under Heaven, he looked up to study the celestial images. He looked down to examine the terrestrial patterns. He contemplated the markings of birds and beasts and how they adapted to their environment. Near at hand he examined his own body, and at a distance he examined other things. He then devised the eight trigrams comprising the bagua. Thus, he was able to communicate with the virtue of the spirits and understand how they regulate the condition of all things."

Master Class

As you learned in Chapter 3, "Divination Chinese Style," Professor Zheng Zhenglang of the Chinese Academy of Social Sciences discovered that hexagrams were originally recorded numerically. Among his findings on oracle bones, pottery fragments, and bronze containers dating to the late Shang and early Zhou dynasties, was a collection of three-term numeric symbols—trigrams. Although his discovery cannot prove that trigrams and hexagrams existed before the late Shang era, it does prove that trigrams and hexagrams co-existed. Also, his discovery does not answer the question of which came first, trigrams or hexagrams. We can only speculate that trigrams preceded hexagrams, because it is easier to construct a complicated system (hexagrams) of divination based on simple parts (trigrams) than it is to create a complex system first and then break it down into parts.

In other words, Fuxi understood that humankind was a microcosm (a small replica) of nature and the cosmos, which make up the macrocosm. By observing how the world operated, he could better understand human nature. (See Chapter 4, "As the Story

Goes: The Historical Origin of the *Yijing*," for a correlation of natural and human aspects.) He could then regulate, order, and harmonize the condition of a person's well-being by communicating with the gods that ruled Heaven. In effect, Heaven (the realm of the spirit world) and earth (his realm) could be linked. The eight fundamental trigrams were the tools that provided the connection.

| Kun | Gen | Kan | Xun | Zhen | Li | Dui | Qian |

Together, the eight trigrams are called the bagua.

The River Map

Legend has it that Fuxi received a gift from Heaven. It was a numeric diagram, a pattern of black (yin) and white (yang) dots on the back of a fantastic dragon-horse that stepped out of the Yellow River. Called the *Hetu* or *River Map,* the pattern represented the ideal, perfect, and balanced world. Let's see how we come to this conclusion.

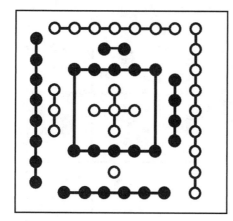

The Hetu or River Map.

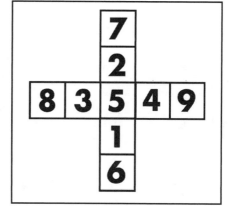

The Hetu Numeric Cross.

First, transcribe the series of black and white dots into their numeric equivalents. For example, the top row of seven white dots corresponds to the number 7. The row of black dots directly beneath the seven white dots corresponds to the number 2. Disregarding the central two groups of five black dots (which forms the number 10), the result is the Hetu Cross, the illustration on the right.

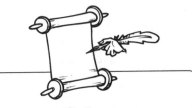

Wise Words

The **Hetu,** or **River Map,** is said to be a gift from Heaven to Fuxi. It is a pattern of black (yin) and white (yang) dots found on a fantastic dragon-horse coming out of the Yellow River. The Hetu symbolizes a perfect, balanced, and motionless world.

Notice how the odd (yang) numbers are perfectly balanced by opposing even (yin) numbers: 1 (yang) is opposite 2 (yin); 3 (yang) is opposite 4 (yin); 6 (yin) is opposite 7 (yang); and 8 (yin) is opposite 9 (yang). Also, notice that all the odd or Heaven numbers (not including the number 5) add up to twenty: 1 + 3 + 7 + 9 = 20. The same is true for the even or earth numbers: 2 + 4 + 6 + 8 = 20.

The Luo River Writing

While some people believe Yu the Great, China's first dynastic ruler, was given both gifts, we will go with the version described in the fifth century B.C.E. text, the *Shangshu (Classic of History)*. It says Heaven bestowed on Fuxi the Hetu, and on Yu, the Luoshu. Also called the *Luo River Writing*, the *Luoshu* is a pattern of black (yin) and white (yang) dots inscribed on a turtle's shell. Yu found the turtle emerging from the Luo Shui River.

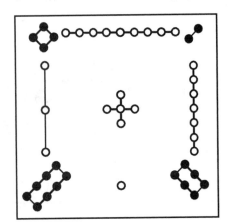

The Luo River Writing.

4	9	2
3	5	7
8	1	6

The Luoshu Magic Square of Three.

As in the Hetu, the dots comprising the Luoshu represent numbers. For example, the four black (yin) dots on the top left side of the diagram correspond with the number 4. To the right of the four black dots are 9 white (yang) dots. Then, 2 black (yin) dots. Unlike the Hetu, the Luoshu symbolizes a world in constant flux and change, a world in motion. While it is beyond the scope of this chapter to explain how the Luoshu numeric sequence moves, we direct you to Chapter 13 of *The Complete Idiot's Guide to Feng Shui* (Alpha Books, 1999).

The Luoshu is called the *Magic Square of Three* because any three cells along a horizontal, vertical, or diagonal line add up to 15.

Knots of Lines

The representation of dots as numbers calls to mind the ancient technique of tying knots on strings as a means of recording data. This technique was used by cultures worldwide (such as the Greeks, Persians, Hawaiians, Africans, and indigenous Indians) before the advent of writing. Georges Ifrah, in his thoroughly researched book, *The Universal History of Numbers* (John Wiley and Sons, 2000) writes about the Incan apparatus called the *quipu.* This elaborate device of knotted string documented "liturgical, chronological, and statistical records, and could occasionally also serve as calendars and as messages."

Today, native Bolivians and Peruvians use the *chimpu,* a knotted string device related to the quipu.

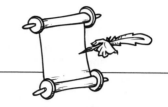

Wise Words

The **Luo River Writing** or **Luoshu** is a pattern of black (yin) and white (yang) dots purportedly found on a turtle shell. When the dots are transcribed into numbers, it yields a diagram called the **Magic Square of Three.** It is considered magical because three cells along any horizontal, vertical, or diagonal line add up to 15. The Luoshu symbolizes a world in motion.

Yi Edicts

Scholars generally agree that counting preceded writing. In her book, *Before Writing: From Counting to Cuneiform* (University of Texas Press, 1992), author Denise Schmandt-Besserat discusses the token system of numeration created by the Mesopotamians as a consequence of the development of agriculture during the Neolithic era (about 8000 B.C.E.). From Mesopotamia (present-day Iraq), the technique of using small clay tokens (in a variety of shapes) to count with and to account for data, spread throughout the Near East. However, her study does not include China. In fact, she states offhandedly that "other scripts developed later, independently, in China and Meso-America."

The ancient Chinese also used knotted string numeration. In fact, Shennong is credited with inventing the system. This calls into question whether Fuxi (who preceded Shennong) received the Hetu diagram. Either knotted numbers were in use before Shennong or, as other texts attest to, Yu the Great (who followed Shennong many centuries later) received both the Hetu and Luoshu diagrams. Despite this mystery, the trigrams could have first been recorded as knots on string. Later, when writing was invented, trigrams (and hexagrams) were recorded as numeric symbols. (Please refer to Chapter 3 for a refresher.) Then, these evolved into the solid and broken lines we are familiar with today.

The following illustration demonstrates the possible evolution from knots to symbols to lines. The commonality is numbers. A knot, the numeric symbol ∧, and a yin line ▬▬ ▬▬ each represent an even or earth number. A space on a string or a string without a knot, the numeric symbol ▬, and a yang line ▬▬▬▬▬▬ each represent an odd or Heaven number.

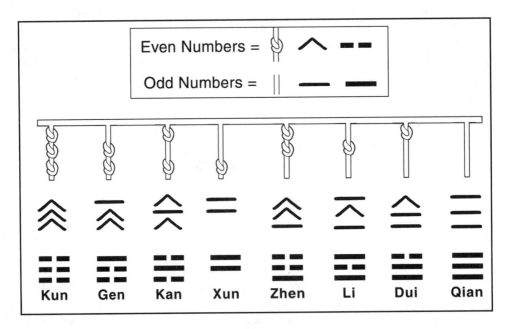

Odd and even numbers recorded by knots, symbols, and lines.

The idea was to extract the meaning of the numbers, which contained the messages from the gods. Regarding the *Yijing*, repeated divination by yarrow stalk over centuries produced a record that matched a six-term number sequence (hexagram) with a resultant human event. Over time, when divinatory interpretation became more complex, numbers weren't just numbers, they were symbols representing a plethora of different things, a kaleidoscope of images. Perhaps this is why line graphs replaced numbers. They were more ethereal. More *un*earthly and more heavenly. After all, the goal of a divination reading is to lead you to a correct path, one bestowing virtuous behavior—attributes of the gods in Heaven.

In Chapter 14, "Learning Yigua Feng Shui," you'll learn about a method of feng shui that uses the eight fundamental trigrams (the building blocks of the *Yijing*) to determine the auspiciousness of your dwelling.

The Bagua Family of Eight Trigrams

In order to figure out how the bagua correlates to the Hetu Cross, you must first call to mind the central theme of the *Yijing*—change. Referring to the following illustration, the eight fundamental trigrams are born out of the dynamic interplay of yin (female) and yang (male). While a full discussion about yin and yang can be found in Chapter 9, "Can You Spare Some Change? The Unchanging Truth About Yin and Yang," for our purposes here, understand that these dynamic forces drive life through perpetual cycles of birth, growth, decay, and death.

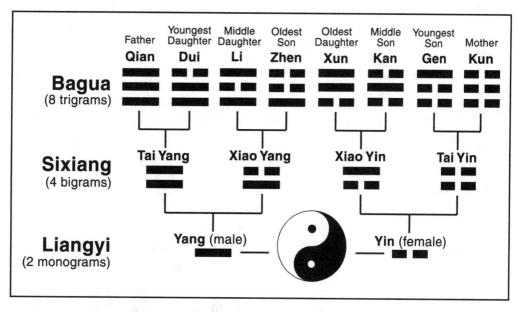

The family of eight trigrams.

Beginning at the bottom, yin and yang are collectively called the *liangyi*, the two monograms. They produce two offspring of their own. With the bottom line corresponding to the parent yin or yang line in question, yin generates *tai yin* and *xiao yin*. Conversely, yang generates *xiao yang* and *tai yang*. The four bigrams are collectively called the *sixiang*. Next, the sixiang produces the eight trigrams. Here, the bottom two lines correspond to the parent bigram in question. The result is the bagua.

Although it is not illustrated, if you multiply the eight trigrams by themselves, the result are the 64 hexagrams comprising the *Yijing*.

Wise Words

Collectively, the two dynamic forces of yin and yang are called the **liangyi,** the two monograms. The liangyi produces the four bigrams, the **sixiang:** *tai yin, xiao yin, tai yang,* and *xiao yang.* The four bigrams produce the eight trigrams, the bagua. The eight trigrams, when multiplied by themselves, produce the 64 hexagrams of the *Yijing.*

The Sixiang and the Hetu

Now that you understand how the bagua family is derived, let's correlate the sixiang (the four bigrams) to the Hetu number pairs. Referring to the following diagram, yang's offspring, tai yang and xiao yang, are matched with the Hetu number pairs, 7/2 and 8/3 respectively. Yin's offspring, tai yin and xiao yin, are associated with the number pairs 6/1 and 9/4.

Correlating the sixiang to the Hetu numbers.

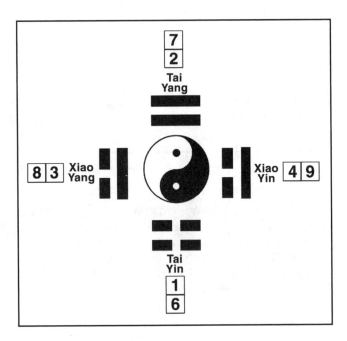

Now, let's add the bagua to our illustration.

The Xian Tian Bagua

Beginning with Qian ☰ and moving clockwise around the taiji (the composite of yin and yang), look at the following illustration. The arrangement of trigrams is called the *Xian Tian*, literally, "prior to the appearance of the phenomenal world." Like the Hetu diagram, the Xian Tian symbolizes a perfectly balanced, motionless world. It can be likened to a bird suspended in mid-air. It cannot move because movement does not exist. In the Xian Tian, father (Qian) is opposite and balanced by mother (Kun); the oldest daughter (Xun) is balanced by the oldest son (Zhen); the middle son (Kan) is balanced by the middle daughter (Li); and the youngest son (Gen) is balanced by the youngest daughter (Dui).

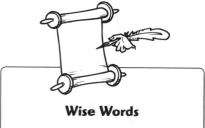

Wise Words

The **Xian Tian** or **Before Heaven** bagua represents a world in perfect balance—a world that is motionless and static, a world where change is nonexistent.

The Xian Tian bagua is also known as the *Before Heaven* sequence of trigrams.

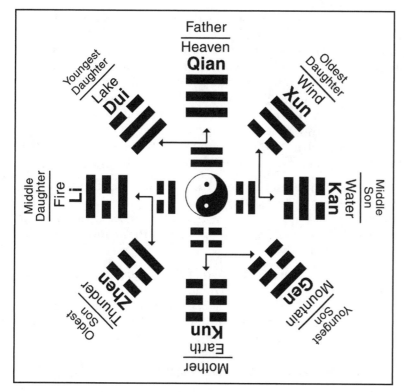

The Xian Tian or Before Heaven bagua.

Pulling the Luoshu Out of the Hetu Hat

Transforming the Hetu Cross into the Luoshu Magic Square requires you to securely fasten your thinking cap. To properly understand complicated traditions like the *Yijing* and feng shui, you must set aside your propensity to analyze and compartmentalize. You cannot allow your mind to become preoccupied with rigid black-and-white thinking. Instead, see the shades of grey. Stretch your imagination.

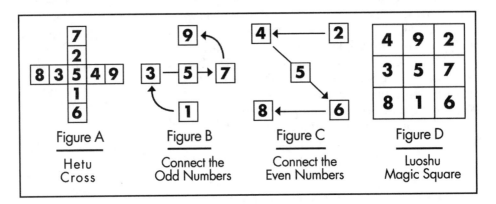

Obtaining the Luoshu from the Hetu numeric diagram.

Scholars of the Song dynasty (C.E. 960–1279) used the description provided in the *Xicizhuan* (the lower commentary to the *Dazhuan*), to reconstruct the Hetu diagram and to correlate it to the Luoshu numeric pattern. Regarding the latter, the Luoshu is derived from the Hetu by connecting the odd numbers and the even numbers in a specific fashion. Let's begin with connecting the odd (Heaven) numbers. Before we proceed, however, understand the numbers 7 and 9 have been switched from their original position on the Hetu Cross (the reason will soon become apparent). Referring to Figure B of the previous illustration, first connect number 1 with number 3. Then, connect number 3 with number 7 (formerly number 9) by passing through the central number 5. Finally, connect number 7 with number 9.

Following Figure C, let's connect the even numbers. However, we must first shift the even numbers clockwise 45 degrees such that the number 2 is stationed at the top left corner (the reason will soon become apparent). Now, connect number 2 with number 4. Then, connect number 4 with number 6 by passing through the central number 5. Finally, connect number 6 with number 8.

Upon closer examination of Figures B and C, notice that the numbers 1 and 3 and 6 and 8 move clockwise while numbers 2 and 4 and 7 and 9 move in a counterclockwise motion. What does this mean? The Song scholars believed that which ascends or revolves clockwise corresponds with the male and future time. On the other hand, that which descends or revolves counterclockwise corresponds with the female and past time. While it is beyond the scope of this chapter to discuss this notion in greater detail, the movement of each number, its inherent nature, and its "age" on the life cycle of birth, growth, decay, and death is the cornerstone of a sophisticated method of feng shui called Xuan Kong (Flying Star). You can learn the beginning level of this interesting technique in *The Complete Idiot's Guide to Feng Shui.*

By combining Figures B and C, the result is Figure D, the Luoshu Magic Square. When the bagua is applied to the numeric diagram, the configuration is called the *Hou Tian* or *After Heaven* sequence of trigrams. Unlike the motionless Xian Tian or Before Heaven sequence that is associated with the Hetu Cross, the Hou Tian depicts a world in motion. A world that follows the ceaseless cycles of birth, growth, decay, and death. How so? Well, in order to understand this, we must shift gears again. This concept cannot be explained using the familial relationships associated with each trigram. We must look to their correlative natural aspects.

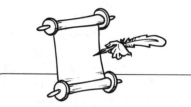

Wise Words

The **Hou Tian** or **After Heaven** bagua is related to the Luoshu. The Hou Tian sequence of trigrams denotes motion, change, and transformation.

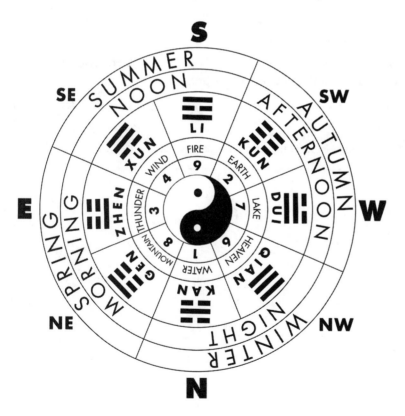

The Hou Tian or After Heaven bagua.

Beginning with the Zhen trigram in the east, spring's new growth is heralded by a clap of thunder. Also, Zhen symbolizes the birth and growth of new ideas, new beginnings, and a renewed spirit. Xun's gentle winds help to foster growth and expansion. Next comes Li. Its intense brightness epitomizes the height of summer's expansion. Fire then consumes it. Summer descends into autumn. The crops are harvested. You have matured and turned inward. It is a time of contemplation, reflection, and assessment. Qian ushers in winter. Everything is still, quiet, and dark. Heaven's bountiful bodies are clear and bright. The cycle has been completed. In Gen, clouds begin to form over the mountains. Rain and thunder herald a new cycle.

In the next chapter, you'll learn how to cast the *Yijing* using two different techniques: the yarrow stalk method and the coin-toss method.

The Least You Need to Know

➤ Heaven bestowed on Fuxi the Hetu diagram, a pattern of black (yin) and white (yang) dots that symbolize a stationary, motionless, balanced world.

➤ Fuxi invented the bagua, the eight fundamental trigrams that represent trasitional stages for all possible cosmic and human conditions.

➤ Heaven bestowed on Yu the Great the Luoshu, a pattern of black (yin) and white (yang) dots that symbolize a world in motion.

➤ The sixiang or four bigrams correlate to the four number pairs on the Hetu Cross.

➤ The Luoshu Magic Square is derived from the Hetu Cross.

Part 3

Learning to Use the *Yijing*

Now that you're knowledgeable about the background of the Yijing, you're ready to learn how to cast your fate. This part will teach you how to prepare mentally for your divination session. You'll learn the proper way to ask a question, and we'll teach you two different methods of arriving at your answer. There's the coin-toss method, where you'll need three like coins; and there's the more complex yarrow stalk procedure that uses 50 stalks from the Achillea plant (don't worry, we'll suggest compatible substitutes for this hard-to-find stalk).

Finally, we provide an amazing case study. Master Joseph Yu (the co-author of the book in your hands) used the Yijing to determine the outcome of the 2000 United States presidential election. If you doubted the Yijing's power, you'll become a bona fide believer after reading the remarkable predictions the oracle provided to Joseph's questions.

Chapter 6

How to Cast the *Yijing*

In This Chapter

➤ Preparing your mind for the divination ceremony

➤ Learning to formulate your question

➤ The yarrow stalk method

➤ The coin-toss method

When you come to a crossroad in your life's path, the *Yijing* can help provide the wisdom to see clearly the road ahead. Be it making a career decision, selecting a mate or business partner, or starting a new project or enterprise, the *Yijing* can provide clarity and insight to your concern, indecision, or problem. It will help you to take action, to "cross the great stream," a directive line appearing quite often in the hexagram texts.

While the Chinese believe their forebears influence the hexagram (the answer) they receive, you may choose to believe your own ancestors lead you to the proper course of action. Or, you may believe your answer is derived from an altogether different source. Perhaps your inner spirit, the collective consciousness of humankind, or God. Regardless from where or from whom the clarity and wisdom come, the *Yijing* produces strikingly accurate forecasts that speak directly to your situation.

In this chapter, we'll introduce two different methods of casting the *Yijing*. But before we begin, a few supplies are required. You'll need 50 stalks of yarrow (roughly 10 inches in length and one-eighth inch in diameter) and 3 like coins (pennies, nickels, dimes, or quarters). While you can reach into your pocket or piggy bank to find the coins, you can obtain yarrow stalks at your local hobby supply store. If the stalks are not readily available, you can use drinking straws (the straight ones), wooden dowels,

or wooden meat skewers (make sure the ends are blunt). If you're very ambitious, search for bamboo stalks at a good nursery or floral shop. Whatever you select, keep the casting tools clean and protected.

Cast Your Fate!

In ancient China, consulting the *Yijing* was reserved for the nobility and the elite. However, by the time of Confucius, all strata of society used the oracle. While those divining information have changed over time, the manner in which the oracle is consulted has not. Even today, the diviner must display the utmost respect and humility. Just as a person entering a place of worship should be appropriately dressed, a person consulting the oracle must be dressed appropriately, but comfortably. He or she must possess a pure mind and a pious attitude. Only then is the diviner ready and able to receive the *Yijing's* invaluable guidance.

Yi Edicts

In the old days of China, before consulting the *Yijing*, the diviner abstained from meat and alcohol for one day. The day of the divination ceremony, he (in ancient China, only men were allowed to divine) bathed, dressed in clean clothes, and then burned incense to create a sacred atmosphere.

Now, while worship services usually take place at a specific site, there is no one place where your divination ceremony must be performed. Simply find a spot away from the hustle and bustle of the busy world. It can be the room where you meditate or read. It can be your bedroom, living room, or garden. Any place that is clean, neat, and quiet, and that has a table or desk on which to perform the casting ceremony will suffice.

Ask and You Shall Receive

The question arises, "How should a question be asked?" Well, in order to obtain an accurate answer, your question must be posed in a precise way. As we discussed in Chapter 1, "Ground Zero: Understanding the Basics About the *I Ching, Book of Changes*," your answer will lead you to a situation that occurred some 3,000 years ago. What transpired in the past will pertain to what is happening to you now, and what could possibly occur in the future. The answer will yield a clear picture, an image you can follow.

It is important to understand that you consult the *Yijing* to gain knowledge about how to properly handle your situation. You do not consult the *Yijing* to receive a direct yes or no answer. Therefore, instead of asking yes or no questions, ones beginning with "is," "will," or "should," ask "what," "why," or "how" questions that inspire a feeling and invoke an innate meaning.

Here are a few examples:

Do not ask: "Should I invest in the stock market?"

Ask: "What will happen if I buy Microsoft stock this week?"

Do not ask: "Will my relationship with Fred work out?"

Ask: "What should I do about my relationship with Fred?"

Do not ask: "Should I ask her to marry me?"

Ask: "What will happen if I ask Susan to marry me tonight?"

Do not ask: "Should I move?"

Ask: "What will happen if I move to Chicago this year?"

Do not ask: "Will a business partnership be advantageous?"

Ask: "What will be the outcome of a business partnership with Henry?"

Do not ask: "Will I be promoted?"

Ask: "How can I get a promotion this year?"

Notice in these examples that the proper questions are specific. You must state about what or of whom you are speaking. Do not ask, "Should I move?" Ask, "What will happen if I move *to Chicago this year?*" Do not ask, "Should I ask her to marry me?" Ask, "Should I ask *Susan* to marry me *tonight?*" Be specific. An ambiguous question will lead to an equally ambiguous answer. But a clear and precise question will lead to a defined course of action.

When you are ready to cast the *Yijing,* wash your hands. Then write your question down on a clean sheet of paper. Close your eyes and meditate on it. Calm yourself, quiet your mind, and focus all of your attention on this question. The goal here is to send your message to the receiver (Heaven, the universal consciousness, your ancestors, your inner spirit, God). Like a computer, you must input accurate information so you can receive valid output data (your answer).

Yi Edicts

The *Yijing* cannot be used for malicious, materialistic, or vengeful reasons. For instance, you cannot ask how to avenge a person's ill will toward you. You cannot ask how to successfully cheat or rob a person. The *Yijing* is used to set you on the proper path, one promoting virtuous and honest behavior. For more information about asking questions, please refer to Appendix E, "Common Questions and Practical Answers About Divining the *Yijing.*"

Holy Stalk!: Casting the *Yijing* Using Stalks of Yarrow

There are many ways to cast the *Yijing.* The traditional and oldest method is by yarrow stalk. From beginning to end, divination by yarrow stalk takes about one hour. If you cannot devote the necessary time to complete this method, we suggest you use the coin-toss technique described later in this chapter, which takes about 15 minutes to perform.

Although divination by yarrow stalk was introduced in the *Dazhuan* or *Great Commentary* to the

Yijing, the instructions for use were inadequately conveyed. The lack of understanding was such that it was impossible to complete a cast. Song dynasty philosopher Zhu Xi (C.E. 1130–1200) solved this problem. He perfected the method that we present here.

Once you have prepared to cast the oracle, place the 50 stalks above the book in your hands (Part 4: "The 64 Hexagrams: A New Interpretation for the 21st Century," is synonymous with the *Yijing*). Set one stalk aside or place it back in its container. This stalk will not be used in the divination. With the remaining 49 stalks, you are now ready to perform the 13-step casting procedure:

1. Divide the 49 stalks into two similar bunches, but don't count them out one by one; just divide them roughly in two. Place one bunch on either side of the *Yijing.*

2. Take one stalk from the bunch on the right and place it above the *Yijing.*

3. Divide the bunch on the right into groups of fours. The last group should have 1, 2, 3, or 4 stalks. Place this last group of stalks above the *Yijing* with the single stalk.

4. Divide the bunch on the left into groups of fours. The last group should have 1, 2, 3, or 4 stalks. Place this last group of stalks above the *Yijing* with the other stalks. There should be a total of either 5 or 9 stalks above the *Yijing.*

5. Pick up the stalks on either side of the *Yijing* and bunch them together in your hands. If there are 5 stalks above the *Yijing,* you should have 44 stalks in your hand. If there are 9 stalks above the *Yijing,* you should have 40 stalks in your hand. Again, divide the stalks into two roughly similar bunches, placing one bunch on either side of the *Yijing.*

6. Repeating Step 2, take one stalk from the bunch on the right and place it above the *Yijing.*

7. Repeating Step 3, divide the bunch on the right into groups of fours. The last group should have 1, 2, 3, or 4 stalks. Place this last group of stalks above the *Yijing* with the single stalk.

8. Repeating Step 4, divide the bunch on the left into groups of fours. The last group should have 1, 2, 3, or 4 stalks. Place this last group of stalks above the *Yijing* with the other stalks. There should be a total either of 9, 13, or 17 stalks above the *Yijing.*

9. Pick up the stalks on either side of the *Yijing* and bunch them together in your hands. If there are 9 stalks above the *Yijing,* you should have 40 stalks in your hand. If there are 13 stalks above the *Yijing,* you should have 36 stalks in your hand. If there are 17 stalks above the *Yijing,* you should have 32 stalks in your hand. Divide the stalks into two roughly similar bunches, placing each bunch on either side of the *Yijing.*

10. Repeating Step 2, take one stalk from the bunch on the right and place it above the *Yijing.*

11. Repeating Step 3, divide the bunch on the right into groups of fours. The last group should have 1, 2, 3, or 4 stalks. Place this last group of stalks above the *Yijing* with the single stalk.

12. Repeating Step 4, divide the bunch on the left into groups of fours. The last group should have 1, 2, 3, or 4 stalks. Place this last group of stalks above the *Yijing* with the other stalks. There should be a total either of 13, 17, 21, or 25 stalks above the *Yijing*.

13. Pick up the stalks on either side of the *Yijing* and bunch them together in your hands. If there are 13 stalks above the *Yijing,* you should have 36 stalks in your hand. If there are 17 stalks above the *Yijing,* you should have 32 stalks in your hand. If there are 21 stalks above the *Yijing,* you should have 28 stalks in your hand. If there are 25 stalks above the *Yijing,* you should have 24 stalks in your hand. If the number of stalks above the *Yijing* does not conform to the number of stalks in your hand, you must begin the entire procedure again.

    Now divide the total number of stalks in your hand by 4: $36 \div 4 = 9$; $32 \div 4 = 8$; $28 \div 4 = 7$; $24 \div 4 = 6$.

Congratulations! You have just determined the first line (out of six) of your hexagram—the answer to your question. You must now repeat Steps 1 through 13 five more times to build a six-tiered hexagram comprised of solid and broken lines. However, before you proceed, you must understand what kind of yin ▬▬ ▬▬ or yang ▬▬▬▬▬▬ line the resulting numbers 6, 7, 8, and 9 correspond to.

Master Class

In 1971, a Han tomb was unearthed at Mawangdui in Changsha (the capital city of Hunan province). In the tomb lay a copy of the *Zhouyi* written on silk cloth. Considered to be the oldest complete divinatory manual found to date, the casting technique described in the text called for 55 stalks of yarrow (instead of the 50 prescribed in the *Dazhuan* or *Great Commentary*). Fifty-five stalks are used because the number represents the sum total of odd (Heaven) and even (earth) numbers from 1 to 10: $1 + 3 + 5 + 7 + 9 = 25$ and $2 + 4 + 6 + 8 + 10 = 30$. Whether you begin with 50 or 55 stalks, only 49 are actually used to divine your hexagram. The extra stalks represent the taiji (or the universe).

Yin, Yang, and Away We Go!

We won't discuss what the concept of yin and yang means here. This discussion is reserved for Chapter 9, "Can You Spare Some Change? The Unchanging Truth About Yin and Yang." For our purposes here, understand the even numbers 6 and 8 represent yin ▬▬ ▬▬ and the odd numbers 7 and 9 represent yang ▬▬▬▬▬. Referring to the following chart, notice the number 6 represents old yin ▬✕▬ and the number 9 represents old yang ▬⊙▬.

Yi Edicts

In Chinese, gua means hexagram; yao refers to one of the six lines comprising each hexagram.

Why are the numbers 6 and 9 old, you ask? Well, following the cycle of birth, growth, decay, and death, old yin and old yang have peaked and are ready to evolve, transform, change, and give birth to their correlative young opposites:

Old yin ▬✕▬ changes into young yang ▬▬▬▬▬.

Old yang ▬⊙▬ changes into young yin ▬▬ ▬▬.

Yarrow stalk numbers and their corresponding lines.

Number of Stalks	Number	Line (Yao)	Name
36	9	▬▬▬⊙▬▬▬	**Old Yang**
32	8	▬▬▬ ▬▬▬	**Young Yin**
28	7	▬▬▬▬▬▬▬	**Young Yang**
24	6	▬▬▬✕▬▬▬	**Old Yin**

The old yin and old yang lines play a significant role in determining which line texts of the hexagram in question you read. Also, the old lines and their subsequent transformations produce an entirely new hexagram, one that represents your future prospects. But let's not get ahead of ourselves. This notion will be fully explained later on in this chapter. For now, just symbolically record your hexagram as being either an old yin (6), young yang (7), young yin (8), or old yang (9) line.

An Example Reading

Now that you've determined the first line of your hexagram, you may wonder if the line represents the topmost or bottommost line of the six-tiered hexagram symbol. A hexagram is built from the bottom up. Therefore, Line 1 or the first cast represents the bottommost line. As you add each successive line, it is as if you are reaching toward the heavens for an answer.

To help you better understand how to assemble your hexagram, let's look at an example:

Master Class

The *Shuoguazhuan,* one of the *Ten Wings* appended to the *Zhouyi,* states: "Heaven 3 and earth 2 generate other numbers." This means that odd, yang, or Heaven numbers count forward to produce other numbers, while even, yin, or earth numbers count backward. For instance, if you count the odd numbers forward beginning with 3 (3, 5, 7, 9), the number 9 (old yang) is the last or oldest number. If you count the even numbers backward beginning with 2 (2, 10, 8, 6), the result is 6 (old yin). For reasons that are beyond the scope of this explanation, the numbers 1 and 4 are not included.

After completing Steps 1 through 13, you are left with 28 stalks. Dividing 28 by 4, the result is 7 or young yang. On the sheet of paper where you wrote your question, record this information as follows:

```
        6
        5
        4
        3
        2
Line 1  (7)  ——— 
```

After completing Steps 1 through 13 a second time, you are left with 24 stalks. Dividing 24 by 4, the result is 6 or old yin. Record this information on Line 2:

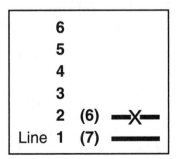

After completing Steps 1 through 13 a third time, you are left with 32 stalks. Dividing 32 by 4, the result is 8 or young yin. Record this information on Line 3:

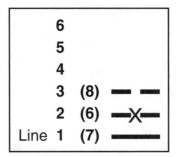

After completing Steps 1 through 13 a fourth time, you are left with 36 stalks. Dividing 36 by 4, the result is 9 or old yang. Record this information on Line 4:

After completing Steps 1 through 13 a fifth time, you are left with 32 stalks. Dividing 32 by 4, the result is 8 or young yin. Record this information on Line 5:

After completing Steps 1 through 13 a sixth (and last) time, you are left with 28 stalks. Dividing 28 by 4, the result is 7 or young yang. Record this information on Line 6:

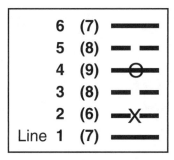

The resulting hexagram looks like this ☲☳, which is the same as this ☲☳ if you omit the "x" and the "o" denoting the line's oldness. Referring to the following Hexagram Identification Key (which can also be found on the front side of the tearcard at the front of this book), you must now identify which hexagram the example's configuration represents. Running your finger across the upper trigram key at the top of the chart, find the trigram that matches the configuration of lines 4, 5, and 6 ☲. These lines correspond to the Li trigram. Next, run your finger down the lower trigram key to determine to which trigram lines 1, 2, and 3 ☳ belong. The first three lines represent the Zhen trigram. Finally, run your finger across the Zhen row and down the Li column until they intersect. The example's configuration of solid and broken lines represents Hexagram 21.

TRIGRAMS UPPER ▶ LOWER ▼	QIAN	DUI	LI	ZHEN	XUN	KAN	GEN	KUN
QIAN	1	43	14	34	9	5	26	11
DUI	10	58	38	54	61	60	41	19
LI	13	49	30	55	37	63	22	36
ZHEN	25	17	21	51	42	3	27	24
XUN	44	28	50	32	57	48	18	46
KAN	6	47	64	40	59	29	4	7
GEN	33	31	56	62	53	39	52	15
KUN	12	45	35	16	20	8	23	2

Hexagram Identification Key

Take this time to determine your own hexagram in the same manner. The example's hexagram and your own hexagram represent your present situation. Let's see how to determine your future outlook.

What the Future Holds

The future hexagram is derived from the present one. Take another look at the example's answer, Hexagram 21:

Your present situation will help determine your future prospects. Here, lines 2 and 4 of the present Hexagram 21 change into their opposites and produce the future Hexagram 41.

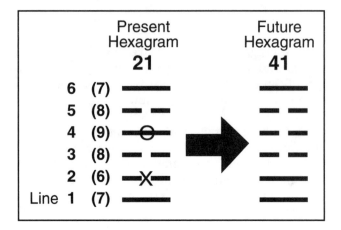

In the example's hexagram, there are two changing lines. They are line 2, old yin (6) and line 4, old yang (9). They must now be changed into their young opposites: Line 2 ─x─ (old yin) changes into ▬▬▬▬▬▬ (young yang); and line 4 ─o─ (old yang) changes into ▬▬ ▬▬ (young yin). The unchanging lines are carried over and do not change. The new configuration yields Hexagram 41 (the upper trigram Gen + the lower trigram Dui = Hexagram 41).

Take this time now to determine your own future hexagram. If your hexagram has no changing lines (in other words, if it is comprised only of a configuration of six young yin and young yang lines), then the hexagram text will describe your present *and* future situation. (You'll learn how to read and interpret a hexagram reading in the next chapter.)

Holy Coin!: Casting the *Yijing* Using Three Coins

The yarrow stalk method is time-consuming and quite complicated. Nevertheless, this is how diviners cast the oracle thousands of years ago. Because most people are impatient to receive an answer, simpler methods were developed over time. One of these is the coin-toss method. Although it is not known who invented the method, we do know it was introduced in the Tang dynasty (c.e. 618–907).

To perform the coin-toss technique, you will need three like coins (three pennies, three nickels, three dimes, or three quarters). As you did in the yarrow stalk method, you must first prepare your mind. On a clean sheet of paper write your question. While you hold the question in your mind, cup your hands around the coins and shake. Cast them on the table. Referring to the following chart, you'll find there are four possible coin combinations. The order in which the coins fall is not important.

Coin Combination	Value
Head + Head + Head	**3 + 3 + 3 = 9**
Head + Head + Tail	**3 + 3 + 2 = 8**
Tail + Tail + Head	**2 + 2 + 3 = 7**
Tail + Tail + Tail	**2 + 2 + 2 = 6**

Assigning a value of 3 to heads and a value of 2 to tails; the sum total of the coins will equal 6, 7, 8, or 9. As in the yarrow stalk method, 6 represents old yin, 7 represents young yang, 8 represents young yin, and 9 represents old yang. This idea is illustrated in the following chart:

Coin Combination	Number	Line (Yao)	Name
3 Heads	9	▬▬▬O▬▬▬	**Old Yang**
2 Heads, 1 Tail	8	▬▬▬ ▬▬▬	**Young Yin**
2 Tails, 1 Head	7	▬▬▬▬▬▬▬	**Young Yang**
3 Tails	6	▬▬X▬▬	**Old Yin**

Coin combinations and corresponding lines.

Toss the coins a total of six times, building your hexagram from the bottom line up. Refer to the Hexagram Identification Key shown earlier to determine your present hexagram, the one representing the current situation. Finally, create your future hexagram by transforming any changing lines (represented by the numbers 6 and 9) into their young opposites. Refer to the Hexagram Identification Key to determine the future hexagram's number.

Now that you understand how to cast the *Yijing* using two different techniques, you are ready to learn how to interpret your hexagram and how to relate it to your question. This is the subject of the next chapter.

Master Class

The coin-toss and yarrow stalk methods yield different probabilities for the four types of lines. In the coin-toss method, there are eight possible ways to arrive at 6, 7, 8, or 9. You have a 37.5 percent or 3/8 chance of drawing young yang (7); a 37.5 percent or 3/8 chance of drawing young yin (8); a 12.5 percent or 1/8 chance of drawing old yin (6); and a 12.5 percent or 1/8 chance of drawing old yang (9). For the yarrow stalk method, there are 16 possible ways to arrive at 6, 7, 8, or 9. You have a 44 percent or 7/16 chance of drawing young yin (8); a 31 percent or 5/16 chance of drawing young yang (7); a 19 percent or 3/16 chance of drawing old yang (9); and a 6 percent or 1/16 chance of drawing old yin (6). In other words, the changing (or old) yin lines are the hardest to draw. Regardless of which method you use, each yields equally accurate results.

The Least You Need to Know

➤ You must prepare your mind before casting the *Yijing* and find a quiet place to perform the divination.

➤ Formulate your question properly. The idea is not to get a direct "yes" or "no" answer, but to get a clear image of how best to handle the situation at hand.

➤ Casting the yarrow stalk involves 13 steps and can take about an hour. It is the original method described in the *Great Commentary* to the *Yijing*.

➤ The three-coin method is much simpler and takes about 15 minutes to perform.

Chapter 7

How to Interpret Your *Yijing* Reading

In This Chapter

➤ Change your ways, change your future

➤ Linking a question to the counsel

➤ Understanding a hexagram's parts

➤ Al Gore or George W. Bush? The *Yijing's* answer

As you learned in the previous chapter, the Chinese believe *Yijing* divination is based on receiving communication from Heaven, their pantheon of ancestors. Adherents submit a question to Heaven, which supplies an answer in the form of a hexagram. The hexagram and its six corresponding line texts tell a story, something that transpired some 3,000 years ago relative to the downfall of the Shang and rise of the Zhou dynasties.

While the scale and nature of events 3,000 years ago may be different today, the pattern of change (the birth, growth, decline, and end of your own life and circumstances) continues. The diviner's goal is to use these patterns made manifest in the changing lines of the hexagram as a guide to understanding the situation at hand, to interpreting their relevance, and to choosing to act upon the advice offered by the line text(s) (or not).

Acting on Change

Once you have determined your hexagram, you're ready to interpret its meaning and relate it to your own situation. Whether you divine by yarrow stalks or coins, the casting procedure yields a hexagram describing your *present* situation at the moment you performed the divination. The present hexagram may generate an entirely new hexagram if it contains 1, 2, 3, 4, 5, or 6 changing lines (represented only by the numbers 6 and 9). This new hexagram describes your *future* outlook, the situation *after* the changes recorded in the line texts are instituted. In other words, by changing your action and attitude according to the prescribed suggestions posed by the line text(s) in question, you can project what the future result will be: If I do this, the result will be this. Of course, you can choose not to accept or implement the advice offered. In that case, you will remain in a stagnant state of indecision and confusion, or the proposed action will lead to an undesirable outcome: If I don't do this, the result will not be this.

Let's begin with understanding how each hexagram is organized. Take this time now to thumb through a few hexagram pages located in Part 4, "The 64 Hexagrams: A New Interpretation for the 21st Century." Using Hexagram 5 as an example, notice the hexagram (and all other hexagrams) is comprised of six parts:

1. **Hexagram Heading:** Reading the graphic bar from right to left, first there's the hexagram number and its corresponding English name. Then there's the Chinese name rendered into Pinyin and its corresponding Chinese character. Finally, there's the hexagram symbol. We include the numbers 1 through 6 running alongside the hexagram to help you match the line text to the correct hexagram line.

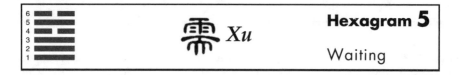

2. **Name:** Here, the name of the hexagram is defined. In this case, Xu means "waiting." You may wonder why Xu is not defined "to wait." Remember, the *Yijing* is all about change, movement, and transformation. "Waiting" is action-oriented. So is "decaying" (versus "to decay," Hexagram 18), "observing" (versus "to observe," Hexagram 20), and "influencing" (versus "to influence," Hexagram 31), and so forth.

> Xu means waiting. Specifically, Xu means waiting with anticipation.

3. **What This Hexagram Is About:** This section describes how this hexagram is relevant to the downfall of the Shang and rise of the Zhou dynasties.

> This hexagram describes how the Zhou leaders moved their tribe several times to find the most auspicious site on which to increase their prosperity. Eventually, they settled in Feng, near present-day Xi'an, where they prepared for the revolution against the Shang. Neighboring tribes joined this much-anticipated endeavor.

4. **Hexagram Statement:** This section offers an overall message, advice about how to react to your situation at hand. While the portion in italics represents a paraphrased translation of the original Chinese text, which is often archaic and nonsensical, the remaining text offers a layman's interpretation, an explanation.

> *With sincerity, there will be brilliant success. With perseverance, there will be fortune. It will be advantageous to cross the great stream.* Wait, watch, and listen. Scope out the situation. Settle in and bide your time. Patience, sincerity, and perseverance will lead you to a bright future. Something fantastic is before you. You will soon cross the threshold, engaging in an important venture (a partnership, marriage, new job).

5. **The Line Texts:** Each hexagram contains a total of six line texts. Here, we show only Line 3 as an example. Like the hexagram statement, the portion in italics represents a translation of the original Chinese text. The remaining text offers an historical perspective, a layman's explanation, and advice. "Nine on Line 2" means the number 9 is located in the second position from the bottom, Line 2. Remember, only the numbers 6 (old yin) and 9 (old yang) are studied. Hence, each line is either designated as a 6 or a 9 line.

> Nine on Line 2: *Waiting on sand will cause minor discontent. Eventually, there will be fortune.* The Zhou once moved to a sandy place near a river. Although water was difficult to retain, it was still a hospitable place. You are full of action. While the result may not be immediate, it will eventually come. Keep up the momentum.

6. **My Yi Journal:** This space is for you to record your *Yijing* divination. Keep notes, monitor your progress, and record the outcome. Only then can you know the power and accuracy of the oracle.

MY YI JOURNAL					
Date	Question	Present Hexagram	Changing Line(s)	Future Hexagram	Notes

Now that you're familiar with the distinct parts of each hexagram, you're ready to implement this information and work toward gaining a resolution to your particular dilemma.

The Lines They Are a-Changin'

Before you proceed, you must have determined your present and future hexagrams according to the instructions provided in Chapter 6, "How to Cast the *Yijing.*" Also, please locate the hexagram pages corresponding to your present and future hexagrams in Part 4. You may wish to paper clip these pages.

Are you ready? Before locating the scenario that best describes your case, we suggest you read this entire section to better understand how to interpret your *Yijing* reading, and any other readings you may conduct in the future.

Case 1: There are no changing lines. In this case, none of the six lines comprising your hexagram contain the number 6 (old yin) or 9 (old yang). Here, there is no distinction between present and future. They are one and the same. Because the hexagram suggests no changes, read *only* the hexagram statement and none of the supporting line texts. Judge by the hexagram statement what you must do to obtain the best result from the situation at hand.

Yi Edicts

In both the yarrow stalk and three-coin methods, you have a 25 percent chance of drawing a changing line and a 75 percent chance of not drawing a changing line. There is an 18 percent chance that your hexagram will contain no changing lines and a 0.02 percent chance that your hexagram will be comprised of all changing lines.

Case 2: There is only one changing line. First, read the hexagram statement corresponding to your present hexagram to gain an overall image of your situation. Then, read the changing line text. For example, if you draw Hexagram 5 and the number 6 is on Line 4, read only Line 4 of the present hexagram. Do not read any of the other line texts! Next, read the hexagram statement corresponding to the future hexagram. Do not read any of its line texts.

Case 3: There are 2, 3, 4, or 5 changing lines. This scenario represents a complicated situation, where changing factors superimpose on one another. First, read the hexagram statement corresponding to your present hexagram. Then, read the line texts corresponding to each changing line. For example, if you draw Hexagram 32 and the number 9 is on Line 2, the number 9 is on Line 3, and the number 6 is on Line 5, then read only Lines 2, 3, and 5 of the present hexagram. Next, read the hexagram statement corresponding to the future hexagram. Do not read any of its line texts.

Case 4: All lines change. Here, all six lines contain a configuration of the numbers 6 (old yin) and 9 (old yang). First, read the hexagram statement corresponding to the present hexagram. Then, read all six line texts. Next, read the hexagram statement corresponding to the future hexagram. Do not read its line texts. There are two special cases: If you draw Hexagram 1, you must also read the section called "All Lines Are Nine." If you draw Hexagram 2, you must also read the section called, "All Lines Are Six."

And the Answer Is ...

The following examples will illustrate how to link the question to the counsel, the proposed course of action:

Example 1

Question: What will happen if I move to Chicago this year?

Casting: Using the three-coin method, you draw Hexagram 3 (signifies accumulating) with no changing lines.

Hexagram statement: "… Whether you're starting a family, a new job, or a business, prepare for a rocky start. Fortify your strength and inner reserve. Appoint capable people who can help foster success. Great care must be taken in any movement. Your enterprise will prove fruitful."

Interpretation: Since the hexagram contains no changing lines, the reading is based entirely on the hexagram statement. The prediction is quite easy to understand. Although you will find the move difficult in the beginning, if you make an effort to adapt to the new environment and find new friends/associates to help you feel more comfortable, the future will be bright.

Example 2

Question: What will happen if Susan and I marry this year?

Casting: Using the three-coin method, you draw Hexagram 14 (signifies great reward) with Line 3 changing. This produces the future Hexagram 38 (signifies misunderstanding).

Present hexagram statement: "… If you have a noble spirit, others will rally to your cause. This is a time of great achievement and prosperity. Your contributions will be recognized and appreciated. However, don't let success go to your head. Accept your reward (promotion, prize, inheritance) with humility."

Line 3: "… You have done a great job! Expect a reward."

Future hexagram statement: "… With diverging viewpoints, a positive outcome can only be had in minor matters."

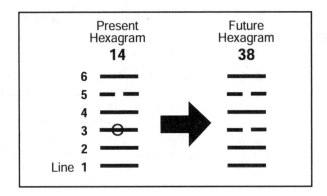

Interpretation: At a glance, the present hexagram statement seems to be irrelevant. You must link the passage to your situation and intuit its meaning. The image indicates success and prosperity. Your courtship has been successful. Your fiancée appreciates your devotion. Do not boast or brag about your good fortune to others. The line text suggests you should move forward with your wedding plans. However, if you proceed as planned, the outcome is made manifest in the future hexagram statement, which implies there will be differing views about how and where the ceremony should be conducted. There will be misunderstandings and different opinions about living as a married couple. Because getting married is not a minor matter, it is best not to act upon the advice of the line text. Postpone the wedding. Enjoy being in love and accept this as your reward. There will be no positive outcome if you marry this year. Seek the *Yijing's* advice next year.

Example 3

Question: What should I do to get promoted?

Casting: Divining with yarrow stalks, you draw Hexagram 28 (signifies a great test) with Line 4 and Line 5 changing. This produces the future Hexagram 46 (signifies rising).

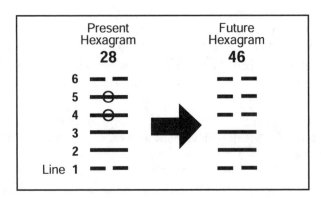

Present hexagram statement: "... The structure (company/relationship) is at its breaking point. Have a plan. Since the sickness has been diagnosed, it will be easy to cure. If your job/relationship is not supporting you, leave."

Line 4: "... The problem you face is not as big as initially assessed. To avoid trouble in the future, handle this dilemma with care."

Line 5: "... Taking action against an ill-prepared and unworthy opponent may be desirable, but it is not noble."

Future hexagram statement: "... Congratulations! You will soon be promoted. With your newly elevated status, you will be assigned an important task or responsibility. Your mission is to solve a difficult problem, mediate a dispute, or install order to a chaotic situation. Don't worry. You're well qualified. The endeavor will prove trouble-free and successful."

Interpretation: Based on this information, the chaotic atmosphere at your workplace suggests you will be promoted to help instill order. The *Yijing* advises that you use political means (which may seem inappropriate to others) to demonstrate your foresight and ability. This will help pave the way to a promotion. If you choose not to accept the *Yijing's* advice, it is best to leave your company.

These examples show how the *Yijing* offers a detailed account of your situation. If you act on the advice, the result is projected in the future hexagram. It is up to you to choose whether or not to accept and implement the changes. In many circumstances, it is advantageous *not* to accept the changes, the advice rendered by the changing lines, because doing so will produce an unfavorable outcome.

The *Yijing* Predicts the New President of the United States

While the *Yijing* is used primarily to help guide the diviner's predicament, it can also be used to provide information not directly related to the diviner. For example, on Tuesday morning, November 6, 2000 (election day in the United States), I (Joseph Yu) used the *Yijing* to determine whether Vice President Al Gore or Texas Governor George W. Bush would win the presidential race. For no particular reason, I chose Al Gore as the focus of the consultation. Let's see what the *Yijing* had to say.

Question: What are Al Gore's chances of winning the presidential election?

Casting: Divining by yarrow stalks, I drew Hexagram 51 (signifies startling) with Line 1 changing. This produced the future Hexagram 16 (signifies contentment).

Present hexagram statement: "... Something will startle your family/company/country. They will talk about it amidst laughter. Although the cause of the startling event will greatly influence your family/company/country, he/she/they will be well aware of the consequences."

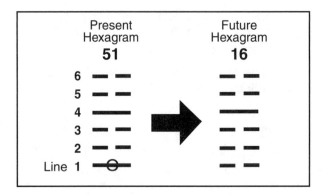

Line 1: "… Take the time to fully understand something before dismissing it."

Future hexagram statement: "… Taking action at the right time will fulfill your mind and spirit. Listen to your instincts."

Interpretation: At the time of the divination, the reading indicates the election result will startle the nation. Does this mean that Al Gore lost? If so, then why talk about it "amidst laughter"? On the other hand, if Al Gore won, then why is the nation startled? What must he "take time to understand"? Why must he "take action"?

The message from Heaven is not conclusive. Obviously, it is not a cut-and-dried situation.

Race to the White House

Of course, at the time, I had no way of knowing what would take place over the next month. I kept notes on the ensuing events to try to understand the *Yijing's* meaning:

➤ *November 8, 2000:* Early this morning, Governor Bush was briefly declared the winner. Vice President Gore called his opponent to concede the election. A short time later, Gore called Bush again to retract the concession. The victory margin in the state of Florida was too close to call. There would be a recount.

➤ *November 9, 2000:* Bush leads Gore by 327 votes in Florida. The final result hinges on the absentee ballots. Gore's legal team demands a hand count of the undervotes, votes rejected by the machines for various reasons.

➤ *November 11, 2000:* After the absentee ballots were added to the Florida tally, Bush was leading by 930 votes. It was in the hands of the Supreme Court of Florida whether to add the hand count results to the overall tally.

The *Yijing's* message begins to unfold as the events startle the candidates and the nation. Following the present hexagram statement, Gore does talk about the situation "amidst laughter." According to the November 20, 2000 issue of *Time* magazine, "When Gore put down the phone, he pumped his arm in victory, the aides around him burst into cheers, and all began to applaud."

Asking Heaven Again ...

While the answer to the first divination still stands, I asked the *Yijing* about the new situation.

Date: November 20, 2000

Question: What is the outlook for Al Gore after the Florida Supreme Court rules on November 21?

Casting: Divining by yarrow stalks, I drew Hexagram 40 (signifies separating) with Lines 2, 3, 4, and 5 changing. This produces the future Hexagram 39 (signifies obstructing).

Present hexagram statement: *"... It is advantageous in the southwest ....* If people hesitate to rally to your cause, don't worry. Your project/idea will be successful. However, if you have a support base from the get-go, you will find rapid success."

Future hexagram statement: "It is advantageous in the southwest and disadvantageous in the northeast .... You are facing a difficult period. Seek guidance and assistance from a trusted friend, counselor, or lawyer. This person will help to shed light on an arduous situation, ending the difficulty at hand. Do not attempt to figure it out on your own."

Interpretation: For space considerations, we do not include the line texts here. You can refer to these on your own. The fact that four changing lines are present, however, suggests a very complex situation. Interestingly, both present and future hexagram statements mention the auspiciousness of the southwest. Does this suggest Bush (who is based in Texas) will win and not Gore (who is based Washington, D.C.—the northeast)?

Despite the directional curiosity, the present hexagram statement indicates the Florida Supreme Court will rule in Gore's favor. Yet, the future hexagram statement is not that optimistic. Upon reading the line texts, Gore will need a strong legal team to help resolve his problem.

Here's how the events unfolded:

➤ *November 21, 2000:* The Florida Supreme Court ruled that the state official would accept the amended tally (which included the hand counts). The unanimous decision by the nine Supreme Court judges delivered a critical boost to Gore's hopes of winning the election. Bush took the case to the United States Supreme Court to reverse the ruling. The legal actions escalated.

➤ *December 4, 2000:* The United States Supreme Court asked the Florida Supreme Court to clarify its ruling permitting recounts to continue past a statutory deadline.

➤ *December 8, 2000:* The Florida Supreme Court, choosing not to reply to the United States Supreme Court's request, ruled that all undervotes not read by the voting machines be hand counted immediately. Bush appealed to the United States Supreme Court.

Unquestionably, Al Gore's legal team was proficient. The decision lay in the hands of the United States Supreme Court.

... and Again

On December 9, 2000, I asked the *Yijing* again about the final outcome of the election.

Question: What will Al Gore do after the United States Supreme Court rules on December 10?

Casting: Divining by yarrow stalks, I drew Hexagram 36 (signifies brightness wounded) with Line 1 changing. This produced the future Hexagram 15 (signifies modesty).

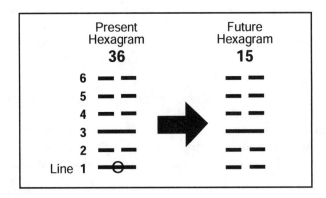

Present hexagram statement: "... Understand that darkness prevails at this time. Mean-spirited and selfish people are in control, wounding the wise and honorable person.

Hide your awareness and shield your insight. Be optimistic and look forward to brighter days. Unfortunately, there is nothing you can do but sit in the dark and wait."

Line 1: "... Don't allow troublesome events and unpleasant people to defeat your spirit. Although your principles are being challenged, maintain a positive attitude. To avoid incurring the wrath of the dark-natured person, lay low."

Future hexagram statement: "... This is a time to set aside your ego and pride. Being second in command enables you to observe, and then outsmart your opponent. Act with dignity. Be gracious and sincere. Your commendable behavior will be rewarded tenfold."

Interpretation: The resolution is crystal clear. The United States Supreme Court will not rule in favor of Gore. He has no choice but to concede graciously.

Here's how the unprecedented battle for the presidency played out:

➤ *December 10, 2000:* The United States Supreme Court stopped the Florida recount.

➤ *December 13, 2000:* The United States Supreme Court ruled that conducting manual vote recounts is unconstitutional.

On December 13, Al Gore gave a moving televised speech. Both Democrats and Republicans agreed that the Vice President acted with dignity and grace. Whether he will be rewarded tenfold remains to be seen.

The point of this exercise demonstrates the power and accuracy of the *Yijing*. Make it a habit to keep a Yi (changes) journal. Ask new questions as new situations arise. While your initial inquiry will always hold, subsequent castings will yield more refined information. Use it to your advantage. Later, when the outcome has been resolved, read your diary to gain a deeper insight and understanding of the oracle. As the saying goes, practice makes perfect.

In the next part, you'll find a new interpretation of the *Yijing*. Use it, learn from it, and respect it!

Yi Edicts

Because I used Al Gore as the subject of the *Yijing* consultation, the reading reflects his point of view. Therefore, the present hexagram statement that "Mean-spirited and selfish people are in control, wounding the wise and honorable person" reflects the opinion of Gore and his supporters. It does not mean the nine judges of the United States Supreme Court are mean and selfish!

The Least You Need to Know

➤ Once you have determined your present and future hexagrams, first read the present hexagram statement, followed by any changing line texts. Then read the future hexagram statement to gain insight about what will happen if you follow the oracle's advice.

➤ The amount of changing lines made manifest in your present hexagram indicates the level of complexity of your situation.

➤ The *Yijing* accurately predicted the result of the 2000 United States presidential race between Vice President Al Gore and Texas Governor George W. Bush.

➤ Keep a diary of your divination and record the outcome of your situation.

Part 4

The 64 Hexagrams: A New Interpretation for the Twenty-first Century

This is what the Yijing is all about—the divinatory text. Here, you'll find the answer to your concern, problem, or dilemma. You'll find wisdom and clarity that speaks to your situation directly. You'll find a direction, a path that will lead you to the proper course of action and virtuous behavior.

Unlike the plethora of other interpretations, ours is unique because we do not muddy our explanations with subjective philosophy. We tell it like it is. We offer a paraphrased translation of the original text and relate it to the events taking place during the decay and death of the Shang dynasty and the rise and fall of the Zhou dynasty. Moreover, we'll relate these events to your situation, enabling you to easily and positively intuit an answer.

Hexagram 1

Power

Name

Qian means power that can be used either constructively or destructively. Representing the sky or Heaven, Qian's impressive and dynamic force exemplifies a great undertaking.

What This Hexagram Is About

Collectively called the Upper Classic, Qian summarizes Hexagrams 3 through 30 chronicling the revolution led by King Wen to overthrow the Shang dynasty.

Hexagram Statement

Something great is about to be born. You will play an important role in this venture. Whether it's the formation of a new business or, on a smaller scale, a family. With careful preparation, you will not encounter unsolvable problems. This venture will continuously evolve, every ending marking a new beginning.

All Lines are Nine: *A group of dragons appear without a leader. There will be good fortune.* When all six lines are old yang (nine), the entire hexagram changes into Kun, Hexagram 2. Read each of the following line texts as well as those comprising Kun. The configuration of six yang lines symbolizes a group of dragons (capable people) waiting for a leader to establish an empire abounding in peace and prosperity.

Nine on Line 1: *The dragon is hidden in deep water. Do not act.* This line refers to King Wen's seven-year house arrest imposed by the tyrant Shang king, Zhou Wang. Now is not the time to begin a project, new business, or family. Wait for the opportunity to develop. In the meantime, get your ducks in a row. Plan and organize.

Nine on Line 2: *The dragon appears in the field. It is time to gather strength for a noble mission. It is advantageous to meet with the great man.* When King Wen was released from seven years of house arrest, a sentence imposed by Zhou Wang of Shang, he returned to his homeland to prepare a military campaign against the Shang tyrant. In the modern world, the assault corresponds to a meaningful project. The great man is one who can help launch it. This person can be a trusted advisor, a business partner, an accountant, and so on.

Nine on Line 3: *The nobleman works with vigor during the day and remains alert at night. If there is danger ahead it will not be damaging.* This line refers to King Wen's military planning against the Shang. Initially, you must work very hard. Examine your work for possible mistakes that could prove costly. By remaining alert and cautious, the end result will be fortunate.

Nine on Line 4: *The dragon is ready to spring from its hiding place and put its plan into action.* The Zhou army captured several outlying Shang castles as a precursor to plunging into a full-fledged war. Once your plan is organized, testing it will help to iron out any wrinkles.

Nine on Line 5: *The dragon flies in the sky. It is advantageous to see the great man.* This line refers to the fall of the Shang dynasty and the rise of the Zhou dynasty. King Wen (the great man) died before his mission was accomplished. His son, King Wu, took the helm and eliminated the Shang king. In the modern world, the scenario suggests it is advantageous to have good successors, especially those you have mentored.

Nine on Line 6: *The dragon is prone to arrogance. He is overbearing. There will be regret.* If King Wu had emulated the cruel Zhou Wang, there would have been much regret. When you are successful, you must act with integrity and fairness. Being dishonest and malicious will cause shame and misfortune.

MY YI JOURNAL					
Date	Question	Present Hexagram	Changing Line(s)	Future Hexagram	Notes

 *Kun*

Hexagram 2

Acquiescing

Name

Kun means acquiescing, complying, submitting, and accepting, qualities associated with yin and Mother Earth.

What This Hexagram Is About

Collectively called the Lower Classic, Kun summarizes Hexagrams 31 through 64, the last 34 hexagrams.

Hexagram Statement

Be firm like a mare. When the nobleman moves, he will be confused in the beginning, but will gain in the end. Like earth's nourishing soil, you are able to make things happen, give rise to things. Like a mare, be loyal and diligent. Be humble and modest. Stick to your principles and learn from your experiences. If the process of events confuses you, don't despair. You will find the right path. Befriend people in the southwest (the Zhou) and turn away from those in the northeast (the Shang).

All Lines are Six: *Persevering opens the way.* In this hexagram, the configuration of six yin lines symbolizes the proper way to serve the king. Loyalty, humility, integrity, and steadfast diligence will propel you to new levels. When all six lines are old yin (six), the entire hexagram changes into Qian, Hexagram 1. Read each of the following line texts as well as those comprising Qian.

Six on Line 1: *Tread on the frost. Gradually, it will become solid ice.* When King Wen served in the Shang dynasty, he remained cautious and composed. Think before you act. Sure-footed persistence will help to establish a solid foundation.

Six on Line 2: *The personality is straight, square, and great. Even though a person may be inexperienced, this is not a disadvantage.* This line probably refers to the Duke of Zhou's (King Wen's son) lack of experience at the beginning of the revolt against the Shang. As long as you have integrity, inexperience will not be an issue. Move forward with confidence.

Six on Line 3: *Virtuous people stick to their principles. A political career is advantageous. He may not be successful, but he will gain recognition for his contribution.* Although the Duke of Zhou was not the true leader of the Zhou, his assistance was accepted and acknowledged. You need not be the chief to be respected and rewarded. Take pride in your current position.

Six on Line 4: *The sack is tied. There will be no blame and no fame.* This line serves as a warning to those close to the king of Shang, Zhou Wang. King Wen was able to survive the Shang king's merciless and cruel wrath by appearing nonthreatening. Like a purse (sack) that conceals valuables, King Wen did not expose his talent. Carefully monitor your speech and actions. While your accomplishments may be small, you will not be defeated or chastised.

Six on Line 5: *Wear the yellow lower garment of high-ranking officers. This marks the beginning of a lustrous career.* This line suggests its author enjoyed a successful political career. Most likely, it refers to the Duke of Zhou (King Wu's younger brother). A bright future is before you.

Six on Line 6: *Dragons fight in the wilderness. The blood is dark yellow.* Referring to the battle between the king of Shang (the old ruler) and the king of Zhou (the new ruler), the dark yellow blood symbolizes the beginning of a new era. King Wu (King Wen's son) killed the Shang king, Zhou Wang, thus establishing the Zhou dynasty. The Duke of Zhou witnessed the assassination. You will witness a power struggle. The winner will make the enterprise successful.

MY YI JOURNAL

Date	Question	Present Hexagram	Changing Line(s)	Future Hexagram	Notes

 *Tun*

Hexagram 3

Accumulating

Name

Tun means accumulating. The image connotes a sprouting seed, which must draw nourishment from the earth and energy from the sun to strengthen and grow.

What This Hexagram Is About

This hexagram describes the initial growth and expansion of the Zhou people. They worked hard to accumulate wealth and formed allies with neighboring tribes to strengthen their power. Although the road to success was not always smooth, the Zhou managed to create a strong empire that lasted for some 800 years (1045 B.C.E.–C.E. 221).

Hexagram Statement

Like the sprout struggling to push through the soil, new things emerge. Expect challenges. Accumulate your strength. Begin anew and push forward. Whether you're starting a family, a new job, or a business, prepare for a rocky start. Fortify your strength and inner reserve. Appoint capable people who can help foster success. Great care must be taken in any movement. Your enterprise will prove fruitful.

Nine on Line 1: *Laying a foundation on solid rock requires persistence and perseverance. It is advantageous to establish a dynasty here.* The Zhou gathered together, mustering strength to found a new empire. It is important to stay focused, keeping your goal in sight. Move forward with your plans. Seek assistance. Allocate responsibility. You will overcome obstacles.

Six on Line 2: *Developing momentum, motivation, and strength is fraught with frustration and difficulty. When a maiden is offered a proposal of marriage, she should decline, even if she must wait 10 years for the next opportunity. The time is not right.* In the beginning, the Zhou had great difficulty establishing a unified empire. Although neighbors (suitors) wished to form alliances, the Zhou declined these offers (proposals), opting to strengthen within. Even if an opportunity seems advantageous, now is not the time to form personal or professional partnerships.

Six on Line 3: *A hunter follows a deer into the forest. The forest ranger is not available to guide the way. If the hunter is an honorable man, he will abandon the chase. If he proceeds, there will be regret.* At the beginning of the revolution against the Shang, the Zhou did not have a military expert to advise King Wen. Without such guidance, if the king had chosen to make advances, he would have been humiliated and defeated. Likewise, do not lose your way. Take heed and understand your motivation before you take action. Obtain competent advice.

Six on Line 4: *A girl sits in her carriage driven by trotting horses. A suitor approaches and proposes marriage. She should accept his offer. There will be no regret.* Once secure and confident, the Zhou united with their neighbors. Forming partnerships will bring fortune. Accept any offers that come your way.

Nine on Line 5: *When fat accumulates in the body, exercise is in order. While small-scale exercises will bring fortune, large-scale endeavors will bring misfortune.* This line refers to the Zhou's accumulation of strength (fat) and how they exercised their power for small gains. Taking small steps will open doors. Taking giant leaps when you are not ready may bring disaster.

Six on Line 6: *The girl sits in her carriage that rumbles forward. She weeps tears of blood.* This line refers to the tragic experience when the eldest son of King Wen, Ji Boyikao, was killed while attempting to rescue his father imprisoned by the Shang king, Zhou Wang. Don't let failure impede your progress. Set aside the bad and focus on the good.

		MY YI JOURNAL				
Date	Question	Present Hexagram	Changing Line(s)	Future Hexagram		Notes

Hexagram 4

Ignorance

Name

Meng means ignorance. It connotes immaturity, youthful unawareness, undeveloped potential, and foolishness.

What This Hexagram Is About

This hexagram describes how the Zhou leaders used the name of Heaven (divine authority) to control, educate, and gain the trust of the common people.

Hexagram Statement

I [the diviner] *am not* asking *the ignorant youth to seek my advice, I am* commanding *them. If my counsel is not followed and he continues to ask the same question, it is foolhardy and disrespectful. I will not advise him again. It is advantageous to be firm.* Make it clear to your apprentices, subordinates, and those under your care that you mean what you say. Implementing structure and rules will yield order, inspiring growth and maturity. You will be respected and admired for your steadfast firmness.

Six on Line 1: *It is most appropriate to use punishment to reprimand the imprudent. However, teaching the right path will help them avoid being shackled. If punishment is overused, it will prove counterproductive.* Although the Chinese used punishment to rehabilitate the wayward, it was not used to avenge a person's wrongdoing. In order to avoid untoward behavior of those under your guidance or care, establish rules and regulations. Make clear the consequences of breaking these. Administer and advise with integrity and honesty. Your words and actions will be followed and imitated.

Nine on Line 2: *It is fortunate to show patience and leniency with the ignorant. It is fortunate to marry a woman and produce children to help support the family.* Be patient with your underlings. Instruct them how to best fulfill their duties productively and honorably.

Six on Line 3: *Do not marry the woman who seeks a rich and powerful man. Such a marriage will bring no advantage.* Marrying a woman (or a man) who desires material gain and has social/professional/political stature will bring regret. When that person finds a wealthier and more influential mate, he or she will leave you. This line also applies to choosing an appropriate business partner.

Six on Line 4: *Enveloping yourself in ignorance brings regret.* This line refers to the people loyal to the Shang empire. They could not accept a change for the better. If you wear blinders, there will be misfortune. Set aside your ego. Be patient. Have an open mind.

Six on Line 5: *Having the innocence and naiveté of a child is fortunate.* It's easier to teach someone who has no knowledge and is willing to learn than someone whose mind is set and can't be changed. Select the inexperienced one. You will not regret your decision.

Nine on Line 6: *Strike at ignorance. It is unfortunate to attack, but fortunate to defend.* Referring to verbal and physical assault, resist the temptation to strike first. If you must defend, know how to counterattack.

MY YI JOURNAL					
Date	Question	Present Hexagram	Changing Line(s)	Future Hexagram	Notes

 *Xu*

Hexagram 5

Waiting

Name

Xu means waiting. Specifically, Xu means waiting with anticipation.

What This Hexagram Is About

This hexagram describes how the Zhou leaders moved their tribe several times to find the most auspicious site on which to increase their prosperity. Eventually, they settled in Feng, near present day Xi'an, where they prepared for the revolution against the Shang. Neighboring tribes joined this much-anticipated endeavor.

Hexagram Statement

With sincerity, there will be brilliant success. With perseverance, there will be fortune. It will be advantageous to cross the great stream. Wait, watch, and listen. Scope out the situation. Settle in and bide your time. Patience, sincerity, and perseverance will lead you to a bright future. Something fantastic is before you. You will soon cross the threshold, engaging in an important venture (a partnership, marriage, new job).

Nine on Line 1: *Waiting in the distant outskirts requires perseverance. There will be no mistake.* The Zhou distanced themselves from the Shang capital, where they were subject to torment by the tyrant Shang king, Zhou Wang. Although they were far enough away to avoid his wrath, there was still much anxiety and anticipation of danger. Stay away from those who pose a threat to you. Wait with patience. For the time being, it is the only thing you can do.

Nine on Line 2: *Waiting on sand will cause minor discontent. Eventually, there will be fortune.* The Zhou once moved to a sandy place near a river. Although water was difficult to retain, it was still a hospitable place. You are full of action. While the result may not be immediate, it will eventually come. Keep up the momentum.

Nine on Line 3: *Waiting in the mud will invite bandits.* Building a capital isolated from neighboring allies was not advantageous for the Zhou. You are exposed to those who will take advantage of your vulnerability; you are secluded from benefactors and allies who can help further your cause. Without the assistance of like-minded people, you are spinning your wheels, going nowhere fast. You are stuck.

Six on Line 4: *Waiting in a hazardous cave is life-threatening.* In ancient China, many people lived in caves. Upon the first rumbling of a landslide, the inhabitants hastened to flee. Danger is imminent! Act quickly. Leave your present relationship. Abandon any undertaking. It is not going to work.

Nine on Line 5: *Waiting with an abundance of food and wine is fortunate only if there is perseverance*. This line refers to the Zhou's final move to Feng, where natural conditions proved favorable. Celebrate! You're in the right place/job/relationship. Wait patiently for further developments. Good things are coming your way.

Six on Line 6: *Go in the cave. Three unexpected guests are coming. Welcoming them with respect will bring prosperity*. Neighboring tribes wished to join the Zhou's revolution against the Shang oppression. You will encounter an unexpected opportunity. Embrace it (a new job, relationship, business partnership/alliance) with open arms.

	MY YI JOURNAL				
Date	Question	Present Hexagram	Changing Line(s)	Future Hexagram	Notes

 **Song**

Name

Song means litigating. The character consists of two components: "speak" on the left side and "public" on the right side. Conflict, dispute, seeking justice, and lodging a complaint are also symbolic of Song.

What This Hexagram Is About

This hexagram describes King Wen's affiliation with the Shang government, where he was summoned to serve as ruler of the vassal state of Zhou. While in office, King Wen publicly opposed the Shang king's wanton cruelty. This led to a seven-year house arrest sentence.

Hexagram Statement

Your sincerity is being obstructed. Do not follow through with legal proceedings. It is advantageous to meet with the great man. It is disadvantageous to cross the great stream. This is not a time to seek justice. Do not start a legal battle or a major dispute. Do not be forceful or insistent. Such actions will cause regret. If the dispute cannot be resolved, compromise or withdraw. By all means, don't let emotions carry you forward. Remain calm. Ally with people who share your viewpoint.

Six on Line 1: *Do not litigate. Although slander may damage your reputation, seeking judicial retribution is a mistake. Voice your complaint publicly. The outcome will be favorable.* Litigation against powerful people or corporations will not lead to satisfactory results. Make your point public and cease further action.

Nine on Line 2: *This is a no-win situation. Withdraw your case. Hide in a small town with only 300 families. There will be no misfortune.* Although justice would have prevailed, many times King Wen held his tongue against the Shang king. Fighting a winless battle against the powerful is unwise. Pick your battles.

Six on Line 3: *Return to your homeland and rally support. Dangerous as the situation may seem, there will be fortune in the end. Continuing to serve the king will yield no reward.* King Wen realized the Shang government was weak. Upon being freed from house arrest, he returned to his homeland to rally support against the Shang king. Start your own business and become a competitor. Give up a relationship and strike a new beginning.

Nine on Line 4: *The case is lost. Submit to Heaven's will. Keep quiet and remain peaceful. There will be good fortune.* King Wen was unable to reason with the Shang king, so he let fate take its course. Do not engage in conflict with the irrational and foolish. They will reap what they sow. They are a lost cause.

Nine on Line 5: *You will win the case. The outcome is fortunate.* Although King Wen did not win the Shang king's verdict, he won the people's support. Make your point of view known. The result will be positive.

Nine on Line 6: *Although you are awarded the leather belt, it will be taken away from you three times in one morning.* Even if King Zhou of Shang bestowed King Wen with honors and gifts for his loyal service, they would have been taken from him repeatedly. You cannot succeed in your situation. Your award (promotion, prize, inheritance) will be revoked three times within a short period.

				MY YI JOURNAL	
Date	Question	Present Hexagram	Changing Line(s)	Future Hexagram	Notes

 *Shi*

Hexagram 7
Mobilizing Troops

Name

Shi means mobilizing troops. In Chinese, the phrase "A mighty shi with one million soldiers" connotes a force to be reckoned with.

What This Hexagram Is About

This hexagram describes how the Zhou leaders (under the Shang flag) conquered enemies of the Shang dynasty, thus gaining the ruler's confidence. These military excursions also helped to unify and strengthen the Zhou people.

Hexagram Statement

With firmness, the experienced leader will make no mistake. There will be fortune. Staunch determination and unwavering commitment is needed to lead any kind of group. Rally your supporters. Organize, control, and instill order. Launch your campaign with unabashed confidence. Leave no room for error. Go for it.

Six on Line 1: *If a military campaign is not organized, there will be misfortune.* King Wen understood that discipline was key to a successful campaign. Without obedience and organization, there is chaos and defeat. Get things under control. Appoint capable people to help carry your effort forward.

Nine on Line 2: *Being the general is advantageous. There will be no blame. The king will assign three important missions to you.* Here, "general" refers to King Wen; "king" refers to King Zhou of Shang. This line indicates the Shang king was pleased with King Wen's military expertise. Your talent is appreciated. You will be entrusted with important assignments.

Six on Line 3: *Corpses are carted away from the frontline. It is disastrous.* Despite being a competent general, King Wen suffered setbacks and human loss. This is an unfavorable divination, suggesting you may have made a disastrous mistake.

Six on Line 4: *The army retreats to the left. There is no mistake.* When the situation looked unfavorable, King Wen led his troops to a safe place to regroup and revitalize. It is unwise to move forward if you or your staff are not prepared. You're only as strong as your weakest link. Take a time out.

Six on Line 5: *There are birds in the field. It is advantageous to bargain for peace. There will be no mistake. If the leader insists on fighting to the bitter end, despite a depleted legion, there will be disaster.* This line exemplifies King Wen's wisdom. After gaining a small victory, he called for a truce. Why continue fighting and jeopardize more lives? Such foolishness only leads to disaster. If you have the upper hand, come to an agreement.

100

Six on Line 6: *When the war ended, the king ordained the victors. It is time to establish states and install feudal families. Do not appoint incapable people.* Because of their military success, King Wen and his men were rewarded with aristocratic titles and allowed to rule the vassal state of Zhou. After the completion of a successful project, you may be promoted. Surround yourself with helpful and knowledgeable people.

		MY YI JOURNAL			
Date	Question	Present Hexagram	Changing Line(s)	Future Hexagram	Notes

 *Bi*

Hexagram 8

Alliance

Name

Bi means alliance. Teamwork, collaboration, and partnership are also indicative of Bi.

What This Hexagram Is About

This hexagram describes how tribes allied with the Zhou after the Zhou conquered the Shang enemies.

Hexagram Statement

Sincerity and integrity will yield positive results. The tribes who are restless will join you. Those who come too late will lose out. Things are coming together. It's a good time to form partnerships and network with people who can help you or your enterprise grow and prosper. Expand your horizons. Make new friends. Connect!

Six on Line 1: *A mistake is not made if an alliance is formed with trustworthy people. When sincerity fills a vessel, there will be unexpected fortune.* King Wen's success in forming alliances was due to his honest intentions, good will, and genuine concern for the welfare of the people. Good things happen to good people.

Six on Line 2: *Forming alliances within the Shang empire is advantageous.* The seeds of rebellion were sown from within the Shang empire, the dukes and earls pledging their allegiance to King Wen. Establish and nourish long-term relationships. Do not burn a bridge.

Six on Line 3: *Seek alliances with bandits.* To avoid trouble, King Wen formed alliances with hostile barbarians who once raided Shang and Zhou villages. Make an enemy your friend. Turn a negative situation into a positive one.

Six on Line 4: *Forming alliances with tribes outside the Shang empire is advantageous.* King Wen sought alliances with tribes outside the Shang domain, their assistance and support proving an integral part of the revolution against the Shang. Make friends with people in other organizations. You may need to ask for their help in the future.

Nine on Line 5: *What is the most effective way to form an alliance? When the king hunts, he directs the game in three directions. The animals that stay in front are allowed to escape.* Similar to releasing immature fish back into the sea, King Wen did not force other tribes to ally with him. Those who were unwilling were allowed their choice. This guaranteed the quality of the alliance. Do not force your opinion on others. You cannot change someone's mind.

Six on Line 6: *If the alliance does not have a leader, there will be misfortune.* King Wen led the revolution against the Shang. Without him, the military assault would have been misguided and subject to failure. Leadership in any partnership is necessary to maintain the focus and strength of the group/company. A leader should appoint a successor to safeguard the longevity of the group/company.

		MY YI JOURNAL			
Date	Question	Present Hexagram	Changing Line(s)	Future Hexagram	Notes

小畜 *Xiao Chu*

Hexagram 9

Small Savings

Name

Xiao Chu means small savings.

What This Hexagram Is About

This hexagram describes the Zhou's inability to expand while under the rule of the Shang empire.

Hexagram Statement

Although the western suburbs were overcast, it didn't rain. The "western suburbs" refer to the Zhou territory, which was located in the western region of the Shang empire. The gathering clouds symbolize the mobilization of troops, and the call to action (rain) refers to overthrowing the Shang. The time to take action is approaching. Be ready!

Nine on Line 1: *After gaining a small victory, the Zhou returned to their homeland. How can this be a mistake? There will be good fortune.* In the beginning, the Zhou could celebrate only small gains. After an assault, they returned home to ground themselves, strengthening their home base. This was the right course of action, the virtuous thing to do. Accumulate wealth slowly and steadily. Buy and hold is the best strategy. In the same way, progress up the corporate ladder. Enjoy each rung. While you should take pride in your accomplishments, by all means, don't brag about them! Stay centered.

Nine on Line 2: *It is fortunate to walk hand-in-hand with your allies.* By sharing his success with his allies, King Wen strengthened their bond. Give credit where credit is due. Praise those who have helped to make you successful. Don't be cheap. Reward your supporters for their efforts. Spreading the wealth will help to raise you to new levels.

Nine on Line 3: *The carriage wheel's brake is released, causing the husband and wife to quarrel.* The Zhou decision-makers could not agree on many issues. Like a runaway carriage, their leadership was out of control. While some favored more aggressive tactics, others wished to be more conservative and cautious. Bickering and discord will ruin your relationship/enterprise. You cannot progress until there is agreement.

Six on Line 4: *Sincerity and awareness of bloodshed will not bring regret.* Loss of human life is inevitable in a revolution. In order to minimize casualties, King Wen proceeded with caution. Although warfare is unpleasant, you must show how it benefits your enterprise. If you install ordinances with sincerity, your followers will not revolt. Like bitter herbs that are unpalatable, they are good for your health.

Nine on Line 5: *Uniting with others will attract support from neighbors who want to share in the wealth.* Those who pledged allegiance to King Wen were unwavering in their devotion. Such support led to a wealth of spirit that enticed others to join his venture. Steadfast determination and enthusiasm will drive your project forward. Expect others to rally to your cause.

Nine on Line 6: *It finally rained, and then stopped. People were mindful of virtues like women who observe chastity. Although the moon was almost full, launching a full-scale attack will bring misfortune.* The Zhou captured several remote Shang castles to test their military skill. Yet, the time wasn't right for a full-scale assault. They needed to rally more support and proclaim their intention to liberate the oppressed. Explain in fuller detail your ideas to those from whom you seek assistance. Although the appropriate time is nearing, it is still too early to launch your project.

MY YI JOURNAL

Date	Question	Present Hexagram	Changing Line(s)	Future Hexagram	Notes

 **Lu**

Hexagram 10

Treading

Name

Lu means treading.

What This Hexagram Is About

This hexagram describes how appropriate actions were taken to oppose the cruel king of Shang, Zhou Wang.

Hexagram Statement

Treading on the tail of the tiger without being bitten by him is fortunate. The tiger symbolizes the tyrant. Treading on his tail enables you to gauge his reaction. By understanding your competition's strengths and weaknesses, you are better able to defeat him. Experience must be gained by testing the waters. Only then are you able to plot the perfect plan.

Nine on Line 1: *Treading forward on the familiar path is not a mistake.* The familiar path refers to the play-it-safe strategy. If you don't draw attention to yourself, the tiger will not place you under suspicion. Creep softly under the barbed wire. A conservative approach is best.

Nine on Line 2: *The path is level and straight. Move forward like a hermit.* King Wen's mission to overthrow the Shang dynasty was on the right path. Like a hermit who is focused, determined, and utterly justified in his decision to separate himself from the world, King Wen concentrated on the mission at hand. In the same way, you must focus on your project/job/relationship. Right now, this is your primary concern.

Six on Line 3: *The blind believes he can see. The lame believes he can walk. To tread on the tail of the tiger and be bitten brings great misfortune. It is similar to a street fighter believing he is an invincible king.* King Wen understood his plan must be fail-safe before launching a full-scale revolution. Visions of grandeur will lead to misfortune. Don't bite off more than you can chew. If your plan isn't sound, revise it.

Nine on Line 4: *Treading with caution upon the tiger's tail will bring eventual fortune.* Proceeding step-by-step, King Wen cautiously tested Zhou Wang's reaction. Because King Wen was prepared, his campaign was won. When it's all systems go, move forward with caution. The fittest will survive. You will be successful.

Nine on Line 5: *He treads with determination. If he is over-confident and inflexible, there will be danger.* In any venture, you must expect challenges and the unexpected. Have a Plan B. Be flexible. Errors come at the most inopportune time. Lack of preparation for the unforeseen invites danger.

Nine on the Top: *Examine the trodden path. The victory will be repeated. There will be a fortunate outcome.* After a successful battle, King Wen reviewed its details. This laid the foundation for future victories. Examine your work with great care. Putting your best foot forward will lead to brilliant success.

		MY YI JOURNAL			
Date	Question	Present Hexagram	Changing Line(s)	Future Hexagram	Notes

 *Tai*

Hexagram 11

Prominence

Name

Tai means prominence. Eminence and abundance are also indicative of Tai.

What This Hexagram Is About

Hexagrams 11 and 12 are opposites. While Tai describes the prosperous beginnings of the Shang dynasty, Pi (Hexagram 12) describes its downfall. Together, they serve as a valuable lesson about the effect of corruption on a nation.

Hexagram Statement

The small gives way to the great. What is insignificant, petty, and unimportant is departing. What is great, important, and magnificent is arriving. Progress yields success. It will be fortunate. This is a time of new beginnings. Although you may have to take one step back to progress two steps forward, don't fret; you're headed in the right direction. Stay focused. Act with integrity and sincerity.

Nine on Line 1: *Remove the weeds that damage the roots. It is a good time to attack.* The elimination of the Xia dynasty's last ruler, the tyrannical Xia Jie, marked the beginning of the Shang era. Disengage from malicious and manipulative people. Subjecting yourself to another's misery causes depression and anxiety. Weed these people out of your life. Such action will bring positive results.

Nine on Line 2: *Gather uncultured people from all directions. Do not neglect capable people who live afar. Employ those who can cross the river without a boat. You may have to disregard some friends. Act with fairness.* These lines capture the strategy of the early Shang leaders. Fairness was secured by giving everyone an equal opportunity to serve in the government. Avoid preferential treatment. Select those who are truly worthy of the task at hand. Such is the quality of a good leader.

Nine on Line 3: *There is no plain without a slope. What has passed will return. Persevere in difficult times. There will be no mistake. Sincerity will bring happiness.* Like any nation, the Shang experienced times of peace and plenty followed by periods besieged with turmoil and discord. With perseverance, a positive attitude, and sincerity, the good days will replace the bad. Hold firm during difficult periods. Appreciate the good ones.

Six on Line 4: *Rich resources are not reliable. Invite neighbors and trust them to work amicably.* The Shang dynasty prospered because they had multitudes of manpower to extract an abundance of natural resources. A fantastic opportunity is before you. Use your connections to help implement your idea. Share your success with those who have helped to pave the way.

Six on Line 5: *The Shang king, Di Yi* (Zhou Wang's father), *married his youngest sister* (Tai Si) *to Ji Chang* (who later became King Wen). *The betrothal marked the beginning of great fortune.* Like his father Ji Li, Chang was betrothed to a Shang princess. The marriage between two powerful tribes was necessary to fortify the Shang ruler's position. Merging with another company, or marrying the appropriate person, will strengthen both parties.

Six on Line 6: *The wall of the castle fell into the moat. Military action should be avoided. The feudal lords do not obey orders. Being firm will bring regret.* Because of the flagrant corruption infesting the Shang government, the entire empire was in turmoil. Therefore, expecting the commoners to trust its leadership was delusional. If there's a problem at home, it needs to be cured from within. If disloyalty and dishonesty plague your workplace, you will lose business. Outsiders cannot trust what is not trustworthy.

MY YI JOURNAL

Date	Question	Present Hexagram	Changing Line(s)	Future Hexagram	Notes

Hexagram 12

Adversity

Name

Pi means adversity, obstruction, misfortune, and great difficulty.

What This Hexagram Is About

Pi suggests impending hardship. Adversity and prominence are two sides of a coin. One cannot exist without the other. This hexagram describes the fall of the Shang dynasty.

Hexagram Statement

Mean people obstruct the way. It is disadvantageous for the honorable man to insist on honesty and integrity. The great is leaving; the small is coming. During the late Shang dynasty, people lived in fear, darkness, and despair. Beset by corruption and cruelty, they allied with King Wen, who promised to liberate them from oppression. Worthless and selfish people, who serve only to insult, humiliate, and obstruct, are blocking your development. Free yourself from their grip.

Six on Line 1: *Remove the weeds that damage the roots. It is important to remain virtuous and persistent.* In the early days of Zhou Wang's rule, he was a virtuous and trustworthy king. He removed the devious, those who would jeopardize the integrity of the throne. Distance yourself from dishonest and malicious people. There will be positive results.

Six on Line 2: *Flattery was gladly received. It was fortunate for the self-serving and mean, and dismal for the honorable person.* Later in his rule, the Shang king began to embrace flatterers. He detached himself from his honorable officers. Flattery is the first sign of darkness in power. Inflating a person's ego leads to a corrupt spirit. Be honest to yourself and to others.

Six on Line 3: *Hiding that which is shameful.* The self-serving person hid his shameful deeds carefully. He did not want to fall out of grace with the Shang king, Zhou Wang. Be wary of the person whose words don't match his of her actions. You are being deceived. Be on guard.

Nine on Line 4: *Act in accordance with Heaven and there will be no mistake. Those who share a noble goal will be fortunate.* King Wen was destined to liberate the people from Zhou Wang's tyranny. Assume a great responsibility. Initiate a radical change. Make the world a better place. You and your followers will revel in the success.

Nine on Line 5: *The obstruction was about to be removed. This proves fortunate for the honorable person. Solidarity will prevail.* This line refers to the rise of King Wen. Other tribes joined the revolution. There is light at the end of the tunnel. Move forward as a cohesive unit and the bright days will come.

Nine on Line 6: *The obstruction was finally removed. Happiness followed distress.* King Wen's son, King Wu, killed the king of Shang, Zhou Wang. The nightmare came to an end. The removal of obstruction leads to a clear path. Success awaits you.

MY YI JOURNAL					
Date	Question	Present Hexagram	Changing Line(s)	Future Hexagram	Notes

Hexagram 13

Assembling People

Name

Tong Ren consists of two characters: On the left side, Tong means union; on the right side, Ren means people. Together, Tong Ren denotes the assembling of people (alliances).

What This Hexagram Is About

This hexagram describes how King Wen assembled tribal leaders to form his military campaign against the Shang. Moreover, it describes his military tactics.

Hexagram Statement

Gathering people in the wilderness is a safe measure. It is advantageous to cross the great stream. It is advantageous for the honorable man to proceed. There will be success. In order not to arouse Zhou Wang's suspicion, King Wen assembled his legions in the backwoods to prepare for the revolution against the Shang. Muster support and form alliances quietly and quickly. With proper preparation, your idea will come to fruition. Be ready for a great adventure.

Nine on Line 1: *Gather outside the gate. There will be no mistake.* King Wen allied with people other than his own. Befriend and partner with acquaintances and strangers. This will broaden your prospects.

Six on Line 2: *Including only those who share the same lineage is a mistake.* Had King Wen allied with only people who were closely related to him, the result would have been shortsighted and regrettable. Partnering with only those with whom you are familiar indicates lack of courage and foresight. You will regret your decision later.

Nine on Line 3: *Hide the army in the bushes. Monitor the enemy on the mound. Look for an opportunity to advance.* Because of the strength of the Shang army, King Wen did not take action against them for three years. Play it safe. Make sure you understand your competitor. Be patient and attack only when you're sure to win.

Nine on Line 4: *Mounted on the enemy's wall, he did not attack.* When King Wen gained the upper hand, he ceased further military action. By doing this, he gained respect and won the people's affection. When you are victorious in battle (litigation, competition), show benevolence. Sportsmanship and goodwill are admirable qualities.

Nine on Line 5: *After the victory, the allies met. They cried first, and then laughed.* After King Wen's allies captured a Shang castle, they rallied to celebrate their victory. When you and your partner(s) have accomplished something great, celebrate your success. It will be a memorable moment.

Nine on Line 6: *The allies met in the outskirts with no regret.* Because they did not want to disturb the Shang commoners, King Wen and his troops gathered away from the captured castle. This display of justice left nothing to regret. When you are the winner, show compassion toward the loser.

MY YI JOURNAL					
Date	Question	Present Hexagram	Changing Line(s)	Future Hexagram	Notes

6
5
4
3
2
1

大 有 *Da You*

Hexagram **14**

Great Reward

Name

Da You consists of two characters: On the left side, Da means great; on the right side, You means reward. Together, Da You means great reward.

What This Hexagram Is About

King Wen (called Ji Chang at this time) led several great battles under the Shang flag. For each victory, the Shang king rewarded him with impressive gifts. However, the conquered people who recognized King Wen as the more honorable leader, bestowed on him the true reward—loyalty.

Hexagram Statement

Great reward indicates that from the beginning, your action was destined to be successful. The gifts bestowed by King Zhou of Shang to King Wen were token rewards. The greater reward was the conquered people's allegiance to him. If you have a noble spirit, others will rally to your cause. This is a time of great achievement and prosperity. Your contributions will be recognized and appreciated. However, don't let success go to your head. Accept your reward (promotion, prize, inheritance) with humility.

Nine on Line 1: *There is nothing wrong with opposition. If difficulty is anticipated, there will be no mistake.* In battle, King Wen expected resistance. Do not underestimate your competition. Be prepared for difficult moments. Such awareness will help you to overcome obstacles.

Nine on Line 2: *Large carriages were loaded with weapons and supplies. The direction to proceed did not matter. There will be no mistake.* In each battle, the Zhou legions had an abundance of supplies. To ensure success, you must have ample support. Replenish your supply cabinet.

Nine on Line 3: *The Son of Heaven* (Zhou Wang, the Shang king) *honored the dukes with a royal banquet. People with no achievements could not expect the same treatment.* When the Zhou leader (posthumously named King Wen) and other officers returned from victory, Zhou Wang honored them with a royal banquet. You have done a great job! Expect a reward.

Nine on Line 4: *If he is not arrogant, there will be no mistake.* Because of King Wen's modesty, the Shang king did not feel threatened. Be humble and you will not be subjected to jealousy, gossip, and other untoward acts.

Six on Line 5: *Sincerity won him the hearts of the people. People looked upon him as a benevolent ruler. It is advantageous.* The conquered returned King Wen's sincerity.

Remember the Golden Rule: Do unto others as you would have them do unto you. Sincerity fosters loyalty.

Nine on Line 6: *Heaven blessed him. Nothing disadvantageous will befall him.* King Wen was destined by Heaven to become a leader. You, too, are destined to lead. Positive results await you.

Date	Question	Present Hexagram	Changing Line(s)	Future Hexagram	Notes

MY YI JOURNAL

 **Qian**

Hexagram 15

Modesty

Name

Qian means modesty. In China, being modest is not only considered virtuous, it is used as a strategic tactic when dealing with other countries.

What This Hexagram Is About

This hexagram describes King Wen's humility. The evil Shang king, Zhou Wang, never felt threatened by such a humble man.

Hexagram Statement

The honorable man will eventually reign victorious. Set aside your ego and pride. Being second in command enables you to observe, and then outsmart your opponent. Act with dignity. Be gracious and sincere. Your commendable behavior will be rewarded tenfold.

Six on Line 1: *The honorable man is humble and gentle. His aspiration is to cross the great stream* (accomplish something great). *There will be fortune.* Admired for his meekness and fairness, King Wen hid his great ambition to overthrow the Shang dynasty. While masking your talent and ambition will help to pave the way for success, boasting of your intentions will cause failure and rejection.

Six on Line 2: *His humility will carry his name far and wide. His determination will bring him great fortune.* People everywhere adored King Wen. While you can relish your stellar reputation, remain humble. This is the correct behavior. You will be blessed with good fortune.

Nine on Line 3: *The honorable man is hard-working and humble. He will be successful.* King Wen was determined. He was a man of action and not words. This led to his success. Work quietly behind the scenes and your efforts will be recognized in the end.

Six on Line 4: *He set the standard for modest behavior. There will not be disadvantage.* King Wen's followers modeled their behavior after his. Following his example is advantageous.

Six on Line 5: *A lack of wealth leads a person to ally with his neighbors. After a successful conquest, let them have their fair share.* The Zhou were not rich. After a successful assault, King Wen shared the wealth with his allies. Such action strengthened the alliance. Be fair to your friends and co-workers and they will support you wholeheartedly.

Six on Line 6: *His humility is well-known. His allies are willing to participate in the military campaign.* Being humble and approachable, King Wen was able to muster the necessary strength to avenge the Shang tyrant, Zhou Wang. Be humble and people will work with you to achieve something great. Have an open-door policy.

MY YI JOURNAL					
Date	Question	Present Hexagram	Changing Line(s)	Future Hexagram	Notes

 *Yu*

Hexagram 16

Satisfying

Name

Yu means satisfying. Yu suggests that if a person follows his or her destiny, that person will lead a satisfied, contented, and harmonious life.

What This Hexagram Is About

This hexagram describes King Wen's skill at taking action at the appropriate time. To do so ensures satisfactory results and impending joy.

Hexagram Statement

When the morale is high, it is time to pursue further military action and establish feudal states. King Wen was an expert diviner, who used his skill to help keep track of the ebb and flow of the people and of the revolution. Because he was able to lead his people at the appropriate time, all were empowered with a sense of accomplishment, satisfaction, and contentment. Taking action at the right time will fulfill your mind and spirit. Listen to your instincts.

Six on Line 1: *Overconfidence leads to arrogance.* King Wen warned his troops not to slack off. Letting their guards down would enable the enemy to take them by surprise. Do not become conceited over an early achievement. Remain diligent and alert. Keep up the good work.

Six on Line 2: *The path is blocked by a large rock. With determination, he found an alternate route by day's end. There will be fortune.* Because the timing of his military assault was crucial to its success, King Wen could not let obstruction delay the mission. Likewise, do not let obstacles hinder your progress. Seek an immediate solution.

Six on Line 3: *He is satisfied with his success. He will be remorseful if he doesn't wake on time.* Do not indulge in the pleasure of success. Begin a new project before you lose your drive and motivation. If you wait too long, it will be too late. Procrastination leads to lethargy.

Nine on Line 4: *There is good reason to be joyful. The success is tremendous. Let the allies celebrate so that they will have no doubts.* Do not doubt your action or decision. You did the right thing. Celebrate and enjoy your victory with friends, family, and associates.

Six on Line 5: *Confidence is the best medicine for disease. With confidence, a person will not die.* King Wen understood that to err is human. However, if a mistake is corrected with sincerity and poise, the outcome will not be disastrous. Stick to your principles. Correct your mistakes and shortcomings. The consequences will not be serious.

Six on Line 6: *The joy and satisfaction will eventually fade. It is time for a new venture. There will be no mistake.* When the excitement of success has subsided, it's time to plan another project. Do not dwell on past glories. Move on.

		MY YI JOURNAL			
Date	Question	Present Hexagram	Changing Line(s)	Future Hexagram	Notes

 *Sui*

Hexagram 17

Following

Name

Sui means following.

What This Hexagram Is About

The revolution against the Shang was in full force, King Wu having taken up the cause after his father passed away. There were many followers. Some were newcomers, and some were opportunists. They would affect the course of events that followed the downfall of the Shang dynasty.

Hexagram Statement

What follows will be progressive success. It is advantageous to stick to your principles. There will be no mistake. The revolution was expected to succeed. By remaining virtuous, King Wu created a dynamic empire without oppression. Follow your destined path. Follow through with an idea or a promise. If you hold fast to your ethics and values, there will be success.

Nine on Line 1: *The officer in charge has changed. Stick to the old principles and the outcome will be fortunate. Finding new associates is beneficial.* These lines suggest that King Wen has passed away. With King Wu (King Wen's son) at the helm, he needed to gain additional allies to ensure the revolution's success. If you assume a leadership position, find outside supporters who can benefit your role. Be true to yourself and you will succeed.

Six on Line 2: *Networking with malicious people will cause the capable ones to leave.* King Wu understood it was disadvantageous to ally with the dishonest, spiteful, and vindictive person. Acknowledging and giving attention to the problematic and unworthy will cause the trustworthy person to become disgruntled, finding suitable attention elsewhere.

Six on Line 3: *Networking with capable people will cause the malicious ones to leave. The latter group will feel they got what they deserved. It is advantageous to remain correct.* King Wu assigned important duties to honorable people. Empowered by their new stature, they served the king productively and proudly. Attract the good, and the bad will avoid your company.

Nine on Line 4: *There are more and more followers. Taking on new ones will lead to misfortune. Clearly explain the reasons for the noble mission and there will not be a mistake.* Success attracts followers with selfish motives. Some even may have been spies of the Shang king, Zhou Wang. To subdue potential troublemakers, King Wu won them over with sincerity. It was the correct thing to do. If you accept new people into your fold, you must first educate them about your mission before you can assign them a job. Be selective.

Nine on Line 5: *Sincerity is appreciated. This is fortunate.* King Wu's followers appreciated his earnestness, integrity, and good will. Your sincerity will move your friends. Proceed without fear.

Six on Line 6: *To keep the multitude of followers under control, it is necessary to establish rules. The king conducts a ceremony on the West Hill.* Before beginning the full-scale military assault against the Shang, King Wu gathered his allies in Zhou territory (in the west). He instituted rules and regulations, binding all as a cohesive unit. Set ground rules. Your great project/relationship/idea is ready to begin.

MY YI JOURNAL					
Date	Question	Present Hexagram	Changing Line(s)	Future Hexagram	Notes

 *Gu*

Hexagram 18

Decaying

Name

Gu means decaying, and the character depicts three worms in an urn. In China, an urn is a vessel for food. When food rots, it becomes infested with maggots and insects.

What This Hexagram Is About

Gu indicates a corrupt enterprise. When the food is rotten, it must be replaced. This analogy denotes a turning point, the moment of change when the Zhou replaced the rotten Shang.

Hexagram Statement

It is advantageous to cross the great stream. The three days before and the three days after the change are the most important. If your job/relationship has soured, it's time to move on. If you assume the position as leader of a corrupt company, work diligently to turn the situation around. Use the three days prior to the new beginning to prepare your mind, body, and spirit. Use the three days after the change to establish new rules, to set goals.

Six on Line 1: *The father left him a corrupt enterprise. If the son is capable, he will correct it. Although the task will be challenging, he will prevail.* Here, "father" symbolizes the Shang dynasty; "son" represents the Zhou dynasty. When King Wu of the Zhou won the empire from the cruel Zhou Wang of Shang, he inherited an administration fraught with corruption. Nevertheless, Wu persevered, correcting past transgressions. The rotten enterprise is in your hands. Take the bull by the horns and right the wrongs. There will be success. On a smaller scale, correcting your bad attitude will open new doors.

Nine on Line 2: *The mother left him a corrupt team. He should replace it.* Here, "mother" symbolizes the corrupt administrators. King Wu removed all the Shang officers, replacing them with a new administration. Out with the old, in with the new. It's time to let go of those associates/friends/entanglements hampering your growth and development.

Nine on Line 3: *There may be regret if one takes over his father's spoiled business and forces him to resign.* At times, King Wu felt guilty about overthrowing the Shang. Don't be remorseful about a broken personal or business relationship that led to your success. You earned your position. You will do well.

Six on Line 4: *Disregarding your father's wrongdoing will cause disdain by others.* King Wu made Zhou Wang's son, Wu Geng, the figurehead of the Shang capital. King Wu then assigned his three younger brothers to monitor Wu Geng's activities. Do not be too trusting of wrongdoers. Install capable people to help keep the wayward in line. Keep an eye on their whereabouts and actions.

Six on Line 5: *To remedy your father's misconduct, you must establish your reputation.* Like his father, King Wu was a benevolent monarch. His edicts were enforced without rebellion. To rectify a situation, you must first secure an honorable reputation. Only then will you gain respect and admiration.

Nine on Line 6: *There are people who will not serve the king and his lords. They choose to pursue a noble mission of their own.* After the revolution and the establishment of Zhou rule, some Shang administrators resigned from their posts. They should be honored. Let them contribute in their own way. If you're promoted, don't expect allies of your predecessor to follow you.

MY YI JOURNAL					
Date	Question	Present Hexagram	Changing Line(s)	Future Hexagram	Notes

 *Lin*

Hexagram 19

Arriving

Name

Lin means arriving.

What This Hexagram Is About

Lin heralds the arrival of the Zhou empire. It also predicts that great misfortune will befall the dynasty in its eighth month. Could this travail refer to an illness or a battle wound King Wu may have incurred? While we can only speculate about the prophecy's meaning, King Wu did, in fact, die two years after the founding of the Zhou dynasty.

Hexagram Statement

If the correct path is taken, prosperity will follow a smooth progression of events. However, in the eighth month there will be misfortune. While your project/career/relationship progresses without a hitch, September (the Chinese New Year begins in February; hence, September is the eighth month) may bring unexpected hardships, challenges, or devastation. Be mindful of your health and finances.

Nine on Line 1: *All have responded to the call. With persistence, it will be fortunate.* The allies responded to King Wu's request to celebrate the founding of the new dynasty. Prepare for a great moment. Expect accolades from your family and friends. Your achievement will be honored.

Nine on Line 2: *All have responded to the call. Nothing will go wrong.* King Wu was concerned that the dynastic transition be smooth. To settle his anxiety, he consulted with Heaven. The divination was positive. Likewise, rest assured you've made the right decision. Prepare for a great moment.

Six on Line 3: *The sweet moment approaches without fanfare. Wait with anticipation and there will be no mistake.* King Wu patiently awaited his coronation. Your time is coming. Patience will temper anxiety. If you're prepared, nothing can go wrong.

Six on Line 4: *The climax has arrived. There will be no mistake.* This line refers to the coronation of King Wu. Congratulations! Your hard work and determination have paid off. (This could be a graduation, wedding, promotion, or the grand opening of an enterprise.)

Six on Line 5: *Wisdom has arrived. It suits the king. There will be fortune.* King Wu displayed his intelligence and insight at his coronation ceremony. Similarly, exhibit decorum. Show respect toward your friends and associates. Putting your best foot forward will yield positive results.

Six on Line 6: *Exhibit compassion and generosity. There will be fortune.* This line refers to King Wu's treatment of the Shang. The best way to win support from the conquered is to be compassionate and kind. In a relationship, be respectful of your partner's parents and siblings.

		MY YI JOURNAL			
Date	Question	Present Hexagram	Changing Line(s)	Future Hexagram	Notes

**觀**Guan

Hexagram 20

Observing

Name

Guan means observing. It connotes contemplation, consideration, and examination, modes of thought necessary to make an important decision.

What This Hexagram Is About

After King Wu founded the Zhou dynasty, his brother, the Duke of Zhou, carefully observed Wu's actions before deciding how best to assist him.

Hexagram Statement

The diviner washed his hands, but was not in haste to present his offering. He gave thoughtful consideration that his next action be immaculate. During the revolution, the Duke of Zhou steadfastly supported and assisted his brother. After King Wu established the new dynasty, it seemed natural that the Duke of Zhou should continue to serve the new king. Yet, the Duke hesitated and carefully considered what position accorded with his talent, ambition, and drive for perfection. Apply for the post best suited to your abilities, wants, and needs. Refrain from making hurried decisions that you may later regret. Keenly observe your associates/prospective mate before establishing a relationship.

Six on Line 1: *Observe the job position with the innocence of a child, even if it is a low-ranking one. For a key position, observe with a keen eye.* When making a career choice or when considering a new job, it is not wise to take into account perks and benefits only. Among many other factors, you must consider whether the position is compatible with your talents. Does it meet your long-term goals? Will it be satisfying? Will it motivate and nourish your self-esteem? Likewise, choose a partner or significant other with the same keen eye.

Six on Line 2: *Peeping only benefits the woman.* In the old days, women were subservient to men. Marriages were arranged. When a suitor came to propose, his prospective bride would peep through the door to examine his appearance, speech, and behavior. If he met with her approval, she would agree to marry him. If you marry someone because of his or her impressive family background, you will play a submissive role. Similarly, joining a prominent organization because of its prestige shows a want of ambition. He or she who "peeps" becomes aware of a situation, acts upon that knowledge, and will be benefited.

Six on Line 3: *Examine my qualifications before making an offer.* The Duke of Zhou was careful to accept a position offered by his brother, King Wu. Eventually, the Duke of

Zhou accepted a post as the Minister of Rites. Know your ability and experience before accepting a job offer.

Six on Line 4: *Observe the beauty of the country. Then, decide if it is propitious to join the government.* If the "beauty" (or spirit) of the people is corrupt, this is a strong indication the government is corrupt, too. Before accepting a post, do some homework about your prospective employer and company. If they have a bad reputation, pass up this opportunity.

Nine on Line 5: *Pay attention to the way I lead my life. If the government is honest, so are the people.* Set a good example for your subordinates/children. Demonstrating honesty, integrity, and fairness is key to developing a good work ethic, healthy self-esteem, and positive attitude among your staff/children.

Nine on Line 6: *Pay attention to the way people lead their lives. The government will know what to do.* Understand your client and competition and you will prosper. Understand your mate/partner and your marriage/business relationship will be fruitful and enjoyable.

MY YI JOURNAL

Date	Question	Present Hexagram	Changing Line(s)	Future Hexagram	Notes

Hexagram 21
Gnawing &
Chewing

Shi He

Name

Shi He consists of two characters: On the left side, Shi means gnawing; on the right side, He means chewing. Together, Shi He symbolizes the importance of maintaining law and order.

What This Hexagram Is About

When King Wen began the revolution against the Shang king, Zhou Wang, Wen's allies came from afar to support his effort. To discourage chaos and ensure order, Wen established rules and regulations for all to abide by. Wrongdoers were promptly punished.

Hexagram Statement

To gnaw and chew indicates smooth progress. It is advantageous to establish law and order. After King Wu won the military campaign, he had to then conquer 99 rival nations that did not wish to pledge allegiance to the Zhou administration, a daunting task by anyone's measure. King Wu took decisive action to ensure his allies worked as a cohesive unit. The laws his father established were strictly enforced. Before you launch an enterprise or establish a business or personal partnership, sign a binding agreement.

Nine on Line 1: *Locking up feet until the toes are inside the cuff serves as a warning to minor offenders. It will work.* In ancient China, the delinquent's feet were locked inside a heavy shoe as retribution for a misdemeanor. If a serious crime had been committed, the punishment warranted a more serious sentence. Lightly punish those who commit minor mistakes so they know they have wronged.

Six on Line 2: *For those who commit serious crimes, biting off the skin by whipping, and breaking the nose by punching are appropriate. There will be no mistake.* A person must suffer the consequences of his or her misdeeds. Be just when judging others. Let your decision be fair. Don't make a mountain out of a molehill.

Six on Line 3: *Biting on preserved meat. It is tough and dry. It is not serious.* Biting on this type of meat symbolizes discovering something dangerous or poisonous. Even if someone is only an accomplice to the crime or offense, that person should be punished as if he or she actually committed the untoward act. Although others may deem the judgment controversial, it is not a mistake. Stand firm. Get rid of those who poison your efforts.

Nine on Line 4: *Biting on preserved meat with bones, one must use a golden arrow. The task is difficult. Insist on justice and there will be fortune.* Sometimes it is difficult to remain steadfast while imposing your judgment. Grasp the "golden arrow" by gaining support from the highest authority (the court, the president of your firm, a family figurehead). Carry out your decision. You have not made a mistake.

Six on Line 5: *Biting meat jerky and finding gold is perilous. Insist on justice and there will be no mistake.* You may be in danger if the one judging you accepts a bribe ("gold") or is biased against you. Likewise, if you are subjected to pressure, don't betray your conscience. Pass on a fair judgment. It is the honorable thing to do.

Nine on Line 6: *Imposing heavy penalties is dangerous.* Although maintaining law and order is important, there must be certain degrees of leniency. Imposing excessively heavy penalties to first-time offenders is unjust. Give people the benefit of the doubt and be lenient. Your kindness will be appreciated.

MY YI JOURNAL

Date	Question	Present Hexagram	Changing Line(s)	Future Hexagram	Notes

 *Bi*

Hexagram 22

Adorning

Name

Bi means adorning. To decorate, embellish, and beautify are also indicative of Bi. While heaven and earth are decorated by the seasons, people decorate their society with intelligence and material gain.

What This Hexagram Is About

The success of the revolution brought great wealth to the Zhou. It was only natural they use their riches to decorate their homes and beautify their country. This hexagram warns that overindulgence is not appropriate.

Hexagram Statement

Construct and adorn. It is good for development. It is advantageous to proceed. Take this time to beautify your surroundings and yourself. Brighten your rooms with a fresh coat of paint. Replace tattered furniture. Purchase a new car. Add to your wardrobe. Learn new words. Take a course that will raise your awareness. Such adornments will build confidence and increase the value of your property.

Nine on Line 1: *Adorn the toes. Give up the carriage and walk.* Adorn your feet with sturdy shoes. Leave your car at home and walk to the store, to work, or to the supermarket.

Six on Line 2: *Adorn your beard.* In the old days, men did not shave on a daily basis. Nevertheless, it was important to trim the beard. Likewise, mind your appearance. A flattering hairstyle, appropriate attire, and impeccable manners will convey a healthy self-esteem. Be the best you can be and you will be noticed.

Nine on Line 3: *Adorn with elegance. Do not forget the principles. It will be fortunate.* The fundamental principles of honesty and sincerity beautify a person's inner spirit. Outwardly, spend time and money on adornments that will beautify your home. However, do not forget that material possessions are the means and not the end to success.

Six on Line 4: *Adorn like a handsome prince riding a galloping white horse. You are going to propose marriage, and not rob.* To decorate your words and actions with flattery will arouse people's suspicion of your sincerity. Your proposal/proposition should benefit both parties. Do not take advantage of your prospective mate/client/competitor.

Six on Line 5: *Adorn your garden with light silk. Although some people will say you are stingy, there will be fortune in the end.* Do not waste money on decorating your home with designer furniture, expensive rugs, and fine art. Frugality and functionality will win. Invest your hard-earned money and reap the rewards.

Nine on Line 6: *Adorn with simplicity. There will be no mistake.* Keep it simple! Less is more. Overindulgence clutters the mind, body, and spirit. Streamline your wardrobe, accessories, and interior design. Let your words and actions be simple and true.

MY YI JOURNAL

Date	Question	Present Hexagram	Changing Line(s)	Future Hexagram	Notes

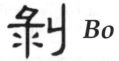 *Bo*

Hexagram 23

Stripping

Name

Bo means stripping, peeling off, shedding, crumbling, or eliminating.

What This Hexagram Is About

The Zhou's glorious victory over the Shang caused the Zhou to become slack. Contentment eroded their vigilance. Bo warns of the detrimental effect of not being alert, of letting down your guard.

Hexagram Statement

It is not advantageous to move in any direction. At this time, a plan will not help matters. Before you can move forward, you must deal with the present moment. Strip old-fashioned ideas, bad habits, and prejudices. Shed what is worn and outdated. Discard things that are not functioning. Concentrate on correcting the problems plaguing your growth and development. Get your business/relationship back on track. Be alert. Take care of yourself. Accept change.

Six on Line 1: *The moisture causes the paint on the feet of the bed to peel. Neglecting the firm foundation is dangerous.* Do not neglect the well-being of your subordinates/children, for this next generation will strengthen the company/family. Without nurturing the future generation's support, the foundation will crumble. Likewise, give proper attention to the grassroots movement.

Six on Line 2: *The moisture affects the leg of the bed. The foundation is in danger of collapsing.* Discontent is spreading to the middle class (mid-level workers, friends). The circumstances have become dangerous and unmanageable. The foundation has become unstable. Act immediately to rectify the situation before all is lost.

Six on Line 3: *Strip it completely. There will be no mistake.* It is too late to correct the situation. Because you cannot do anything, let it go. The business/partnership/romance is not repairable. Detach and make room for new opportunities.

Six on Line 4: *The water has rotted the entire bed. The skin of those who have slept in the bed is also infected. It is very dangerous.* Corruption has affected all strata of the business/society/family/partnership. Chaos, arguments, gossip, and untoward behavior reign supreme. You are in a dangerous situation. Do not hang on to a rotten business/job/romance. To do so will cause permanent damage to your physical and mental well-being.

Six on Line 5: *Like a school of fish, those favored by the king found shelter in the palace. It is not disadvantageous.* The Zhou who have not been corrupted gathered in safety to discuss how best to resolve the situation. Stay away from people who seek to damage your self-esteem, position, reputation, and spirit. Plan how to get out from under their perverse grasp.

Nine on Line 6: *The great fruit has not been eaten. Honorable men will sit in carriages. Mean people will be stripped of their houses.* Referring to the core of the Zhou government, the "great fruit" has not been damaged. The people supported those who maintained honor and integrity. Stay firm and correct and you will be recognized and rewarded.

MY YI JOURNAL

Date	Question	Present Hexagram	Changing Line(s)	Future Hexagram	Notes

渡 *Fu*

Hexagram 24

Returning

Name

Fu means returning, with an underlying meaning of recovering from a difficult period.

What This Hexagram Is About

In the previous Hexagram 23, the Zhou leaders began their rule on the wrong path, their overconfidence leading to corruption and chaos. In this hexagram, realizing they have erred, the Zhou returned to the proper path.

Hexagram Statement

Obstacles will not hinder movement. Each direction brings fortune. Return on the seventh day. "Seven days" indicates you will rebound quickly, that you require only a short time to recuperate from a period fraught with difficulty and frustration. Congratulations! Very soon your life will be back on track.

Nine on Line 1: *If one has not traveled the wrong path for a great distance and returns to the right course, there is no need to repent. Begin anew. This is fortunate.* The Zhou empire started on the wrong path. Fortunately, they corrected their ways before it was too late. Don't waste time crying over spilled milk. Take immediate measures to correct your mistake. Move forward with confidence and dignity.

Six on Line 2: *Rejuvenate before returning to the proper path. There will be fortune.* Take a deep breath. Rest, relax, and re-energize yourself before starting fresh. Forgive and forget. You will be blessed.

Six on Line 3: *Mistakes may be repeated. As long as the right path is sought, there eventually will be fortune.* Do not be disheartened by treading the wrong path time and again. As long as your mistakes are corrected, you will not be faulted. Keep trying. Sooner or later, you'll get it right!

Six on Line 4: *While walking with other people, he returned alone.* The majority is not always right. If you understand they have made a bad choice or an incorrect judgment, go your own way. Don't concede to their will.

Six on Line 5: *Return to the proper path with sincerity.* Admitting your mistake is an honorable act. There is nothing to be ashamed of.

Six on Line 6: *Losing your way in a return to the proper path is dangerous. There will be misfortune. If troops are lost, they will be defeated and the king will be in imminent danger. For 10 years, he will be unable to win a battle.* If you do not discover the mistake in time, it may be too late to recover your loss. For 10 years, you will suffer irreparable damage to your business/career/relationship.

MY YI JOURNAL				
Date	Question	Present Hexagram	Changing Line(s)	Future Hexagram	Notes

Hexagram 25

Wu Wang

Without Wrongdoing

Name

Wu Wang consists of two characters: On the left side, Wu means without; on the right side, Wang means wrongdoing. Together, Wu Wang means being subjected to misfortune without having done anything wrong.

What This Hexagram Is About

This hexagram refers to what transpired after King Wu met an untimely death. Wu's young son, Cheng Wang, became the new emperor with his uncle, the Duke of Zhou, as his advisor. Despite the groundless rumors intended to damage his reputation and motive, the Duke of Zhou continued to help his nephew rule with stately righteousness.

Hexagram Statement

In the beginning there will be steady progress. If there is determination, there will be fortune. If there is an unjustified motive, then all actions are inappropriate. The arrangement of installing the Duke of Zhou as Cheng Wang's advisor proved trouble-free in the beginning. However, the partnership was challenged when the Three Monitors (Guan, Cai, and Huo, the Duke of Zhou's brothers), for their own selfish reasons, tried to undermine the arrangement. Disengage from troublemakers. Do not become entwined in the misdeeds of others. Stay on the high road and you will be rewarded.

Nine on Line 1: *If there is nothing wrong, proceed. There will be fortune.* The Duke of Zhou had no hidden motive as Cheng Wang's advisor. No one thought ill of the relationship. If you believe you are doing the right thing, proceed with courage and confidence.

Six on Line 2: *Don't expect a bountiful harvest without first plowing the field. Don't expect a harvest upon sowing the seeds. When there is a purpose, the action will be rewarded.* The Duke of Zhou did not expect his young nephew to rule without first being trained. With integrity and honesty, the Duke of Zhou took it upon himself to teach Cheng Wang about proper decorum, military strategy, and governing. Likewise, don't bite off more than you can chew. Set realistic goals. Seek assistance. Find a mentor.

Six on Line 3: *Calamity can come without reason. For example, someone ties his ox to a tree. A passerby takes the ox. Someone in the neighborhood is accused of stealing the ox. Without evidence, this is an inappropriate accusation.* Although you may not have done anything wrong, misfortune has befallen you. Hold your head high and proceed as planned. Stay calm. The discord with soon pass.

Nine on Line 4: *With determination, insist on the right path. There will be no mistake.* The Duke of Zhou did not pay attention to rumors. Instead, he concentrated on assisting his nephew, the king. Have faith. Your name will be cleared.

Nine on Line 5: *He ailed without fault. He is cured without medication. He is happier than before.* If you suffer unfounded slander, your reputation will not be hurt. Do not take malicious and baseless rumors personally. Moreover, do not combat the perpetrators. Although it is difficult now, when the dark cloud passes, you will find happiness.

Nine on Line 6: *Unanticipated misfortune comes. It will be disadvantageous to act.* You do not have to err to become entwined in an unfavorable situation. Stay put. Wait for the appropriate time to take action.

MY YI JOURNAL					
Date	Question	Present Hexagram	Changing Line(s)	Future Hexagram	Notes

6 5 4 3 2 1

大畜 *Da Chu*

Hexagram 26

Great Gains

Name

Da Chu consists of two characters: On the left side, Da means great; on the right side, Chu means gains. Together, Da Chu means great gains, great reward, and great achievement.

What This Hexagram Is About

This hexagram tells how the Duke of Zhou was able to carry out his ideas despite the groundless rumors spread by the Three Monitors, his brothers. By contributing wholeheartedly and unselfishly to help set the government on the proper path, the Duke of Zhou felt greatly rewarded.

Hexagram Statement

It is advantageous to be firm. It is disadvantageous to enjoy luxury and leisure at home. It is advantageous to cross the great stream. It is time to capitalize on your idea. Focus your energy on making your dream come true. Do not think about it; do it! Have courage and step into the "great stream." It will propel you forward. If you procrastinate at home or spend leisure time with friends, you will have missed an opportunity to achieve something great.

Nine on Line 1: *The situation is perilous. It is advantageous to remain calm and wait.* Peace can be deceptive. The danger has not been completely eliminated. Remain cautious. Do not be taken by surprise.

Nine on Line 2: *The strap controlling the carriage wheels has been removed.* This line refers to the Duke of Zhou being given full authority to institute his ideas. Your talent will not be restrained. You are free to go forward with your plan.

Nine on Line 3: *Although it is no easy task, ride a good horse to pursue a goal. With steadfastness and determination, the result will be positive. If there is time, sharpen your defensive skills. Any direction will prove fortunate.* You are prepared to carry out your plan. Stay abreast of the latest news/competition/inventions that will hone your craft/ idea/project. Your endeavor will be met with success.

Six on Line 4: *Protect the young bulls. Tie them by the horns. From the beginning, there will be fortune.* Check your work and check it twice. Pay attention to details. If you are meticulous, you will accomplish your task and achieve something great. Your idea (young bulls) will come to fruition.

Six on Line 5: *The castrated boar shows its tusks without aggression. It is fortunate.* Although his tusks are threatening, a castrated boar is harmless. This line speaks of the gossip and trouble besieging the Duke of Zhou. Because he gained the upper hand, the ne'er-do-wells were all bark and no bite. Do not pay attention to gossip or rumors. Remember, you're in control!

Nine on Line 6: *You are on the road carrying Heaven's will. It is fortunate.* Heaven mandated great responsibility to the Duke of Zhou. Congratulations! You have been chosen to accomplish a noble task.

MY YI JOURNAL

Date	Question	Present Hexagram	Changing Line(s)	Future Hexagram	Notes

 *Yi*

Hexagram 27

Jaws

Name

Yi means jaws. It reflects nourishing (nurturing) and being nourished (nurtured) by good food, good words, and good deeds.

What This Hexagram Is About

This hexagram tells how the Duke of Zhou benefited (nourished) the country by establishing educational standards and training opportunities, two bulwarks for a prosperous society.

Hexagram Statement

Observe how and what a person eats and you will know his health. There will be fortune. Be mindful of what comes in and goes out of your mouth and the mouths of others. Nourish yourself with proper food. Nourish your hopes and dreams. Nourish the growth and development of others. Make sure your speech is articulate and sincere. Filling yourself with good food, having a positive attitude, and doing good deeds are both healthful and beneficial for you and for those with whom you associate.

Nine on Line 1: *Instead of watching the sacred turtle, you come to admire me eating. It is unfortunate.* The ancient Chinese believed the turtle to be a wise creature capable of communicating with Heaven. Admiring those with special talents and accomplishments will bring misfortune. Envy and jealousy lead to a weakened spirit. Do not compare yourself to others. Be content with your achievements.

Six on Line 2: *Nurturing only the privileged is dangerous.* Provide opportunities to those who possess great potential, not to those who are privileged and less motivated. Join an organization that empowers you.

Six on Line 3: *If the selecting process is not fair, danger lurks. Capable people will not come for 10 years.* When recruiting people to join your company/organization/school, selection should be based on merit. In romance, do not base your selection on your prospective mate's financial status, career choice, and other superficial considerations. You will neglect your nourishment. You will not attract capable workers/suitors for 10 years.

Six on Line 4: *Correct the way you recruit people and there will be fortune. Although the privileged will glare and pounce at you like a tiger, there will not be much trouble.* Stick to your principles. Ignore those asking for special considerations and unjustified favors. Do not let them pressure or influence your decision. There will be no mistakes and no regrets.

Six on Line 5: *Nurturing the underprivileged instead of the privileged goes against accepted rules. Insist on idealism and there will be fortune. However, it is not time to cross the great stream.* You are going against the grain, doing what most people will not do. You will find success only if you stay put for the time being. Now is not the time to begin a new romance/job/project/business.

Nine on Line 6: *The recruitment plan is correct. Although it may be fraught with difficulty, the result will be fortunate.* Your years of persistence and hard work have paid off. You have assembled a capable team. It is time to put your ideas into action. Make your dream come true. You have the means and support.

		MY YI JOURNAL			
Date	Question	Present Hexagram	Changing Line(s)	Future Hexagram	Notes

Name

Da Guo consists of two characters: On the left side, Da means great; on the right side, Guo means passing. Together, Da Guo indicates a great test a person must pass.

What This Hexagram Is About

This hexagram describes how the Duke of Zhou handled the rebellion led by his brothers, the Three Monitors. This was a time of crisis and turmoil for the Duke of Zhou and for the empire as a whole.

Hexagram Statement

The ridgepole of the house sags. It is advantageous to find a direction. Upon King Wu's death, the newly founded dynasty was on the verge of collapsing. The king's brother, the Duke of Zhou, shouldered many responsibilities in an effort to support the sagging empire. You are exposed to danger. Your company/relationship/project is on the verge of collapsing. However, since the sickness has been diagnosed, it will be easy to cure. If your job/relationship does not support your well-being, it's time to find greener pastures.

Six on Line 1: *With sincerity, place the offering on a mat made of white rushes. There will be no mistake.* The Duke of Zhou made clear to other high-ranking officials his sincerity about assisting the young emperor, Cheng Wang. From the get-go, demonstrate your genuineness and good intentions. Gain the support and trust of others. Be humble.

Nine on Line 2: *New shoots sprout from a decayed willow. It is like an old man marrying a younger woman. There is nothing disadvantageous.* The Duke of Zhou did not want to use military force against the uprising led by his three brothers. The crisis aroused his courage and tenacity, demonstrating that an old man was still capable of solving difficult dilemmas. Although the situation is trying, you can overcome any obstacles.

Nine on Line 3: *The ridgepole is crooked. It is dangerous.* Wu Geng, son of the tyrant Shang king, Zhou Wang, grasped the opportunity of discord within the Zhou administration to rebel against them. Chaos prevails. This is a dangerous time. Be careful!

Nine on Line 4: *The crooked ridgepole bulges upward. This is fortunate, albeit inconvenient.* The Duke of Zhou easily thwarted the rebellion led by his brothers, the Three Monitors. Likewise, the problem you face is not as big as initially assessed. To avoid trouble in the future, handle this dilemma with care.

Nine on Line 5: *The decayed willow blooms again. It is like an old woman marrying a younger man. There is no blame and no fame.* Using military force to achieve peace and harmony is like an old woman marrying a younger man. While not wrong, such a match is inappropriate and unseemly. Similarly, taking action against an ill-prepared and unworthy opponent may be desirable, but it is not noble.

Six on Line 6: *Wading through the water until his head is submerged is dangerous. There will be no mistake.* The Duke of Zhou displayed his wisdom and courage by putting down the rebellion led by his three brothers. He took calculated risks, which proved successful in the end. With perception, perseverance, and fearlessness, you will pass a difficult test.

MY YI JOURNAL

Date	Question	Present Hexagram	Changing Line(s)	Future Hexagram	Notes

 Kan

Hexagram 29

Cavern

Name

Kan means cavern or falling into a cavern—a dangerous situation. Since this hexagram is comprised of two like trigrams, it implies double danger.

What This Hexagram Is About

This hexagram narrates the danger the Duke of Zhou faced during the first three years he assisted his nephew, the new king, Cheng Wang.

Hexagram Statement

He falls repeatedly into perilous situations. Faith and sincerity provide a connection to the hearts of others. His action is noble and benevolent. While the Duke of Zhou's three brothers prepared for a coup d'état, the son of the Shang king (whom they were assigned to monitor) prepared his own rebellion by allying with small neighboring tribes. The situation was extremely dangerous. Yet, because the Duke of Zhou gained the trust of the people, he was able to restore order. Accept the challenge and confront the danger. Remove any barriers impeding your path. Seek assistance from those loyal to you. Take charge of the situation and move forward with confidence.

Six on Line 1: *He falls repeatedly into the deep and becomes trapped inside the cavern's deepest recess. There is danger.* Any attempt to climb out of danger places you in even greater peril. All you can do is adapt to the present situation. Bide your time and wait out the storm.

Nine on Line 2: *Danger lurks in the cavern. Advance with small steps.* The Duke of Zhou first gained the support of other senior officials before launching a full-scale attack against his brothers. Walk softly, proceeding in small steps. Patience and perseverance are the keys to getting out of danger's way.

Six on Line 3: *Perilous situations come one after the other. It is progressively dangerous. Do not act.* Enemies (gossipers, devious individuals, war) surround you. Whatever direction you take will lead to greater danger. Stay calm. Do not dance to their tune.

Six on Line 4: *Even for ceremonies, wine is contained in simple earthenware and rice in bamboo baskets. Everything is conducted with extraordinary modesty. In the end, there will be no mistake.* Now is not the time to be extravagant. Do not spend beyond your means. Be frugal. Keep things simple.

Nine on Line 5: *The water in the cave has not overflowed yet. It is only up to ground level. There will be no mistake.* The danger/problem you face is still under control. It will not become a monumental menace. Soon, it will be over.

Six on Line 6: *He is tied up with ropes and thrown into a thicket of thorns. He is unable to release himself for three years. It is very dangerous.* The cruel Shang king, Zhou Wang, caused many to distrust the leader and government. The Zhou had great difficulty convincing the commoners otherwise. Your problem is deep-seated. It will take three years to cure this painful and troublesome situation.

MY YI JOURNAL					
Date	Question	Present Hexagram	Changing Line(s)	Future Hexagram	Notes

 *Li*

Hexagram 30

Brightness

Name

Li means brightness and radiance. Since this hexagram is comprised of two like trigrams, it means extreme brightness radiated by the sun during the day and the moon during the night.

What This Hexagram Is About

This hexagram describes how the Duke of Zhou's stalwart efforts to conquer the 99 tribes that refused to acknowledge the Zhou rule helped to build a strong empire lasting over 800 years.

Hexagram Statement

It is advantageous to be steadfast. There will be prosperity. It is fortunate to raise cows. The Duke of Zhou succeeded in conquering the 99 nations because he won the support of the commoners, who were revolting against their leaders. Like cattle, they were hardworking and tame. Clarify and make known your intentions. Let your radiance illuminate your idea. Your future is bright, free of obstructions. Being aware of your purpose will bring great success.

Nine on Line 1: *The new followers come in all kinds of shoes. Remain alert and there will be no mistake.* When the Duke of Zhou began his military venture, many people allied with his army. They represented all strata of society. As long as you do not lose sight of your objective, acquaintances and new associates will not hinder your development.

Six on Line 2: *The newcomers who wear yellow will bring fortune.* To the Chinese, the color yellow is analogous to humility and hard work, qualities associated with people who have simple demands. People who are modest, diligent, and conscientious will form the backbone of your project.

Nine on Line 3: *Those who act like the setting sun must be aroused with songs and drumming. If not, they will be like aged people who have become the burden of the empire. It is dangerous.* When recruiting people to join your project/company/cause, you may encounter some who have passive spirits. Make them dance to the beat of your drum or they will immobilize your effort.

Nine on Line 4: *Some people arrive like a flash of light, their radiance quickly dying out. Discard them.* When you recruit people to join your project/company/cause, there will be some whose enthusiasm burns out. Likewise, if a romance comes suddenly, lighting up hot and quick, it will die out as quickly as it came.

Six on Line 5: *Some people come in tears and sorrow. It is fortunate.* Some people who have joined your project/company/cause may have been mistreated by their previous employer. Or, their talent was not appreciated or recognized. You are fortunate to find them. In a romance, take care to nurture your mate's feelings. Illuminate his or her spirit. You will find success.

Nine on Line 6: *By the order of the king, you are on a punitive expedition. Execute the leaders of the rebellion, but release his legions to show benevolence. There will be no mistake.* Punish the ringleader thwarting your spirit/development/project. Be lenient towards the others. Your kindness will be appreciated.

	MY YI JOURNAL				
Date	Question	Present Hexagram	Changing Line(s)	Future Hexagram	Notes

 *Xian*

Hexagram 31

Influencing

Name

Xian means influencing. Conjoining, bringing together, and connecting are also indicative of Xian. Specifically, it describes how a man woos or influences a woman.

What This Hexagram Is About

This hexagram uses the analogy of courtship to explain the art of making friends and acquiring beneficial associates. During the revolution against the Shang, the Duke of Zhou brought people together by rallying support for his brother, King Wu. He carefully watched and listened to potential allies in an attempt to understand their wants and needs.

Hexagram Statement

He who woos the girl with perseverance will be fortunate. The Zhou leaders courted prospective partners, ensuring that a marriage between tribes would lead to peace and prosperity. Understand your mate/partner/competition by studying them. Win their love/friendship/loyalty with integrity and truth.

Six on Line 1: *Watch the movement of his big toe.* A person's gait is led by his big toe. Observe how people lead their lives. By understanding their intentions, you can decide if a particular individual would make a good mate/partner.

Six on Line 2: *Watch the movement of his calf. It is dangerous.* To watch a person's calf means he/she is capable of kicking or hurting your reputation, self-esteem, or objectives. Approach with caution. Do not befriend this person until you fully understand his or her motives.

Nine on Line 3: *Follow the movement of his thighs. It is regretful.* Following someone without first understanding his or her motive and ideals is foolhardy. Do not accept other people's opinions blindly. Investigate the truth. Follow the right movement.

Nine on Line 4: *Do not be remorseful. Do not hesitate. You will lose friends. Be firm and there will be fortune.* Do not waste time repenting past transgressions. Also, if you are indecisive, how can you expect others to follow your ideas and support your goals? Have a plan and stick to it.

Nine on Line 5: *Pat him on the back. There will be no regrets.* Friends/co-workers/subordinates/loved ones need your support and encouragement. Cheer their accomplishments. Make them proud. This is the right course of action.

Six on Line 6: *Watch his jaws, cheeks, and tongue.* Understand others by observing their speech and facial expressions. Do they look you in the eye when they speak to you? Are their words well-chosen and sincere? Developing a mutual understanding is essential to a meaningful friendship/partnership.

		MY YI JOURNAL			
Date	Question	Present Hexagram	Changing Line(s)	Future Hexagram	Notes

 *Heng*

Hexagram 32

Constancy

Name

Heng means constancy, stability, and permanence. To continue and persevere are also indicative of Heng.

What This Hexagram Is About

During the Zhou revolution, the Duke of Zhou's effort to secure stable relationships with potential allies was met with frustration. Although his motive and intention were positive, the result was not. Likewise, while the hexagram as a whole is fortunate, the line texts are not. The diviner who receives this hexagram must be positive and optimistic about the situation at hand.

Hexagram Statement

Persevere without fault. It is advantageous to find a direction. There will be fortune. Develop stable relationships and friendships. With a solid support base, any avenue you pursue will be advantageous and rewarding.

Six on Line 1: To force a consistent relationship from the outset is dangerous. There is no advantage. Stable relationships cannot be instituted from the beginning. To expect one will invite insult. Let the friendship/partnership/romance develop and mature. Give your mate/client/partner space.

Nine on Line 2: Forget about the regrettable relationship. Forget about that which was a mistake from the beginning. Forget about the unhappy outcome and begin fresh. Let go of the past and new doors will open.

Nine on Line 3: He does not insist on being virtuous. To make him a friend is shameful. To continue the friendship brings regret. Unfortunately, there are those who have low morals and substandard principles. They have no respect for others, living their lives selfishly and without sincerity. It is not advantageous to establish a relationship with such persons. It will bring only humiliation.

Nine on Line 4: There is no game on the hunting grounds. The Duke of Zhou tried with earnestness to hunt for allies to support his father's (King Wen's) cause. However, his effort did not bring desirable results. When a project/cause/romance is not worth your effort, it is just a waste of time. Continue to search and you will find that person who will rally to your support.

Six on Line 5: To insist on maintaining a relationship with someone is fortunate for a woman, but dangerous for a man. Traditionally, a married woman would be considered virtuous by remaining loyal to her husband, no matter how disrespectfully he treated her. On the other hand, for a man to remain married to a disloyal wife would be considered cowardly. Make a wise decision when befriending an ally or prospective mate.

Six on Line 6: *To break a steady relationship is risky*. The Duke of Zhou understood some alliances were not promising. Instead of persevering, he took the risk and severed the relationship. When a partnership/romance is not working, sever the tie. It is the right move.

		MY YI JOURNAL			
Date	Question	Present Hexagram	Changing Line(s)	Future Hexagram	Notes

 *Tun*

Hexagram 33

Retiring

Name

Tun means retiring—specifically, to step back, withdraw, or retreat from action in order to prepare for advance later.

What This Hexagram Is About

Frustrated with the slow and unsatisfying progress of forming strong alliances to support the revolution against the Zhou, the Duke of Zhou temporarily retreated to prepare for his next move.

Hexagram Statement

Retire. There will be success. Use this time to assess your progress, your goals, and your dreams. Go on a retreat. Take a vacation alone. Prepare a plan, a new vision of your future. Also, evaluate your friends. There is no need to maintain relationships with those who do not bring you joy or support your goals.

Six on Line 1: *Retreating at the last moment is perilous.* As long as you do not advance, it is still safe. Even if you are the last one to leave, you will still reach safety. But, why wait? If your job/relationship is not satisfying, leave now.

Six on Line 2: *Tie up your decision with the hide of a yellow cow. There is no way to let go.* Make up your mind in an unbiased manner and activate your decision. Do not look back.

Nine on Line 3: *A barrier blocks your retirement. The situation is seriously dangerous. Pretend to indulge in the company of a new concubine.* People are determined to seek your assistance. This can be very exhausting. Pretend you are not interested. Pretend to be preoccupied with a new romance. Let others underestimate your ability and you will be left alone.

Nine on Line 4: *Honorable men retreat without looking back. It is fortunate. Common people cannot make up their minds to leave. It is unfortunate.* It is time to pull back from the relationship/situation/job. Act now. Do not hesitate. If you are doubtful, your indecision will lead to catastrophe.

Nine on Line 5: *The retreat is correct and beautiful. It is fortunate to persevere.* Withdrawing from the company of a person(s) whom you do not enjoy gives you fresh air. Do not waste your time. You will find peace in your decision.

Nine on Line 6: *Great reward follows the noble retreat. It is advantageous.* Leaving bad company, a bad relationship, or a bad situation is a courageous act. Doing so will lift a tremendous weight off your shoulders. Regardless the angle from which you view it, you've made the right decision.

Date	Question	Present Hexagram	Changing Line(s)	Future Hexagram	Notes

MY YI JOURNAL

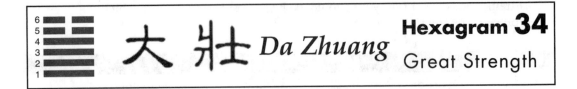

Name

Da Zhuang means great strength. It consists of two characters: On the left side, Da means great; on the right side, Zhuang means strength. Together, Da Zhuang suggests the power of nature.

What This Hexagram Is About

Upon pulling back from seeking competent allies to help defeat the Shang, the Duke of Zhou had time to gather his strength, arming himself with knowledge and determination. Like thunder's powerful clap, the Duke of Zhou gained momentum, fame, and respect. With such a stellar reputation, he was able to make manifest his ideas.

Hexagram Statement

It is advantageous to be firm in correctness. You have a good reputation. Your attention to detail, thoroughness, integrity, and fortitude have been noticed by others. Institute your idea. Let your purpose carry you forward. Your admirers will support your effort.

Nine on Line 1: *The strength is in the toes. It is not advantageous to conquer. Build sincerity.* The Duke of Zhou understood he must build a solid support base before he could move forward with the rebellion against the tyrant Shang king, Zhou Wang. Without gaining the trust and respect of your associates/clients, you cannot advance to a higher level. This is not a time to be modest. Display your talent.

Nine on Line 2: *It is fortunate to insist on correctness.* Take a stand. Do not budge. Eventually, you will win.

Nine on Line 3: *Common people use their strength inappropriately. Honorable people will not. Using strength unwisely is like a ram butting against a fence and getting his horns entangled.* Do not waste your time and energy pursuing futile activities. Instead, focus on finding rewarding opportunities that will lift your spirit, fortify your mind and energize your body.

Nine on Line 4: *It is fortunate to be firm with correctness. Regrettable moments will soon be forgotten. When the fence is broken, it will not entangle the ram's horns. If the wheel's axles are tied safely, the great carriage can move forward.* Wait for the appropriate moment to proceed. When there are no barriers and when you have gathered enough strength, make your move with confidence.

Six on Line 5: *When luck turns, a ram may be lost. There is nothing to regret.* Even though you may have great courage and mental and physical prowess, it does not mean you're invincible. If you suffer a setback, it is not a big deal. Sometimes you must take one step back to take two steps forward.

Six on Line 6: *Like a ram butting the fence with its horns entangled, you cannot advance or retreat. There is no advantage. Realize there is difficulty ahead and there will be fortune.* You are trapped between a rock and a hard place. No matter what you do, you cannot advance. Stay put. Patiently wait it out. You will realize a positive result eventually.

Date	Question	Present Hexagram	Changing Line(s)	Future Hexagram	Notes
MY YI JOURNAL					

6
5
4
3
2
1

Jin

Hexagram 35

Promoting

Name

Jin means promoting, the hexagram suggesting career advancement or an award received. The image symbolizes the rising sun emerging on the horizon.

What This Hexagram Is About

The Duke of Zhou was praised and rewarded by his father for his committed efforts in the revolution against the Shang king, Zhou Wang.

Hexagram Statement

The earl, who helped to rule the country, was bestowed gifts of horses by the king. He received the award three times within one day. Here, "earl" probably refers to the Duke of Zhou. Like the sun rising to meet the new day, your radiance shines. Congratulations! You will be promoted, the higher position bringing you greater prosperity, authority, and enlightenment.

Six on Line 1: *You are promoted. Slander hurts you. Remain firm and there will be no fault.* Upon receiving an award (inheritance, prize) or being promoted, expect others to be jealous of your gain. Although you may be subjected to gossip, ignore the tittle-tattle. Be generous and forgiving. There will be positive results.

Six on Line 2: *Worry accompanies promotion. Persevere. Accept the blessing from your grandmother.* While problems arise as a result of your promotion or receipt of an award (inheritance, prize), don't fret. By all means, don't let your emotions dictate your actions. Use your head! Your good luck is a gift from your ancestors.

Six on Line 3: *Receive applause from the crowd and all unhappy events are forgotten.* Slowly and steadily, you will win the trust, appreciation, and confidence of your associates/family. Such praise will erase past transgressions and misfortunate events.

Nine on Line 4: *Some liken your promotion to a giant rat assigned duties he is incapable of performing. The situation is perilous.* To the Chinese, the "giant rat" is also known as the five-skill rat: It can fly, but it cannot touch the roof; it can climb, but it cannot reach the treetop; it can swim, but it cannot cross the river; it can run, but it cannot be faster than others; and it can dig, but the hole is not deep enough to burrow. Some people thought the Duke of Zhou was promoted only because he was the son of the king. While it may be difficult in the beginning, once you display your talent, you will be accepted by the suspicious.

Six on Line 5: *There is nothing to regret. Do not bother with success or failure. Do what needs to be done. It is advantageous.* Your position is stable. Therefore, don't fret about trifling gains or losses. Ups and downs come with any situation. Focus on performing your duties to the best of your ability and you will find further prosperity and enrichment.

Nine on Line 6: *Expect promotion to the horn's tip. Conquer the rebellious barbarians. The situation is perilous, but it will be fortunate and faultless. However, if excessive punishment is used, it is shameful.* The tip of an ox's horn is the highest position on the mammal. This is analogous to your status. In order to maintain your high-level position (in a company, or as head of the family), be authoritative. Exercise your power by punishing the wrongdoers. However, do not overstep your boundaries. Excessive action leads to shame and humiliation.

MY YI JOURNAL

Date	Question	Present Hexagram	Changing Line(s)	Future Hexagram	Notes

Name

Ming Yi consists of two characters: On the left side, Ming means brightness; on the right side, Yi means wounded. Together, Ming Yi means hiding one's brilliance to deflect unwanted hardship.

What This Hexagram Is About

This hexagram describes what transpired during the reign of the tyrant Shang king, Zhou Wang. Honorable and wise people serving the king lived in darkness, a time of oppression and danger.

Hexagram Statement

Wounded brightness. Persevere in adversity. Understand that darkness prevails at this time. Mean-spirited and selfish people are in control, wounding the wise and honorable person. Mask your awareness and shield your insight. Be optimistic and look forward to brighter days. Unfortunately, there is nothing you can do but sit in the dark and wait.

Nine on Line 1: *Righteousness is defeated and flees like a wounded bird with drooping wings. Mourning the defeat, honorable people refuse to eat for three days. No matter what is done, the master will not be pleased.* Don't allow troublesome events and unpleasant people to defeat your spirit. Although your principles are being challenged, maintain a positive attitude. To avoid incurring the wrath of the dark-natured person, lay low.

Six on Line 2: *The left thigh is wounded. The strong horse saves his master. It is fortunate.* The reign of darkness has disabled you. You are being subjected to groundless gossip. Let your allies save you.

Nine on Line 3: *Wounded while launching an attack in the south, he captured the enemy's leader. The full-scale war will be won with patience and perseverance.* Here, "south" is equated with darkness. In the beginning of the Zhou revolution, they battled against southern (and eastern) tribes loyal to the Shang. Confront the unpleasant person oppressing you. Wage war against his mean-spiritedness. Don't be passive. Do something about your dire situation. Persevere and you will win.

Six on Line 4: *Entering the left side of the belly of the enemy, he captured his heart and learned about his evil plans. He escaped through the gate.* The Chinese refer to the heart as the mind, the place where a person's consciousness resides. Hateful people are conspiring against those who disagree with their management. Leave before you get hurt.

Six on Line 5: *Ji Zi (Zhou Wang's uncle) pretended to be insane to protect his dignity. It is advantageous to be firm*. Ji Zi admonished the Shang king for his cruelty and immorality. This irritated the tyrant, who sought to punish his uncle. However, Ji Zi escaped his sentence by feigning insanity. Hide your wisdom. See no evil, speak no evil, and hear no evil. Be patient.

Six on Line 6: *The master cannot distinguish between brightness and darkness. He may promote you to a sky-high level or plunge you into the ground*. King Wen and his son, the Duke of Zhou, understood the Shang king, Zhou Wang, was a poor ruler. When he was pleased, he would promote you to a high position. When he was displeased, he would demote you to the lowest one. When the management is not sound, do not be elated if you're advanced. Be cautious.

MY YI JOURNAL

Date	Question	Present Hexagram	Changing Line(s)	Future Hexagram	Notes

6
5
4
3
2
1

家 人 *Jia Ren*

Hexagram 37

Family

Name

Jia Ren consists of two characters: On the left side, Jia means family. On the right side, Ren means people. Together, Jia Ren means people comprising a family.

What This Hexagram Is About

In this hexagram, the family is a microcosm of the country. The father figure is the king, and the wife his officers. The Duke of Zhou used the model of an ideal family to project a model of an ideal country.

Hexagram Statement

It is advantageous for women to be correct in household affairs. In traditional Chinese society, a man's place is outside the home while a woman's place is inside the home. The man works to support his family and the woman keeps the home and family members in good order. Understand your position in your family/company. Perform your assigned duties with integrity and dignity. Do not overstep your boundaries.

Nine on Line 1: *Avoid regrettable incidents by setting up rules and regulations for the family to follow.* An ounce of prevention is worth a pound of cure. Avoid unnecessary chaos by establishing and enforcing house rules (or regulations for workers to abide by).

Six on Line 2: *A woman must take no active role outside. She must stay within and prepare food. Perseverance brings positive results.* Tradition dictates that a man can focus on his career if his wife looks after him well. Likewise, a king/president can gain international recognition if his officers enforce law and order within the country. If your internal affairs are in order, then you (or the breadwinner) can concentrate on external advancement.

Nine on Line 3: *Family members are cold and stern toward each other because the master has established strict rules. Nevertheless, it is fortunate. If the women and children act silly and foolish, it is shameful.* Firm rules force all to work harder. Without them, a person is less motivated and tends to procrastinate. Nothing gets accomplished. Although there is little laughter, the outcome is fruitful. Work hard. Don't dawdle.

Six on Line 4: *The family becomes rich. There is great fortune.* When everyone works together as a cohesive unit, there is success, prosperity, and satisfaction. Remember, you're only as strong as your weakest link.

Nine on Line 5: *If the internal affairs of a country are run like a rich family, there will be prosperity.* Administer your family as if you were the king governing his country. Take pride in your duties and you will succeed.

Nine on Line 6: *Rule with sincerity and dignity. Eventually, there will be fortune.* For a family, the master of the house should demand obedience. In exchange, he will be fair and sincere. For a country, the king/president should rule with authority. In exchange, he should be benevolent. This idea applies to running a company or even for establishing a relationship.

		MY YI JOURNAL			
Date	Question	Present Hexagram	Changing Line(s)	Future Hexagram	Notes

 *Kui*

Hexagram 38

Misunderstanding

Name

Kui means misunderstanding. Specifically, it means to view things differently, which causes a misunderstanding, opposition, or disagreement between parties.

What This Hexagram Is About

This hexagram describes the difficulties King Wen faced at the beginning of the revolution he led against the tyrant Shang king, Zhou Wang. Of all the hexagrams, the line texts comprising Kui are the most visual.

Hexagram Statement

There is fortune in small matters. When people hold opposing views, it is difficult to agree on important matters. However, in small matters, people can agree and cooperate. While people suffered Zhou Wang's reign of terror, some were of the opinion that a civil war was necessary. Others sought to correct the corruption threatening the government. With diverging viewpoints, a positive outcome can only be had in minor matters.

Nine on Line 1: *Forget about regrettable things. When a horse is lost, do not look for it. It will return by itself. When you meet a mean-spirited man, he is harmless.* If there are disagreements within your organization/family/relationship, people may leave out of frustration. Do not waste time trying to win them back. They will return on their own accord, realizing the disagreement was only a misunderstanding. If you encounter a mean-spirited and odious individual, you will not be harmed. You will recognize his or her bad attitude and malicious intentions.

Nine on Line 2: *Meeting the master in the lane does not give rise to embarrassment.* Here, "master" refers to King Wen. His son, the Duke of Zhou, comforted people who had disagreements with his father. He advised that they should not feel embarrassed if they met him unexpectedly. Likewise, if you have a disagreement with your boss, do not feel uneasy if you meet him or her at a social function. It is an opportunity to remove the misunderstanding.

Six on Line 3: *The carriage has stopped. The ox has pulled away. The man in the carriage is angry like a person who has suffered tattooing on the forehead and amputation of the nose. The beginning is horrible, but the ending is fortunate.* In ancient China, a convicted criminal was maimed, the disfigurement insulting his dignity. The Duke of Zhou used this analogy to explain King Wen's anger about being placed under house arrest by the Shang king, Zhou Wang. Your ideas are rejected and your power is stripped. Despite the humiliation, the outcome will be positive.

162

Nine on Line 4: *Betrayed, you feel isolated. You will meet an honorable man who is sincere to you. The situation is perilous, but there will be no mistake.* King Wen had sympathizers in the Shang court who joined him in opposing Zhou Wang. Yet, despite this, when King Wen spoke out, no one supported him. King Wen felt betrayed. That is, until Jiang Ziya stepped forth to fill the void. Jiang Ziya was King Wen's personal advisor and military consultant. A wise man, he helped the king win the revolution. Although you may feel isolated, detached, and without support, you will soon meet a trustworthy person who will capably advise you. You will not make a mistake in this difficult period.

Six on Line 5: *Forget that which you regret. Being betrayed by a person you trust is like being bitten. While it is painful, move forward.* When King Wen voiced his opinion against Zhou Wang's tyrannies, he gained no open support. As a result, he felt betrayed. Yet, he chose to forgive and forget. Do the same. Do not hold a grudge. Get on with your life.

Nine on Line 6: *Isolated, you see a pig covered with mud pulling a cart filled with devils. You draw your bow. When you are about to shoot, you tell yourself to relax. These devils are not robbers. They are coming for a wedding.* The "pig covered with mud" is actually a dirty man pulling a cart filled with foreigners. These lines refer to King Wen forming alliances with distant tribes. If you encounter a stranger, do not be alarmed. He or she comes in peace and seeks to befriend you.

	MY YI JOURNAL				
Date	Question	Present Hexagram	Changing Line(s)	Future Hexagram	Notes

 *Jian*

Hexagram 39

Obstructing

Name

Jian means obstructing, to face great difficulty and adversity.

What This Hexagram Is About

This hexagram describes the various difficulties the Zhou faced at the beginning of the revolution against the Shang.

Hexagram Statement

It is advantageous in the southwest (Zhou) and disadvantageous in the northeast (Shang). It is advantageous to see the great man. With perseverance, there will be fortune. Here, "great man" refers to King Wen. You are facing a difficult period. Seek guidance and assistance from a trusted friend, counselor, or lawyer. This person will help to shed light on a strenuous situation, ending the difficulty at hand. Do not attempt to figure it out on your own.

Six on Line 1: *To advance will bring difficulties. To wait will bring fame.* Take action at the appropriate time. When it is not suitable to advance (find a new job or mate, ask for a raise or promotion), wait patiently and you will see positive results. Do not act hastily.

Six on Line 2: *When the king is in danger, the officials should try to save him at the expense of their own lives.* It is important to be loyal to your country (or marriage) and its leader (your mate). Even if you must suffer, remain true to your country's founding principles (marriage vows).

Nine on Line 3: *To advance will bring difficulties. To wait will reverse the situation.* King Wen waited three years to launch his attack against the tyrant Shang king, Zhou Wang. Bide your time. The appropriate opportunity will come. Although your situation isn't bright now, there will be light at the end of the tunnel only if you wait.

Six on Line 4: *To advance will bring difficulties. It is beneficial to form alliances before striking.* When your workload is overwhelming, it is advantageous to ask for help. Find a partner, nanny, housekeeper, or assistant. Being a martyr invites frustration and possible failure. In romance, before you become committed, seek advice from those you trust.

Nine on Line 5: *In deep trouble, his friends rescue him.* If you have proven yourself to be worthy, respectful, and sincere, your friends/associates will come to your aid. Don't be afraid to ask them for help.

Six on Line 6: *To advance will bring difficulties. To stay behind will bring great achievement. It is advantageous to see the great man.* You are not yet prepared to move forward with your plan (a cause, marriage, project). You must first meet your advisor/mentor/leader, who can assess your situation, hone your ideas, and help present your plan.

		MY YI JOURNAL			
Date	Question	Present Hexagram	Changing Line(s)	Future Hexagram	Notes

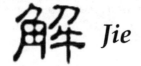 *Jie*

Hexagram 40
Separating

Name

Jie means separating or releasing yourself from a difficult situation. Initially, Jie meant to butcher an ox.

What This Hexagram Is About

This hexagram advises how the Zhou overcame the adversity that is described in Hexagram 39.

Hexagram Statement

It is advantageous in the southwest (Zhou). *There is fortune in nonaction. If there is advancement, fortune will come more quickly.* Whether the people supported King Wen's cause to end (or separate from) the oppressive Shang rule is a moot point. The revolution was destined by Heaven to be successful. If people hesitate to rally to your cause, don't worry. Your project/idea will be successful. However, if you have a support base from the get-go, you will find rapid success.

Six on Line 1: *There will be no mistake.* There is no mistake in separating yourself from an arduous situation or onerous relationship. Like a blade of grass emerging from the frozen winter soil, the task is difficult, but not impossible. Proceed with courage and confidence. It is meant to be.

Nine on Line 2: *Three foxes are hunted. The golden arrow is recovered. It is fortunate to be firm and correct.* Here, "hunting" refers to small military excursions. Recovering the "golden arrow" means no troops were lost in battle. Nourish your enterprise/relationship in incremental steps. As long as you have integrity, your endeavor will prove successful.

Six on Line 3: *Filling the carriage with treasures will attract bandits. If you insist on doing this, it will be regrettable.* Do not put all your eggs in one basket. Diversify your portfolio. Investing too heavily in one sector can endanger your hard-earned savings. You will regret such misguided action.

Nine on Line 4: *Free your toes. When friends arrive, they will trust you.* You are ready to move! Your friends recognize your confidence and zeal and will rally around your cause. Take action now. You're about to embark on a great adventure.

Six on Line 5: *When the honorable man is released from bondage, it is fortunate. Even the commoners will trust and follow him.* This line refers to King Wen being freed from seven years of house arrest imposed by the cruel King Zhou of Shang. Upon Wen's release, the commoners assembled to support his rebellion against the tyrant king. You are free to execute your idea. Many will enthusiastically come to assist you. Accept their help.

Six on Line 6: *The duke successfully shoots the falcon perched on the high wall. There is no disadvantage.* King Wen removed all obstacles hindering the success of his revolution against the Shang. Likewise, liberate yourself from those who have betrayed you. Clear your path of problems and concerns and proceed with confidence.

MY YI JOURNAL

Date	Question	Present Hexagram	Changing Line(s)	Future Hexagram	Notes

 *Sun*

Hexagram 41

Decreasing

Name

Sun means decreasing, diminishing, and lessening.

What This Hexagram Is About

This hexagram describes the Zhou government's economic strategy. Specifically, it describes how they reduced spending in an effort to elevate the people's well-being, providing them with necessary financial aid.

Hexagram Statement

Sincerity is the origin of fortune. The government can assist on its principles. There will be no fault. The policy can be implemented. With a tight budget, what can be offered to Heaven? Two bamboo baskets filled with simple offerings are sufficient. If you cut your enterprise's budget while taking pains to avoid impacting your employees, they will remain devoted if you are sincere. On a smaller scale, evaluate your spending habits. Cut out frivolous luxuries. Tightening your belt will enable you to realize your dream.

Nine on Line 1: *Suspend your affairs and hasten to your friend's aid. There is no mistake. Contribute what you can.* King Wen gained friends by being unselfish. He wholeheartedly made donations, contributing within his means. A friend in need is a friend indeed. Do not hesitate to assist a friend to the best of your ability. You will gain much more than you lose.

Nine on Line 2: *It is advantageous to assist on the right policy. Instituting new taxes and reducing welfare are dangerous.* Because the Zhou were not yet prosperous, increasing taxes would not improve their financial outlook. It is better to cut unnecessary expenses and increase the people's (your employees) wages. Set aside money for investment, future expansion, and retirement. On a smaller scale, draw up a budget and stick to it.

Six on Line 3: *When three people walk together, there is one too many. When a person walks alone, he will gain a friend.* When you have too much, you will lose some. When you do not have enough, you will gain some. Too many cooks spoil the broth. Work alone and someone will lend a helping hand.

Six on Line 4: *When the sickness has diminished, it is joyous. There will be no mistake.* The right policies can cure the sick economy (your company/relationship). When there are signs of recovery, everyone benefits. Monitor the changes and celebrate any improvement.

Six on Line 5: *When the people's wealth is increased, they offer the king 10 pairs of turtle shells. How can the king refuse such a kind gift? It is fortunate from the beginning.* Under your leadership, your employees/children will prosper. To show their appreciation, they will bestow gifts on you. Accept them with gratitude. You deserve the attention.

Nine on Line 6: *Instead of decreasing revenue, it is time to increase taxes. There will be no mistake. It is advantageous to proceed in any direction. The people are patriotic and will place their country's interest before their own.* When your business is thriving, your staff will not mind contributing more time and energy. They share your pride. In a relationship, expect reciprocal attention. Remember, the love you give will be rewarded by the love you receive.

MY YI JOURNAL

Date	Question	Present Hexagram	Changing Line(s)	Future Hexagram	Notes

Yi

Hexagram **42**

Increasing

Name

Yi means increasing.

What This Hexagram Is About

This hexagram describes how the Zhou government benefited from increasing its revenue by taxation and spending the surplus wisely.

Hexagram Statement

It is advantageous to proceed in any direction. It is advantageous to cross the great stream. In Hexagram 41, the government helped its people prosper by decreasing taxation and increasing welfare. Here, it is the opposite. When you enjoy prosperity, it is time to put into action that which you did not have the means to do before. Begin a new business, advance your education, make a generous donation to a charity. Step into the great stream and let your drive carry you forward. Invest in your future.

Nine on Line 1: *The people make use of government aid for agriculture. The harvest is bountiful. There is fortune from the beginning. There is no mistake.* When money is well spent, you can see the results. Do not be stingy. Contribute wholeheartedly to a good cause.

Six on Line 2: *When the people prospered, they offered the king 10 pairs of turtle shells. How can the king refuse such a kind gift? It will be fortunate to maintain the right policy. The king offered the turtle shells to Heaven.* Show your appreciation for your good fortune by giving back to the community. Volunteer. Become a mentor. Make a generous donation to a worthy charity or cause. You will be rewarded.

Six on Line 3: *When the country is devastated by natural phenomena or war, taxation must be increased. There will be no blame. The dukes must be officially informed.* Messengers for the Zhou government were sent bearing new tax policies to officers administering the dynasty's outer regions. When more capital is needed to carry forth your enterprise/ education, ask your partners/parents to contribute. A well-prepared report (or a glowing report card) will guarantee their support.

Six on Line 4: *Tell the dukes to follow the appropriate course of action. The increased revenue may be used to relocate the capital.* Advise your managers to prepare for relocation or an altered course of directive. On a smaller scale, now is the time to seek new avenues of interest or plan a career change. You may have to relocate.

Nine on Line 5: *As long as they are sincere and they benefit the people, there is no need to divine the auspiciousness of your actions. Proceed as planned.* It is not necessary to ask God or a higher power for guidance. If what you seek to do is carried out with integrity, sincerity, and fairness, you will be blessed.

Nine on Line 6: *Some dukes refuse to increase taxes. They even attack the policy makers. Some dukes do not collect the taxes. It is perilous.* Some people oppose your ideas. Some even attack your credibility and intention. Others cannot decide. Your situation is troublesome, awkward, and danger-prone. Be careful.

		MY YI JOURNAL			
Date	Question	Present Hexagram	Changing Line(s)	Future Hexagram	Notes

 *Guai*

Hexagram 43

Severing

Name

Guai means severing a relationship.

What This Hexagram Is About

This hexagram describes a moment of political turmoil within the Zhou administration. Upon King Wen's death, his son, King Wu, succeeded him, with Wu's brother, the Duke of Zhou, helping to administer the flailing empire. Considered a reformer, the Duke of Zhou, had ideas not always accepted by the conservative leaders. As a result, he severed relationships with those opposing reform.

Hexagram Statement

Appeal for support in the king's court. There is danger. You must warn your allies. It is disadvantageous to declare war. It is advantageous to communicate. These lines vividly describe the Duke of Zhou's angst, his passion about his beliefs. Plead your case to your opposition before taking drastic measures. If you cannot convince them to accept your opinion, you may have to litigate.

Nine on Line 1: *Keeping the toes strong is not enough to bring victory. It is regrettable.* Although the Duke of Zhou won the commoners' (toes) support, it was insufficient to sway the leaders. Similarly, you can succeed only if you win support from people of influence (a judge, high-ranking managers, senior relatives). Without their support, the outcome will not be satisfactory.

Nine on Line 2: *Be on the alert. Do not slacken even at night and there will be no accidents.* When a political or legal battle is inevitable, you must remain extremely cautious and vigilant. Only then will you not err. Do not provoke your opponent(s).

Nine on Line 3: *Show you are determined to sever the relationship. The honorable man who severs ties with his opponents is like a man walking alone in the rain. Although he may be annoyed with his soaked clothes, it will be harmless.* Those with whom you have severed ties will slander your name. Ignore their untoward behavior. It is one reason you have separated yourself from them. Eventually, the unpleasantness will subside, leaving your virtuous reputation intact.

Nine on Line 4: *Having had the skin on your buttocks stripped, you walk slowly in pain. You do not listen when someone advises you to guide the ram from behind rather than leading him from in front.* You have been stripped of your authority and power. Learn from your mistakes and seek competent advice before taking action. You can't afford to be rammed by your opponents again.

Nine on Line 5: *Like removing weeds from your lawn, sever your relationship with those who oppose you. This is appropriate. There will be no mistake.* Weed the unprincipled characters from your life. Who needs to associate with people who deplete your inner spirit? This applies to a boss, a soured romantic relationship, and disagreeable friends. Do it amicably, and no harm will come.

Six on Line 6: *Your call for help does not yield response. In the end, there will be danger.* You cannot secure support for your idea/cause/project. Try again at another time or delay your plans and go back to the drawing board.

MY YI JOURNAL				
Date	Question	Present Hexagram	Changing Line(s)	Future Hexagram	Notes

 *Gou*

Hexagram 44

Meeting

Name

Gou means meeting—specifically, to meet with people.

What This Hexagram Is About

This hexagram describes the various kinds of people the Duke of Zhou encountered as he assembled them to help assist in instituting his reforms for the new Zhou administration.

Hexagram Statement

Do not marry the strong women you meet. In this line, "women" refers to the uneducated and ignorant, qualities not associated with political, entrepreneurial, and philanthropic leaders. Do not judge a person by his or her appearance. Intelligence, not beauty, is what is important. Forming friendships/relationships with intelligent people will help to stimulate your mind and elevate your spirit.

Six on Line 1: *A metal braking system is installed in the carriage. If the brakes are released, there will be danger. It is like meeting lean and hungry bears. Perseverance brings positive results.* The "carriage" represents the capacity to assemble capable people to help administer the Zhou empire. The carriage's "brakes" represent the controlled method of choosing the appropriate people. The "lean and hungry bears" represent power-hungry but incapable people. Choose your friends/significant other wisely.

Nine on Line 2: *The fish are kept in the sack. There will be no mistake. It is disadvantageous to let the fish come near the guests.* The "fish" represent mean-spirited and hateful people, who must be kept in check. Avoid their company. They seek to pollute the minds of others, contaminating a person's confidence, motivation, and good intentions. (Note: Some sinologists translate "fish" as sex addicts. Sex without love should be avoided.)

Nine on Line 3: *People whose buttocks have been stripped walk with great difficulty. It is dangerous, but there will be no mistake.* Symbolizing criminals who have been whipped with a cane, these lines tell us it is dangerous to associate with those who have a corrupt history. However, if a person has redeemed him- or herself, give that person a second chance. Keep a watchful eye and you will not be harmed.

Nine on Line 4: *There are no fish in the sack. It will give rise to evil.* The "fish" (mean-spirited and hateful people) must have escaped and returned to the river. When these unscrupulous individuals are loose and out of control, it signals the beginning of trouble. Left unsupervised, they will spread their delusions, infecting others with their malice and negativity. This marks the beginning of worrisome times. Be careful. (Note: Some sinologists translate "fish" as sex addicts. "No fish in the sack" means you have no love life. Such repression can give rise to unscrupulous behavior.)

Nine on Line 5: *Using willow twigs to wrap a melon is like concealing your ability. Watch the mean people fall like meteors in the sky.* Surround yourself with intelligent, like-minded people. But, by all means, don't boast about your connections. It is time for you to take action when those hindering your progress fall by the wayside.

Nine on Line 6: *Meeting people who blow their horns is shameful. There will be no harm.* Using individuals who toot their own horns (brag about their accomplishments) for your gain is shameful. Sometimes it can't be helped. You will not be faulted.

MY YI JOURNAL

Date	Question	Present Hexagram	Changing Line(s)	Future Hexagram	Notes

 *Cui*

Hexagram 45

Gathering

Name

Cui means gathering together. Assembling and uniting are also indicative of Cui.

What This Hexagram Is About

This hexagram describes what happened when King Wu assembled his supporters at a sacrificial ceremony, where he asked his ancestors to approve his decision to conquer the 99 nations refusing to pledge alliance to the new Zhou administration.

Hexagram Statement

The king goes to the ancestral temple to make offerings to his ancestors. It is fortunate to offer a large sacrifice. It is advantageous to meet the great man. It will be advantageous to proceed in any direction. Persevere and the outcome will be positive. Assemble people to help forward your cause. Work together to create something great. The result will prove successful.

Six on Line 1: *Sincerity did not bring the desired result. Chaos reigns and the people gather. He raised his fist and spoke. He smiled. There is no worry. There will be no mistake.* King Wu assembled his people, asking them to help him restore order to the floundering empire. You are about to lead or participate in an important venture. The morale is high. Nothing will go wrong.

Six on Line 2: *The king leads his people to prosperity. At the sacrificial ceremony, the ancestors accept his sincerity.* You are doing something important. Your sincerity is appreciated. Proceed as planned and you will be blessed.

Six on Line 3: *Although the people gathered, they were not unified. The differences are not severe. It is a shame.* The Zhou were not convinced that military action against the 99 nations was necessary. Likewise, you have not convinced your supporters of your plan. While your idea/cause/project has not been met with strong objections, you must approach your opposition from a different angle. Putting yourself in their shoes will enable you to understand their concerns.

Nine on Line 4: *Great fortune. Nothing to blame.* What you seek (partnership/new enterprise/job) is promising. Proceed and you will succeed.

Nine on Line 5: *The gathering unifies ideas. There will be no mistake. Some are not confident. Persevere and there will be no remorse.* You have gained the majority vote. While some people may have abstained or cast a nay vote, eventually you will win them over.

176

Six on Line 6: *Some people sigh, some people weep. Yet, there is no reason to blame them.* Although some people do not agree with your decision and have expressed their displeasure, proceed as planned. Prove your position.

		MY YI JOURNAL			
Date	Question	Present Hexagram	Changing Line(s)	Future Hexagram	Notes

 *Sheng*

Hexagram 46

Rising

Name

Sheng means rising. It denotes being promoted.

What This Hexagram Is About

This hexagram narrates how the Duke of Zhou was promoted by his elder brother, King Wu. The Duke of Zhou became the king's diviner and military advisor in the mission to conquer the 99 nations that remained loyal to the Shang.

Hexagram Statement

The great man will appoint you to an important position. Do not fear. It is fortunate to conquer the south (the 99 nations). Congratulations! You will soon be promoted. With your newly elevated status, you will be assigned an important task or responsibility. Your mission is to solve a difficult problem, mediate a dispute, or install order to a chaotic situation. Don't worry. You're well-qualified. The endeavor will prove trouble-free and successful.

Six on Line 1: *Your solid reputation has led to your promotion. There will be great fortune.* In Hexagram 43, the Duke of Zhou severed relationships with those who opposed him. His courageous action, righteousness, and eagerness to help his people advanced his career. Your sincerity and virtuousness has caught the attention of the powers that be. You will be promoted.

Nine on Line 2: *Display your gratitude and make an offering to your ancestors. There will be no mistake.* Throw a party to celebrate your promotion. Let others share in your joy. It is well-deserved.

Nine on Line 3: *You are promoted to head an empty city.* An "empty city" is something devoid of problems. You are starting from scratch. Your task is to assemble a capable team for a special purpose. You are free to recruit a team of your liking.

Six on Line 4: *The king celebrates on Mount Qi. It is fortunate. There will be no mistake.* King Wu of Zhou makes an offering to the ancestors in his homeland on Mount Qi. The ceremony is held to obtain blessings for the forthcoming military assault against the 99 rebel tribes. You are the key person in an important project. Prepare, prepare, prepare. Your endeavor will be met with success and further promotion.

Six on Line 5: *There is fortune in persistence. You are rising to a higher level.* You are climbing the corporate ladder smoothly, steadily, and with great determination. But don't let your success go to your head. Stay grounded.

Six on Line 6: *Having risen to a level that makes you feel dizzy, it is advantageous to maintain a solid work ethic.* Overjoyed at your rapid advancement, you find it too good to be true. Stay focused. Keep on track. Don't let your success lead you astray.

		MY YI JOURNAL			
Date	Question	Present Hexagram	Changing Line(s)	Future Hexagram	Notes

Kun

Hexagram 47

Confining

Name

Kun means confining. Being oppressed and fatigued is also indicative of Kun.

What This Hexagram Is About

This hexagram describes how the Duke of Zhou and his troops were trapped by the rebel tribes that would not pledge allegiance to the new Zhou government.

Hexagram Statement

It is fortunate for the superior man. Even though his words are not respected, there will be no blame. Unfortunately, you are not being taken seriously. These are trying times. Oppression rules. But don't worry. Optimism will help you overcome these frustrating obstacles. Remain noble and the bad will give way to the good.

Six on Line 1: *Upon entering a gloomy valley, he sits on a tree stump feeling oppressed. The sun will not rise for three years.* Due to your lack of preparation and unfamiliarity with the situation at hand, you have made a drastic mistake. The gloomy circumstances have darkened your spirit. You will not be able to right the wrong for three years.

Nine on Line 2: *The mistake is caused by overeating and drinking. The scarlet kneepads have arrived. It is advantageous to use them at the sacrificial ceremony. It is dangerous to launch an attack. The situation will change for the better.* The "scarlet kneepads" denote the rank of a duke. Overindulging in food and drink implies the Duke of Zhou made hasty decisions about the military attack against the 99 tribes. His eagerness clouded his clarity of mind. As a result, he lost the first battle. Your zeal has caused you to make a mistake. In the future, do not make casual decisions about an important matter. Calm down. Take a deep breath and think things through logically and thoroughly.

Six on Line 3: *It is distressing to be trapped among stones, your movement confined by thorns. Entering the palace, you fail to find your wife. It is dangerous.* In a difficult situation, a man finds comfort from his wife. Because you cannot find proper counsel, you must deal with an arduous situation alone. Use your discretion wisely.

Nine on Line 4: *The chariot's heavy metal wheels slow the army coming to the rescue. It is shameful. Yet, the rescue effort will eventually arrive.* King Wu sent his troops to rescue the Duke of Zhou and his legions, who were trapped by rebel tribes refusing to recognize the Zhou government. You're in a precarious situation. Wait patiently, and the much-needed assistance will arrive in time.

Nine on Line 5: *Those wearing red kneepads threatened to impose punishment by cutting off a person's nose and feet. He accepted his sentence peacefully and sacrificed to Heaven for good fortune.* Here, "red kneepads" symbolize aggressive ministers, who avenge misdeeds. You have made a dreadful mistake. You may be fired or asked to leave your post. Do not retaliate. It was meant to be.

Six on Line 6: *Oppressed by creeping vines on unsteady ground, any movement will bring remorse. Acknowledge the mistake and continue on. The result will be fortunate.* You are in an unstable situation/relationship. Carefully evaluate your next move. You do not want to make the same mistake twice. If you take the high road, the result will be positive.

MY YI JOURNAL					
Date	Question	Present Hexagram	Changing Line(s)	Future Hexagram	Notes

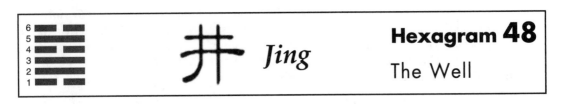

井 *Jing*

Hexagram 48

The Well

Name

Jing means a well, the storage place of the most valuable resource—water.

What This Hexagram Is About

This hexagram emphasizes the importance of labor or, to be exact, human resource. After King Wu conquered the 99 nations, he questioned how to use the abundant resources wisely.

Hexagram Statement

The town can change its ownership, but the well cannot change its function. Although the well's water will not be drained, it will not be replenished either. People arrive to enjoy the water. If the bucket is drawn up and the rope is entangled around it, or the bucket is broken, it brings misfortune. Although new governors were installed throughout the 99 nations, King Wu did not change the acting officers. Had they been excluded from the new administration, the misguided action would have initiated great tumult. This is a time to communicate and network with people. Draw from the great well of knowledge and elevate your intelligence and status.

Six on Line 1: *The water is muddy and cannot be consumed. The old well is useless.* In some countries, the government is so corrupt that restoring order is hopeless. If you acquire a company and discover the senior staff is corrupt, then replace them by choosing someone from your pool of resources. If there is no one qualified to fill the position, then abandon this post.

Nine on Line 2: *There are fish in the well. If you shoot them with an arrow, you may cause the water bucket to crack.* These lines warn to make good use of your human resources. Treat your staff/children/significant other fairly, honorably, and respectfully. Abuse the system and your company/project/relationship/family will fall apart.

Nine on Line 3: *The mud in the well has been removed. The water is now clear and good for consumption. If the water is not used, it is wasted. If the king is wise, he will use the good water for his benefit.* The Zhou removed the corrupt officers administering the 99 nations, leaving the capable ones to help them restore order. Good people possessing a solid work ethic and determination will support you. Neglecting them is wasteful and shameful.

Six on Line 4: *Repair the well's lining. There will be no mistake.* Restructure your organization/relationship to benefit your wants and needs. The efficiency will improve.

Nine on Line 5: *The well is purified. The cool water is good for drinking.* Your organization/relationship is back on track. It is productive, satisfying, and empowering to your intellect and spirit.

Six on Line 6: *Do not cover the well with a lid. Mutual trust will bring fortune.* Do not limit the talent and capabilities of your workers. Do not keep them under your thumb. Trust them and they will demonstrate their devotion to you.

MY YI JOURNAL					
Date	Question	Present Hexagram	Changing Line(s)	Future Hexagram	Notes

 *Ge*

Hexagram 49

Reforming

Name

Ge means reforming. Specifically, Ge symbolizes the hide of an ox that is transformed into leather, the tanning process denoting reform.

What This Hexagram Is About

This hexagram describes how the Duke of Zhou helped King Wu reform the Zhou empire into a prosperous, efficient, and united nation. The Duke of Zhou became the Minister of Rites, a position that established ceremonial rites and the appropriate music for certain occasions (such as weddings and burials).

Hexagram Statement

To gain the trust of the people, the ruler must be determined to reform. It will be smooth from the beginning and fortunate in the end. Minor inconveniences will be forgotten. Old ideas must be discarded to make way for the new. Reform is inevitable. Although some people may balk at your progressive ideas, ignore their stubbornness and short-sightedness and continue on your path. You are not making a mistake.

Nine on Line 1: *To be strong, use the hide of a yellow ox.* To make fine leather, the choice of raw material is essential. Likewise, in order for reform to be successful, it must be based on practical ideas and carried out by capable people. Make sure your idea is well-thought-out, well-planned, and well-researched. You can't go wrong.

Six on Line 2: *Sufficient time has passed. It is time to institute changes. There is fortune in perseverance.* The time is ripe. Put into action your plan/idea/project. With persistence and perseverance, your endeavor will prove successful.

Nine on Line 3: *There is resistance. It is dangerous. Persistence will overcome obstacles. The plans must be examined and reexamined three times before further action is taken. Eventually, the people will concede.* You must explain and present your idea/plan many times before it is accepted. While the time-consuming task is frustrating, the leg work will pay off in the end.

Nine on Line 4: *The situation is resolved. Everyone is confident about the reform. There will be fortune.* Mistakes are unavoidable. Identify and correct them early on and you will be respected for your attention to detail, honesty, and determination. Your idea has been accepted. Proceed as planned.

Nine on Line 5: *The superior man changes like a tiger changing its stripes. Divination is not needed. The people will change.* The "superior man" refers to King Wu and his brother, the Duke of Zhou. They led the reform just as naturally as a tiger takes to hunting. You are a capable leader. You do not need approval to implement your ideas. Everything will go according to plan.

Six on Line 6: *Honorable men change like a leopard changes its spots. Inferior men only appear to accept the change. Misfortune lurks behind the scenes. Persevere. There will be fortune.* While some people will wholeheartedly help to carry out your ideas, some will only pretend to. Actually, they work behind your back to sabotage your endeavors. Fortunately, these unscrupulous individuals represent the minority. Proceed at full strength and there will be success.

MY YI JOURNAL					
Date	Question	Present Hexagram	Changing Line(s)	Future Hexagram	Notes

 *Ding*

Hexagram 50

The Caldron

Name

Ding represents a bronze caldron, the character depicting a cooking pot having four legs, two ears (handles), and one eye (the opening or the lid). The king used the caldron to prepare food as offerings to Heaven. In exchange, Heaven granted him ears, eyes, and legs to make him clever and able.

What This Hexagram Is About

This hexagram describes what happened when the Duke of Zhou installed the new Zhou administration.

Hexagram Statement

There will be a good beginning, smooth progress, and great fortune. The new administration introduced by the Duke of Zhou began on the right foot. Put into action your progressive plan, novel idea, or newfound insights. Any obstacles hindering the implementation will serve only to sharpen and perfect your endeavor.

Six on Line 1: *The caldron is overturned. It is advantageous to throw away the food rotting inside the vessel. The concubine gives birth to a son. There will be no blame.* Referring to the Shang dynasty, the "rotting food" was replaced by a fresh administration, the Zhou. The new empire claimed legitimacy as if the wife was barren and the concubine gives birth to a son. Now that you are in charge of the situation at hand, rid your organization of outdated ideas and incompetent people. On a smaller scale, your sense of empowerment drives you to shed bad habits, filling your spirit with productivity and renewed self-confidence.

Nine on Line 2: *The caldron is filled with food. The enemy is weak and cannot oppose the ruler. There will be fortune.* While the new Zhou administration was solid and filled with capable people, its opposition was weak and caused no harm. Ignore individuals who degrade your ideas. Your opinion is the only one that counts.

Nine on Line 3: *The caldron's ear is lost. It cannot be lifted. The fat pheasant cannot be eaten. The rain will come to cool the caldron. Eventually, there will be fortune.* Like a plump pheasant, the new Zhou government is ready. However, the loss of the caldron's "ear" (handle) suggests that there are few people who can carry out the new system. The "rain" removes the frustration. It takes time to get a new enterprise/relationship up and running. Expect to ride out a few rough waves before you sail smoothly to success.

Nine on Line 4: *The caldron's leg is broken. The food reserved for the nobles has spilled. The scene is ugly. There will be misfortune.* Because the capable Zhou people could not shoulder the immense responsibility of administering a new government, they fell by the wayside leaving the incapable ones in charge. Work to correct your situation before it turns into disaster.

Six on Line 5: *The caldron's ears are replaced by brass ones decorated with gold rings. It is advantageous to be firm and correct.* The corrupt people governing the newly formed Zhou administration were eventually replaced by people dedicated to installing honesty and fairness. Negative, selfish, and imprudent people impede your progress. Rid yourself of them.

Nine on Line 6: *The caldron is decorated with jade. There will be great fortune. There is no disadvantage.* While bronze is hard, jade is soft. Each balances the other. A well-balanced system brings harmony and good fortune. Executing your orders with strictness and benevolence will guarantee success.

Date	Question	Present Hexagram	Changing Line(s)	Future Hexagram	Notes

MY YI JOURNAL

 *Zhen*

Hexagram 51

Startling

to disturb suddenly by surprise.

Name

Zhen means startling, in particular being surprised or shocked by the sound of thunder.

What This Hexagram Is About

This hexagram describes how the Zhou people reacted to the new government.

Hexagram Statement

Thunder comes with a startling "quak-quak" causing the people to laugh, "ya-ya." The thunder shocks a hundred li. The diviner did not drop his spoon. The new Zhou administration startled everyone far and wide (100 li). Once the shock wore off, they laughed about it. Here, "diviner" refers to the Duke of Zhou. Because he orchestrated the system, he was not startled and kept his composure (the spoon). Something will startle your family/company/country. They will talk about it amidst laughter. Although the cause of the startling event will greatly influence your family/company/country, they will be well aware of the consequences. (Note: Li is the Chinese mile.)

Nine on Line 1: *Thunder comes with a startling "quak-quak" causing the people to laugh, "ya-ya." There will be fortune.* When radical ideas are introduced or implemented, it shocks all involved. Once people get used to the new idea/organization/relationship and understand its fundamental basis, they will laugh with joy. Take the time to fully understand something before dismissing it.

Six on Line 2: *The shock is frightening. Some people give up their precious shells and hide in the hills. Don't look for them. They will return in seven days.* In ancient China, seashells were used as money. If a friend/loved one/associate leaves because he or she is overwhelmed by new circumstances, don't worry. He or she will not be gone for long.

Six on Line 3: *The thunder awakens everyone. However, no one is hurt by the shock.* Wake up and accept new ideas. They will not harm you.

Nine on Line 4: *The shock causes some people to sink in the mud.* Some people are not ready for change and cannot adapt to it. They will become stuck in their old ways, unable to keep pace with the changing world.

Six on Line 5: *Some people come and go amidst the startling movement. It will be risky. There is gain and no loss.* Be on the alert to accept a risky position. Remember, nothing ventured, nothing gained.

Six on Line 6: *Some people are so startled they pant and gaze with confusion. It will be dangerous to proceed in any direction. If the shock does not affect you, but affects your neighbor, there should be no complaints. However, his friends may speak against him.* Those who do not accept change tend to be anxious and unhappy. Do not act against change. If your friend/loved one/associate reacts to change in an unusual way and receives taunts from others, do not blame him or her.

		MY YI JOURNAL			
Date	Question	Present Hexagram	Changing Line(s)	Future Hexagram	Notes

 *Gen*

Hexagram 52

Stopping

Name

Gen means stopping, with an underlying meaning of reaching the final destination.

What This Hexagram Is About

This hexagram describes how an officer should give proper advice to the king. It describes the art of politics.

Hexagram Statement

Stopping a person at his back cannot effectively halt the body's motion. It is like walking into a courtyard without being noticed. There will be no blame. While everyone needs competent advice, it should be offered directly to the person and not spoken behind his or her back. First, you must get the attention of the person whom you wish to advise.

Six on Line 1: *Stop at the toes. There will be no mistake. It is advantageous to be firm.* Offer your advice before a person acts. Warn your friend/partner to think before he or she leaps.

Six on Line 2: *Stopping his calves while he is moving will displease him because you should be following him.* You cannot stop what has already started. You will be blamed if you attempt to do this. Your relationship will be spoiled. Taking action at the proper time is most important.

Nine on Line 3: *Stopping a person's forward movement at the loins will pull his muscles. It causes injury and pain. His heart will be infuriated.* When something is in full force (for example, a relationship or the restructuring of a company), and you seek to bring it to an abrupt stop, it will cause harm. He or she will be angry.

Six on Line 4: *Stopping the entire body without causing him to lose balance will not be a mistake.* If the action/relationship can be stopped safely, it will not prove problematic.

Six on Line 5: *Stopping the jaws so that a person's speech is orderly will not cause remorse.* Plan and organize your speech (or that of a friend/associate) before delivering it. Understand that words can be either constructive or destructive. Think before you speak. You do not want to regret what you say.

Nine on Line 6: *Nobility in stopping a person's wrongdoings will bring fortune.* Act with integrity and honesty when advising a person to reconsider his or her intended actions. Be diplomatic.

MY YI JOURNAL					
Date	Question	Present Hexagram	Changing Line(s)	Future Hexagram	Notes

 *Jian*

Hexagram 53
Gradually
Progressing

Name

Jian means gradually progressing, moving forward, and advancing in incremental steps.

What This Hexagram Is About

This hexagram tells how the Zhou empire gradually progressed to become a prosperous and united nation under the leadership and guidance of King Wu and the Duke of Zhou.

Hexagram Statement

A betrothed woman must prepare her wedding step by step for it to be fortunate. It will be advantageous to be firm. The preparation of a wedding is a tremendous undertaking. It must be done slowly, with great thought and care. To rule a country or manage an enterprise is no less complicated. Attention to detail, staunch determination, and unwavering commitment will ensure a successful venture. Progress gradually and capably.

Six on Line 1: *The wild swan gradually lands by the river's edge. It is like a young man in danger of being spoken against. There will be no mistake.* When the Zhou empire was established, the king was weighed down by widespread discontent. You are just beginning a career/relationship. Approach with care and humbly accept constructive criticism. There is always room for improvement.

Six on Line 2: *The wild swan gradually lands on a large rock. He eats and drinks happily. There will be fortune.* Your company/project/relationship is on firm ground. Your staff/partner is content. Congratulations! You are on the right track.

Nine on Line 3: *The wild swan gradually lands on the dry plateau. It is like a husband going to war with an unknown return date. It is also like a pregnant woman losing her unborn baby. There will be misfortune. Defend against intruders.* The swan landing on barren soil symbolizes the new Zhou empire taking a wrong turn (as indicated in Hexagram 43). You are going in the wrong direction. Stop what you are doing. Defend yourself against misfortune.

Six on Line 4: *The wild swan gradually lands in the woods. There, he finds branches on which to rest. There will be no mistake.* It is safer to be in the treetops than on the ground. Find a safe place to rest, regroup, and re-energize before taking off on a new venture/relationship. Be sure of your next move.

Nine on Line 5: *The wild swan gradually lands on high ground. It is like a woman who fails to conceive in three years. Finally, misfortune leaves. The wish is fulfilled.* When King Wu conquered the 99 rebel nations, his people could rest. Although conceiving an empire of peace and plenty was difficult, it proved successful in the end. You have accomplished your mission. You are ready for something new.

Nine on Line 6: *The wild swan gradually flies above the clouds. The feather that falls to the ground is used in a ceremony. There will be fortune.* Although King Wu died two years after the founding of the Zhou dynasty, he laid a foundation that lasted for some 800 years. When you have accomplished something great, it is time to aspire to an even higher, more ambitious goal. When you have successfully established a relationship, why not consider partnership/marriage?

MY YI JOURNAL				
Date	Question	Present Hexagram	Changing Line(s)	Future Hexagram	Notes

Name

Gui Mei consists of two characters: On the left side, Gui indicates a marriage ceremony; on the right side, Mei means a younger sister. Together, Gui Mei means the marrying of the younger sister.

What This Hexagram Is About

This hexagram describes how Di Yi (Zhou Wang's father) had his younger sister married to Ji Chang (King Wen). Another maiden, usually a younger sister, accompanied the bride as the king's concubine. This role served an important purpose. If the wife was barren, hopefully the concubine could provide heirs to the throne. The Chinese were fond of using the partnership of husband and wife to symbolize the relationship between the king and his ministers. The Duke of Zhou (King Wen's son) used the marriage of Di Yi's sister to represent his situation after his brother, King Wu, died. As the country's caretaker, he supervised the empire, acting on behalf of his young nephew, Cheng Wang, the king.

Hexagram Statement

Any direction proves dangerous. There will be no advantage. The Duke of Zhou sensed his position as acting head of the empire was dangerous. Whether it is your rightful position or not, you are in charge. Unfortunately, even though you perform your duties with the utmost sincerity and integrity, your situation will not bring a favorable outcome.

Nine on Line 1: *The concubine accompanying the elder sister to her wedding is like a lame person limping. There is no advantage.* While you may be acting on behalf of your superior, it is still more advantageous to be the one in charge.

Nine on Line 2: *A person's eyesight is not totally lost if he is blind in only one eye. It is advantageous for a hermit to keep his lifestyle.* Turn a blind eye to unpleasant happenings.

Six on Line 3: *A maiden's marriage is important. However, she must accompany her elder sister as a concubine.* The Duke of Zhou's position as advisor to the young king, Cheng Wang, was at times frustrating. As the acting head, you may not like to implement your ideas, for there will be those who are suspicious of your motives. There is no need to be sheepish. Hold your head high and carry on.

Nine on Line 4: *The wedding ceremony is delayed. It is better late than never.* As a result of King Wu's death, the coronation of his young son and the appointment of the Duke of Zhou as the country's caretaker were probably delayed. The announcement of your promotion/engagement will be delayed.

Six on Line 5: *When Di Yi arranged his younger sister's marriage, the bride's wedding garment was not as beautiful as her sister's dress. The moon is almost full. There will be fortune.* King Wen's concubine (Di Yi's younger sister) probably gave birth to both King Wu and the Duke of Zhou. Although you may win something by default, do not feel ashamed. Use your newfound position/inheritance/prize to the best of your ability. You will shine.

Six on Line 6: *The lady carries an empty basket. The gentleman slaughters the ram, but there is no blood. There will be misfortune.* The young king's coronation ceremony was not extravagant. Because he was too young to rule, the Duke of Zhou became the country's caretaker, a challenging position fraught with obstacles and frustration. There are difficult times ahead. Maintain the proper decorum. Sharpen your political acumen.

MY YI JOURNAL					
Date	Question	Present Hexagram	Changing Line(s)	Future Hexagram	Notes

 **Feng**

Hexagram **55**
Overshadowing

Name

Feng means overshadowing, with the underlying meaning of problems brought about by prosperity.

What This Hexagram Is About

This hexagram describes an eclipse, which symbolizes impending corruption overshadowing honesty. The Duke of Zhou admonished his young nephew, Cheng Wang (the king), about the ill effect of being extravagant.

Hexagram Statement

The king watches his people enjoy prosperity. He is like the sun at its brightest. There is no worry. The Zhou empire gained an abundance of riches left behind by the Shang. The young king rejoiced in his people's extravagant lifestyle. Like the noonday sun, he felt radiant and proud. He was not aware of the lurking ramifications of sudden prosperity. Enjoy your good fortune while you can. Remember, money is the root of all evil. Be wise about spending it and boasting about it.

Nine on Line 1: *Getting along with the destined master, nothing goes wrong for the first 10 days. What follows will be revealed as time progresses.* When you meet your new boss or prospective mate, there is always an enjoyable honeymoon period where everyone is on his or her best behavior. What comes later remains to be seen.

Six on Line 2: *The eclipse casts a large shadow on earth. The polestar [north star] is seen at midday. There is mistrust and suspicion. If sincerity prevails, it will be fortunate.* Rumors spread far and wide that the Duke of Zhou wanted to be king. Gossip envelopes you. Take the high road and do not react against the groundless accusations. The outcome will prove positive.

Nine on Line 3: *The sun is eclipsed. Even the faintest stars can be seen at midday. Someone broke his right arm in the dark. It is not too bad after all.* Like the sun's brightness being suddenly blocked, the Duke of Zhou's radiant spirit was depressed by baseless rumors. Yet the accusations were not fatal. If you have not committed a wrongdoing, the rumors besieging you will not be serious. Eventually, your innocence will shine through.

Nine on Line 4: *The eclipse holds fast. The polestar can still be seen at midday. You will meet a like-minded person. There will be fortune.* The baseless rumors still hover around you. Don't fear. Your partner/significant other/superior has confidence in you. The sun will soon come out, making your days brighter.

Six on Line 5: *The official document arrives. It clears your name. There will be good fortune.* The truth will set you free! You will be officially recognized. Congratulations.

Six on Line 6: *An elegant mansion is hidden in the dark because its owner does not want to expose his wealth. If you peep inside the door, you cannot see anyone. If the situation continues for three years, there will be danger.* The Duke of Zhou warns his young nephew, the king, about the effects of extravagance and distancing himself from his people. Do not flaunt your good fortune. You will alienate your family and friends.

MY YI JOURNAL

Date	Question	Present Hexagram	Changing Line(s)	Future Hexagram	Notes

旅 *Lu*

Hexagram 56

Traveling

```
6 ▬▬ ▬▬
5 ▬▬ ▬▬
4 ▬▬▬▬▬
3 ▬▬▬▬▬
2 ▬▬ ▬▬
1 ▬▬▬▬▬
```

Name

Lu means traveling, with the underlying meaning of journeying through life.

What This Hexagram Is About

This hexagram is meant to be a lesson given by the Duke of Zhou to his young nephew, King Cheng Wang. It teaches him how to live the life of a benevolent ruler.

Hexagram Statement

Persevere through small achievements. A person encounters small memorable moments during his life journey. Cherish these. Although you may encounter bumps in the road, your life becomes meaningful and smooth if it is led with sincerity, honesty, and determination.

Six on Line 1: *If a traveler concerns himself with pettiness, it will bring misfortune.* Be generous. Give your time, talent, and energy to others. Understand that stinginess, small-mindedness, and meanness accumulate to cause harm later. What goes around, comes around.

Six on Line 2: *During the journey, there is sufficient money to find a good inn and a young servant.* Sometimes life is devoid of problems and filled with comfort and joy. You are blessed.

Nine on Line 3: *The inn has burned down. The young servant flees. The situation is perilous.* The Duke of Zhou warned his nephew to control his temper. The burnt inn symbolizes misfortune. Because of it, the traveler may lose his temper and punish his servant, who then leaves. In an arduous situation, maintain your composure. Your kindness will be rewarded.

Nine on Line 4: *Upon finding a campsite, I am still unhappy even though I have an axe and a means of livelihood.* Sometimes life is not what we want it to be. As long as you have the means to continue your sojourn, you can look forward to a better tomorrow.

Six on Line 5: *The pheasant is killed with one arrow. This will bring fame.* Use your talent and determination to find new opportunities that will make your name known and respected.

Nine on Line 6: *The bird's nest is burnt. The traveler laughs at first, and cries later. It is unfortunate that he loses his ox.* Here, the Duke of Zhou tells a different story from the one he tells in Line 3. The "bird's nest" refers to the inn; the ox, the young servant.

Upon seeing the devastated inn, the traveler laughs because it is not his property. When he realizes the indiscretion, his servant has already left. Remorseful, the traveler cries. Showing compassion is virtuous. Do not make fun of another's misfortune. It could be you.

		MY YI JOURNAL			
Date	Question	Present Hexagram	Changing Line(s)	Future Hexagram	Notes

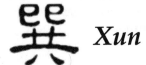 *Xun*

Hexagram 57

Penetrating

Name

Xun means penetrating.

What This Hexagram Is About

Like Hexagram 56, this one is also meant to be a lesson given by the Duke of Zhou to his young nephew, King Cheng Wang. It teaches him how to penetrate the hearts and minds of his subjects by being earnest.

Hexagram Statement

It is advantageous to proceed in any direction. It is advantageous to see the great man. The Duke of Zhou advised Cheng Wang to spread his message like the wind penetrating the hills and valleys. It is important to voice your opinions/objectives/goals. Assemble your staff/children and communicate your wants and needs. Be heard!

Six on Line 1: *Deciding whether to advance or retreat is like having the firmness of a military leader.* Determination will carry your cause/career/relationship forward. You cannot afford to be hesitant.

Nine on Line 2: *Communicate the message while kneeling before an alter. Employ diviners and exorcists. There will be fortune without fault.* In ancient China, rulers used the name of Heaven to communicate their wishes to the people. When you preach your ideas to your associates/friends/family, show your sincerity as a clergyman would.

Nine on Line 3: *Penetrating too deep will bring disrespect.* Do not beat people over the head with your opinion/cause/concern. Such action is disrespectful. Do you want to be known as a fanatic or zealot?

Six on Line 4: *Forget about regrettable events. Hunt and you will find bountiful game.* You must not let setbacks and unfortunate happenings bother you. By all means, don't dwell on them! Do something constructive to curtail your misfortune and you will see positive results.

Nine on Line 5: *Find fortune in persevering. It is advantageous to forget about remorseful events. Although the beginning is not favorable, the ending is. Before taking action, ponder for three days. Upon taking action, watch the result for three days.* Carefully think through your decision before putting it into action. While the outcome may bring difficulties in the beginning, you have not made a mistake. Monitor the progress of your decision.

Nine on Line 6: *Even though you kneel before the alter to communicate your message, if you have lost your means, it will be evil to persist.* Here, "means" refers to losing the trust of your partner/staff/friends/family. If you do not follow through on your promises, you will gain a bad reputation. No matter how sincere you appear this time, you will not gain any support.

		MY YI JOURNAL			
Date	Question	Present Hexagram	Changing Line(s)	Future Hexagram	Notes

Dui

Hexagram 58

Pleasing

Name

Dui means pleasing.

What This Hexagram Is About

Like Hexagrams 56 and 57, this hexagram is also meant to be a lesson given by the Duke of Zhou to his young nephew, King Cheng Wang of Zhou. It teaches him how to please his subjects by making them feel content and satisfied.

Hexagram Statement

Progressive smoothness. It is advantageous to be firm and correct. As king, Cheng Wang learned that pleasing others is reciprocated by unwavering loyalty, peace, and prosperity. Being benevolent is the correct approach to leading/parenting. Persisting with this attitude will inspire harmonious relationships among your staff/family.

Nine on Line 1: *Pleasing people with agreeable gestures is fortunate.* A pleasant demeanor conveys your sincerity, good will, and good intentions. Smile! Look people in the eye when you speak to them. Uncross your arms and legs. Appear open and comfortable. Your radiance will comfort others.

Nine on Line 2: *Pleasing people with sincerity is fortunate. Regrettable events will be forgotten.* If a misunderstanding has caused tension between you and your friends/family/staff/associates, iron it out with sincerity. It is the only way to remove a grudge and hurt feelings.

Six on Line 3: *Pleasing people with empty words brings misfortune.* Pleasing or placating your friends/family/staff/associates with flowery language and superficial intent will backfire. You will shoot yourself in the foot. Be true to yourself and to them.

Nine on Line 4: *Pleasing people through discussion sometimes brings disagreement. In order to resolve the problem, find its cause.* Discussion often brings out differing opinions. Mediate the conversation. Taking the middle road will help lead to a resolution.

Nine on Line 5: *Trusting someone who seeks to hurt you is dangerous.* Trusting a wolf in sheep's clothing is foolhardy. Know who your friends and foes are before you confide in them.

Six on Line 6: *Please people through temptation.* Entice your supporters. Seduce your mate. Place a carrot stick in front of them and they will leap to help you. Reward a job well done.

MY YI JOURNAL					
Date	Question	Present Hexagram	Changing Line(s)	Future Hexagram	Notes

 *Huan*

Hexagram 59

Dispersing

Name

Huan means dispersing. Dissolving, dissipating, and eliminating are also indicative of Huan.

What This Hexagram Is About

King Cheng Wang's three uncles (Cai, Guan, and Huo) were assigned to monitor the Shang king's son, Wu Geng. They were intensely jealous of the Duke of Zhou's position as the young king's advisor. They spread baseless rumors that the Duke of Zhou intended to eliminate Cheng Wang so that he could become king. This had a negative effect on the people's morale, and their loyalty and enthusiasm began to dissipate. This hexagram describes how the Duke of Zhou rectified the situation.

Hexagram Statement

Progressive smoothness. The king goes to the ancestral temple. It is advantageous to cross the great stream. It is advantageous to persevere. With the new Zhou empire in turmoil, Wu Geng grasped this opportunity to begin a rebellion against them. The Duke of Zhou accompanied the young king to the temple to ask for a blessing. Afterwards, they effectively thwarted Wu Geng's rebellion. Say a prayer, grasp the bull by the horns, and eliminate any obstacles hindering your development.

Six on Line 1: *Rescuing the country with strong horses is fortunate.* "Strong horses" refers to quick military action. Nip the problem in the bud. Act quickly and with determination. Do not hesitate.

Nine on Line 2: *Sit at the table while people disperse. The moment for repentance will leave.* To "sit at the table" means to act calmly amid chaos. Don't panic. Take a deep breath, clear your head, and rectify the situation with great thought and care.

Six on Line 3: *Humbly ask the dispersing people to return. There will be nothing to regret.* Your group has disbanded. Out of frustration and disappointment they have abandoned your project/cause/company. Humbly plead with them to reconsider. Promise you will resolve the problem at hand. Do not be ashamed. Your determination will prove fruitful.

Six on Line 4: *The dispersed people return in multitudes. It is unbelievable.* People are coming to support you in droves. The response is overwhelming. It is a sight to behold.

Nine on Line 5: *Dispersion is like a person sweating a fever. The king disperses his wealth to those supporting him. There will be no mistake.* When a person is sick, cooling the fever by sweating is the natural cure. Likewise, if discontent plagues your inner spirit, make a donation to a worthy charity. Become a mentor. Volunteer for a noble cause. You will strengthen your weakened spirit and fortify your mind. If you lead a company, share your profit with your employees. Your thoughtfulness will be returned tenfold.

Nine on Line 6: *Dispersing greater calamity by causing bloodshed is inevitable. Learn the lesson. There will be no further mistakes*. The rebellion led by Wu Geng was suppressed by military action, effectively eliminating any further threat of Shang resistance. The root of your problem has been eliminated. Although you may have paid a hefty price (emotionally or physically), it is worth it.

MY YI JOURNAL

Date	Question	Present Hexagram	Changing Line(s)	Future Hexagram	Notes

 *Jie*

Hexagram 60

Regulating

Name

Jie means regulating your spending.

What This Hexagram Is About

After the civil war caused by the Three Monitors was squelched, the Duke of Zhou regulated national spending. This hexagram explains his philosophy of governing the Zhou reserves.

Hexagram Statement

There is smooth progression. Overregulating is disadvantageous. Once the war against the Duke of Zhou's three brothers was thwarted, it was necessary to reduce the budget in an effort to replenish their reserves. Yet, making drastic cuts would impede the country's progress. This is a time to tighten your belt. Frugality will set you back on track. However, don't be too strict. An occasional indulgence is just and appropriate.

Nine on Line 1: *Staying inside the house to avoid unnecessary spending is no mistake.* Regulate spending by eating in more. Entertain yourself with a good book, intelligent television programs, and a relaxing bath. Write a letter or play a game. Just stay home!

Nine on Line 2: *Staying inside the house when opportunity knocks at the door will bring misfortune.* When a great opportunity presents itself, invest in it. Do not allow frugality to lead to stinginess. You cannot gain anything by hoarding your savings.

Six on Line 3: *If spending is not regulated, complain and grumble. There will be no mistake.* If your mate or business partner is overspending, bringing it to his or her attention will not cause a problem.

Six on Line 4: *If being frugal suits you, your progression will be smooth.* A penny saved is a penny earned. Spend within your means. Build up your nest egg and reap the benefits.

Nine on Line 5: *If you enjoy regulating your life, there will be fortune. Your name will be respected for living a noble lifestyle.* Spending less will make you healthier, wealthier, and wiser. You will enjoy spiritual satisfaction rather than material abundance.

Six on Line 6: *Being stingy is dangerous. Cease being miserly and you will forget about these miserable days.* Frugality is virtuous. But living a miserly life is not. Spend when needed and you will be a happier person.

Date	Question	Present Hexagram	Changing Line(s)	Future Hexagram	Notes

MY YI JOURNAL

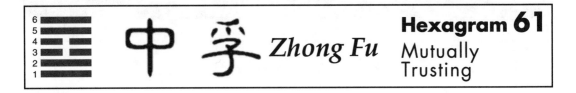

Name

Zhong Fu consists of two characters: On the left side, Zhong means central; on the right side, Fu means sincerity and trust. Together, Zhong Fu means being mutually trusting, being sincere from the bottom of the heart.

What This Hexagram Is About

The rebellion created by the Three Monitors was caused by a lack of trust between them and their brother, the Duke of Zhou. This hexagram describes how the Duke of Zhou handled the delicate situation.

Hexagram Statement

Offering simple sacrifices like piglets and fish will bring fortune. It is advantageous to cross the great stream. It is advantageous to insist on the correct path. Sincerity cannot be measured. True friendship is not gained by lavishing expensive gifts on people. As long as there is mutual trust between you and your mate/associates/business partner, you can work together to create something great.

Nine on Line 1: *Being in harmony is fortunate. If hidden motives exist, people will not dine together.* If ulterior intentions and suspicions lurk beneath the surface of your relationship, how can you enjoy your partner's/friend's/associate's company? Do not be paranoid. Have faith in the relationship.

Nine on Line 2: *The mother crane calls out to her children from the shade. They respond immediately. I have fine wine. Will you join me?* The "mother crane" refers to the Duke of Zhou. The "children" are the Zhou people. The "wine" represents the just policies that helped to make the country prosper. The Duke of Zhou asked his people to trust him. Have faith in the management. Everyone will share in its success.

Six on Line 3: *An enemy appears. For an instant, you want to go to war. The next moment, you do not. Sometimes you want to cry and sometimes you want to sing.* These lines refer to the Duke of Zhou's indecision about waging war against his brothers, the Three Monitors. You are at a crossroad. You must make an important decision. Use the utmost discretion. Carefully think through the ramifications of your decision.

Six on Line 4: *The moon is almost full. The horse is lost. There will be no mistake.* The Duke of Zhou realized his brothers were working against him and not with him. It has become clear that your friend(s) has turned against you. Now that the situation has come to light, do something about the unpleasantness.

Nine on Line 5: *When friends love each other like brothers, there will be no mistake.* The Duke of Zhou was able to convince his brother, the Duke of Zhao, that the rumors spread by their three brothers were groundless. The Duke of Zhao agreed to launch a military attack to restore peace and order. Gain the trust and support from your most important partner. There will be no mistake.

Nine on Line 6: *The rooster crows, its voice rising to Heaven. To persist will bring misfortune.* A rooster cannot fly. It can only hope its crow will reach far and wide. Words without action bring misfortune. The Duke of Zhou realized this and set out to thwart the rebellion led by his brothers. Don't just talk about it, do it!

MY YI JOURNAL

Date	Question	Present Hexagram	Changing Line(s)	Future Hexagram	Notes

| 6 |
| 5 |
| 4 |
| 3 |
| 2 |
| 1 |

小過 *Xiao Guo*

Hexagram 62

Small Testing

Name

Xiao Guo consists of two characters: On the left side, Xiao means small; on the right side, Guo means test. Together, Xiao Guo means small testing—passing a small test.

What This Hexagram Is About

Many people were suspicious of the Duke of Zhou's intentions when he agreed to assist his young nephew, King Cheng Wang. This hexagram describes the small tests the Duke of Zhou had to pass in order to win the confidence of the people.

Hexagram Statement

There is advantage in small matters, but not for important ones. The flying bird's squawk can reach only earth and not Heaven. There will be great fortune. It is advantageous to be firm. The Duke of Zhou understood he must accomplish small tasks first. His orders are like the bird's, which must reach the officers and not the king, the Son of Heaven. For the time being, it is better to take care of small matters. Tie up loose ends. You cannot tackle an important issue until your desk is cleared.

Six on Line 1: *The bird ascends. There will be danger.* The Duke of Zhou could not go above the young king's head and mandate unrealistic ordinances that could not be fulfilled. Likewise, understand your job position. Trying to implement rules/ideas that can be done only by your superior will bring an unfavorable outcome.

Six on Line 2: *Missing the ancestor, he meets the ancestress. Unable to meet the king, he meets the minister. There will be no mistake.* These lines refer to the situation after King Wu died. Since his son was too young to govern, everyone counted on the Duke of Zhou to administer the new empire. In unusual circumstances, you must take on exceptional responsibilities. Don't complain. It is an opportunity to display your talent, determination, and loyalty.

Nine on Line 3: *Without taking extraordinary precaution, it is easy to get hurt. The situation is dangerous.* Sometimes the Duke of Zhou was too harsh with King Cheng Wang, his young nephew. This gave many the idea that he sought to replace the king. You are in a sensitive position. Act within your rank. Do not overstep your boundaries.

Nine on Line 4: *There will be no error if the superior is not bypassed. Avoid danger. Do not perpetually insist.* As long as you do not overstep your boundaries, you will not encounter any problems. Doing so would endanger your name.

Six on Line 5: *Although dense clouds gather over the western suburbs (Zhou), it does not rain. The duke shoots with a tethered arrow and hits the game in a cave.* The Duke of Zhou successfully suppressed the rebellion led by his three brothers, thereby dispersing the dark cloud hovering over the empire. Although your situation seems to be disastrous, it is not. Take action and resolve the matter at hand.

Six on Line 6: *Passing by without meeting the target is like a bird soaring. It will bring disaster and danger.* Going over the head of your superior will lead to him or her resenting you. You will have to suffer the consequences of your action. Do not overstep your boundaries.

MY YI JOURNAL					
Date	Question	Present Hexagram	Changing Line(s)	Future Hexagram	Notes

 *Ji Ji*

Name

Ji Ji consists of two characters: On the left side, Ji means already; on the right side, Ji means crossing the river. Together, Ji Ji means already crossing the river, already accomplishing something.

What This Hexagram Is About

This hexagram summarizes the rise and fall of the Shang dynasty. It concludes with the Zhou overthrowing the Shang administration. That which is already accomplished is the establishment of Zhou rule.

Hexagram Statement

Progressive smoothness. It is advantageous to persevere in small matters. There will be fortune in the beginning and chaos in the end. Upon establishing a new enterprise or relationship, expect smooth sailing at its onset. As time progresses, you may encounter uncertainties and problems, which may lead to an unfortunate and chaotic ending. Proceed in incremental steps.

Nine on Line 1: *Like a fox crossing the river and getting only his tail wet, he carefully brakes his carriage's wheel. There will be no mistake.* Although unpleasant events (misunderstandings, arguments, misfortune) may dampen your enterprise/relationship, they will not hurt your accomplishment.

Six on Line 2: *A woman loses her hair ornament. There is no need to search for it. In seven days, it will be found.* Whatever you have lost will soon be returned.

Nine on Line 3: *Gao Zong* (Shang King Wu Ding) *spent three years conquering the Gui Fang* (a northern barbarian tribe). *Incapable people should not be employed.* As a result of incompetent generals leading the Shang legions, it took an inordinate amount of time and a heavy loss of life to conquer the barbarians. If you are determined to win (a campaign, a new job, litigation), then surround yourself with knowledgeable people who can help foster your success. You will win.

Six on Line 4: *The fine cotton clothing turns to rags. Be alert all day.* The three years spent battling the northern tribes proved exhausting. The Shang people felt ragged. They lost their trust in others. Likewise, don't be too trusting.

Nine on Line 5: *While the eastern neighbor slaughters an ox for his sacrifice, the western neighbor can afford only a humble offering. Nevertheless, the western neighbor is blessed.*

Here, "east" refers to the Shang; "west" refers to the Zhou, the less prosperous tribe. Despite your financial circumstances, endeavor to succeed to the best of your ability. Heaven helps those who help themselves.

Six on Line 6: *The head is submerged in water. It is dangerous.* The defeat of the Shang empire by the Zhou can be likened to a man drowning. The Shang could do nothing to save themselves. Congratulations! You have defeated your enemy/competition. Your mission has been accomplished.

MY YI JOURNAL

Date	Question	Present Hexagram	Changing Line(s)	Future Hexagram	Notes

未 濟 *Wei Ji*

Hexagram 64
Not Yet
Accomplished

Name

Wei Ji consists of two characters: On the left side, Wei means not yet; on the right side, Ji means crossing the river. Together, Wei Ji suggests the goal has not yet been accomplished.

What This Hexagram Is About

This hexagram warns the Zhou that history may repeat itself.

Hexagram Statement

There is smooth progression. The little fox has not yet crossed the river, but its tail is already wet. Nothing is gained. The "little fox" refers to Ji Li, King Wen's father, who was killed because he posed a threat to the Shang empire. This event marked the beginning of the dynastic change. Change is in the air. Step into it with courage and confidence. Ji Li did not act in time. Look about you. Do not be afraid. Persevere.

Six on Line 1: *The little fox got its tail wet. It is a shame.* The "little fox," Ji Li, was not capable of defeating the Shang king, Wu Ding. You cannot yet defeat your competitor or advance to a higher position. Take this time to hone your skills and strengthen your inner reserve without being noticed. Keep a low profile.

Nine on Line 2: *Brake the wheels. Persevere in persistence. There will be fortune.* Play it safe! This is no time to take unnecessary risks. Being cautious is the right course of action.

Six on Line 3: *The great river has not yet been crossed. However, it is advantageous to cross it. Danger lurks.* It was risky business attempting to overthrow the Shang. Yet, the Zhou persevered to achieve this goal. Your project/job is going to be very difficult. Yet, do not give up. It is a terrific opportunity to achieve a great accomplishment.

Nine on Line 4: *It is fortunate to be firm. All unhappy events will be forgotten. Join the Shang to help conquer Gui Fang* (a northern tribe). *In three years, the big country will bestow gifts and accolades on you.* The Shang king, Wu Ding, invited the Zhou to help him conquer the northern barbarians. In so doing, the Zhou gained valuable military experience. Learn from your superiors and competition. It will pave the way to success.

Six on Line 5: *It is fortunate to be firm. It is honorable to be noble. Gaining the people's trust brings great fortune.* Sticking to your principles will help foster a noble reputation. It is the first step toward success.

Nine on Line 6: *Toasting your success is not a mistake. If you become addicted to drink later, then it will damage your reputation.* The Shang leaders drank to excess and led lavish lifestyles. The heady intoxicating taste of success colors the mind and threatens resolve. The Duke of Zhou feared his people would follow in the Shang's footsteps and succumb to debauchery. He fought against this. Be mindful of addiction. It is difficult to break a habit. The best thing to do is to fight it before it gains too firm a hold.

	MY YI JOURNAL				
Date	Question	Present Hexagram	Changing Line(s)	Future Hexagram	Notes

Part 5

Understanding the Principles of the Chinese Cosmos

This part will enlighten you about the esoteric concepts of qi and yin and yang. While qi is the "stuff" of the universe, the vital force at the heart and development of all things, yin and yang are the two dynamic forces driving life through perpetual cycles of birth, growth, decay, and death. Although the terms are not included in the Yijing, the concept was probably understood. Some 500 years later, when the Ten Wings (the seven commentaries in 10 parts) were attached to the oracle, the concepts were solidified, given names, and used to interpret the oracle assembled by King Wen and his son, the Duke of Zhou. In fact, understanding the principles of qi and yin and yang have become fundamental to practicing many Chinese traditions including the Yijing, feng shui, and acupuncture.

Chapter 8

The Mystery of Qi

In This Chapter

➤ What is qi?

➤ The history of qi

➤ The Western notion of qi

➤ The methodical Western mind

What do the *Yijing,* Chinese medical traditions (like acupuncture, acupressure, and herbs), Chinese martial arts (like qigong and taiji), and feng shui (the art and science of living in harmony with your environment) have in common? Okay, they're all Chinese traditions that improve your well-being. What else? Well, each is based on the purported existence of an underlying and united, nourishing and vital, physical and metaphysical force called qi. "Purported" is the key word. This is because the existence of qi has not been scientifically proven. Also, this is the primary reason that Western medical and scientific communities have largely ignored Eastern traditions. That is, until recently.

In this chapter, you'll find out what qi is. You'll learn it is not a concept unique to the Chinese, but a belief shared by cultures worldwide. Also, you'll learn how the West *is* coming closer to identifying a unifying force that governs our bodies and environment. Could this be qi? Will this fundamental tenet of Chinese medicine and philosophy be proven scientifically? Will its existence compel the conventional medical stronghold to reevaluate a system of healthcare based on isolation and fragmentation?

There's much to ponder. So, let's get into qi!

The Essence of Qi= energy

No word in the English language can accurately describe *qi* (pronounced chee). In popular mythology, qi is synonymous with "energy," a natural or intellectual power that exerts activity. For example, there's solar energy. The sun's rays give light, provide warmth, and help to foster growth. Natural energy resources like oil and gas provide fuel for industry and transportation, and heat for our homes. Nutrition affords us physical energy. With sustenance we thrive and feel energetic. Without it, we are drained of our energy. And then, we have electromagnetic energy, one of the fundamental forces of nature, galvanizing and unifying the growth and development of all living forms. So, is qi a source of energy "discovered" by the ancient Chinese? No, qi is not a mysterious energy.

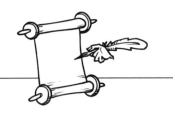

Wise Words

Qi is the underlying and unifying, nourishing and vital, physical and metaphysical ("beyond the physical") life force at the center of all things.

Energy, in all of its various forms, is just one aspect of qi we understand through sensory perception (the five senses of sight, smell, taste, hearing, and touch). Actually, qi underlies energy. Qi is an information field that gives energy its impetus to move and change. In fact, qi is the underlying, holistic, and vital force at the center of all things—hyperspace, the sun, a seashell, your pet, and you. If we describe qi as an energy flow, we deny its metaphysical qualities (since these are not recognizable to sensory reality). Intuition, fate, dreams, and hunches—surely, we agree these things are real, but can we prove their existence?

Qi can best be characterized as "life breath" or "cosmic breath." The following are some qualities the Chinese attribute to qi that will help to foster a better understanding of this enigmatic concept:

➤ Qi is the holistic and underlying vital force and substance of everyone and everything.

➤ Qi is the nonmeasurable and imperceptible breath permeating, connecting, and uniting the cosmic and earthly realms.

➤ Qi is physical. It's the life force acupuncturists seek to activate with their needles and the power martial artists channel to split bricks.

➤ Qi is metaphysical. It is your luck, destiny, and fate. It's your intuition, the sixth sense you feel when you're "on to something," the "vibe" you get about a particular person, place, or thing.

➤ Qi is your spirit, your soul.

The concept of qi hasn't always encompassed such a broad range of qualities. Like anything else, it has evolved and changed over time. Unlike Western science's reliance on logic, reason, and direct experimentation to understand nature's truths, the ancient Chinese primarily used intuitive knowledge, looking within nature's pattern of change.

The Changing Concept of Qi

The first documentation of the word qi can be found in the *Shuoguazhuan (Explanation of the Trigrams)*, one of *the Ten Wings* attached to the *Zhouyi* during the Warring States Period (or as early as the late Spring and Autumn Period). As noteworthy as the *Shuoguazhuan* is, another text defining qi is considerably more interesting. Purportedly written by an historian named Zuo Qiuming in 541 B.C.E., the *Zuozhuan* is a superlative narrative describing six types of Heaven qi that descend to earth: yin, yang, wind, rain, darkness, and brightness. When an imbalance occurs, the excess is made manifest as one of six types of bodily illness. For instance, an excess of yin can cause low blood pressure, resulting in insufficient blood flow and the feeling of being cold and weak; an excess of yang can cause fever; high winds can cause arthritic conditions; constant rain can cause stomach ailments; extreme darkness can cause hallucinations; and extreme brightness can cause heart disease. (The concept of yin and yang is the subject of the next chapter, "Can You Spare Some Change? The Unchanging Truth About Yin and Yang.")

Notable Quotable

"When the essence of matter transforms, life is born. [When the transformation takes place] on earth, grain grows. [When the transformation takes place] in Heaven, galaxies form. When [qi] flows between Heaven and earth, it becomes ghosts and spirits. When [qi] is stored in the body, a person becomes a sage. Regarding the birth of men, Heaven contributes the essence; earth contributes the form. When essence and form combine, it becomes man. When there is balance and harmony, there is life. When there no balance and harmony, there is no life."

—*Guanzi*, fifth century B.C.E.

As the concept evolved, qi extended beyond the earthly (meteorological) and human (physiological) realms to include the influence of the cosmos. This belief was first recorded in the 431 B.C.E. text called the *Zhouyu*, assembled by Bo Yangfu, the Grand Historian of the state of Zhou. Bo Yangfu relates qi to the downfall of the Zhou dynasty: "The qi of Heaven and earth must not lose their proper order. If they extend beyond the proper order, there will be chaos .... There will be an earthquake." In other words, Heaven caused an earthquake to communicate its displeasure with the king. The king's inability to promote harmony and balance within his empire caused chaos and discord, which led to the end of Zhou dynastic reign.

The *Guanzi* is another significant text. Purportedly written by Guan Zhong (d. 645 B.C.E.), the prime minister of the state of Qi, this manuscript gives qi spiritual attributes. Called "essential qi," it provides humankind with wisdom and intelligence to be strengthened by moral character and righteous living.

According to the book *Confucianism, Buddhism, Daoism, Christianity and Chinese Culture* by Tang Yi-Jie (The University of Peking Council for Research in Values and Philosophy 1991), by the end of the Eastern Han dynasty (C.E. 25–220), three texts emerged that further define qi:

➤ The *Zhuangzi*. Written by Zhuang Zhou (356–286 B.C.E.), this great Daoist work informs us that people should "keep their form perfect and replenish their spirit to be merged into one with Heaven and earth."

➤ The *Lushi Chunqiu*. Attributed to Lü Buwei (d. 235 B.C.E.), this text discusses the "preservation of good health." It offers this advice: "Qi should be made to flow constantly within the body ... [and] with essential qi renewed daily, the vicious qi will go and a full life span will be reached; this is called truth."

➤ The *Huainanzi*. Compiled by Liu An, King of Huainan (d. 122 B.C.E.), this encyclopedic work explains the origin of qi. It says that the universe was a shapeless void filled with original qi. The interaction of its positive (yang) and negative (yin) forces produced life as we know it.

And the Qi Plays On

Of course, these aren't the only texts that describe the nature of qi. Many others exist that are equally important and interesting. For example, consider the *Book of Burial* or *Zangzhu*. Attributed to Guo Pu (C.E. 276–324), this manual explains how to locate auspicious sites for burial of the dead. It's all about locating the "dragon's lair," the common point on the geophysical plane where qi intersects. In fact, the *Book of Burial* provides the underlying theories of Form School feng shui, the first and oldest school of feng shui, which studies how terrestrial shapes and watercourses effect your well-being. You can learn more about feng shui in Chapter 13, "Increasing Your Health, Wealth, and Relationships with Feng Shui," and Chapter 14, "Learning Yigua Feng Shui."

Also, there's the *Neijing, The Yellow Emperor's Classic of Internal Medicine*. Written by scholars in the second or third century B.C.E., the *Neijing* summarizes the theoretical and practical knowledge of medical practitioners.

The Yijing's Qi

By the time the *Ten Wings* or commentaries were attached to the *Zhouyi* (the compilation being renamed the *Yijing*), the concept of qi was transformed into an all-encompassing vital force at the heart and development of all things. The *Dazhuan* (*Great Commentary*) explains it like this: "The essence and qi combine to form living things; the wandering spirit [qi] causing change [between life and death]." This passage suggests a living person is able to communicate with the spirit of the deceased because of and through the common binding component of spirit qi. The deceased uses the commonality to manipulate the stalks of yarrow or coins used as divinatory tools to help guide the diviner.

Qi Around the World

The idea that there is a holistic and interactive force of nature is not just an exclusive Chinese concept. In fact, cultures all over the world believe in an imperceptible and nourishing force that underlies life. Each culture has its own term. For instance, the Indians call a vital force "prana." It is known as "ankh" to the Egyptians; "ruah" to the Hebrews; "tane" to the Hawaiians; and "arunquiltha" to the Australian aborigine.

The following is how several celebrated historical figures of the Western world defined a vital force that influences our well-being:

➤ Pythagoras (560–500 B.C.E.), a Greek philosopher and mathematician, believed our spirit and the air we breathe are connected to "the unlimited." The air is a vital and healing force called "pneuma." The words pneumatic and pneumonia are derivatives of pneuma.

➤ Isaac Newton (1642–1727) in his 1687 book, *Principia,* promoted the idea of a "subtle spirit," an electrical vital force governing humankind and the environment.

➤ Luigi Galvani (1737–1798), an Italian physician and physicist, accidentally "discovered" a steady current of electricity (the only type known then was of the static variety, sparks caused by friction) while performing experiments on frog legs. Galvani proposed that a bioelectric vital force, called "animal electricity," was hidden in the nerves of living organisms. Today, words like galvanize, galvanic, and the galvanoscope pay tribute to his work.

➤ Dr. Hans Driesch (1867–1941), a German vitalist and embryologist, was convinced that life had a special inherent process that could not be detected by physical laws. He called this "entelechy," from the Greek word entelecheia, a nonmaterial agent intrinsic to living substances.

➤ Dr. Harold Saxton Burr (1889–1973) taught anatomy and neuroanatomy at Yale University School of Medicine from 1914–1964. In 1935, with Dr. F.S.C. Northrup, they developed the electrodynamic theory of life. This theory postulates that electrical energy is "the unifying characteristic of the universe." That bioelectrical phenomenon underlies the growth and development of all living forms. Burr called the connective electric fields "L-fields" (life-fields). Also, he was convinced the state of one's mind could affect the state of the body's L-field.

➤ Dr. Bjorn Nordenstrom (1920–) gained recognition for treating tumors with electrical probes. Nordenstrom postulates an intricate electrical network exists within the body that controls organ functions. In 1979, he assembled decades of research into a book, *Biologically Closed Electrical Circuits: Clinical, Experimental, and Theoretical Evidence for an Additional Circulatory System* (Nordic Medical Publications).

➤ Dr. Robert O. Becker (1923–) is a pioneer in the field of regeneration, the study of how the body restores or revitalizes itself after injury. Like Burr, Becker believes electricity is the key to understanding life processes. He proposes that electrical currents are connected to the body's nervous system, the organ group that coordinates, receives, transmits, and stores information throughout the body.

Yi Edicts

Kirlian photography is a photographic technique that captures electromagnetic fields on film. It offers visible and measurable proof of qi's physical aspects. Many people call these images *auras*. Two Russian scientists, the husband-and-wife duo of Semyon and Valentina Kirlian, developed Kirlian photography.

After reviewing the preceding historical suggestions of qi, you'll notice the notion of a pervasive, unified, and healing force becomes less mystical and incomprehensible and more accepted, understood, and quantifiable. Through various precise measurements and scientific experiments, many Western medical pioneers have come to believe that electromagnetic energy is the holistic and curative dynamic behind biological processes. Although space prohibits a full accounting of other modern theories pertinent to qi, understand that the physical and quantifiable presence of electromagnetism (and anything else) describes only one aspect of qi. Remember, the notion of qi has other qualities incapable of being measured through sensory perception. But the door has been opened. The acknowledgement and inclusion of holistic healing does represent forward movement in science and medicine.

The Newly Expanded Western Mind

The biggest problem we Westerners have in viewing the world is our mindset. It limits us. Let's face it, we're a rational lot. We say, "This is not logical." "What's the reason behind this?" "Prove it!" This rational insistence dates to the ancient Greeks. We can thank Pythagoras (560–500 B.C.E.) and Aristotle (384–322 B.C.E.) for developing the scientific methods of *deductive* and *inductive* reasoning. Isaac Newton came along some 1,000 years later and reinforced this methodical standard. He established laws about how the universe functioned. Laws that did not extend beyond sensory reality. Laws that limited. Newton's universe was black and white, cause and effect. The universe was seen as predictable, linear, and coherent. Logic could provide an answer to everything. It made sense.

A New View for a New Millennium

The twentieth century proclaimed a new scientific paradigm. Einstein's theory of relativity proved matter to be an illusion, just a masked form of energy. The subatomic world of quantum physics determined the system of isolation, separate and distinct attention to the component parts, to be an invalid method of gaining knowledge of the whole. Our mindset was becoming less rigid, our view of reality more open to alternative possibilities.

In fact, new sciences have surfaced such as psychology and chaos theory, challenging our sensory perception. These new sciences emphasize holism, a connectivity with our environment and with other people. For instance, noted psychologist Carl Jung was instrumental in developing archetypal patterns in dreams. He understood the inner psyche to be a "collective living mirror of the universe." As you have learned, this notion is reminiscent of the Chinese microcosmic-macrocosmic concept. In Chapter 11, "Science, Synchronicity, and the *Yijing*: Understanding a Holistic Universe," you'll read about theoretical physicist David Bohm. He "softened" physics by integrating psychology, philosophy, religion, and biology into a new holistic worldview.

Indisputably, the West is slowly coming to grips with the fact that not everything can be quantifiably and precisely measured. After nearly 3,000 years of linear and fragmented thinking, we are expanding our mindset to include nonlinear and holistic interpretations. We are allowing ourselves to think the unthinkable. We're broadening our horizons to include seeing the forest *and* the trees.

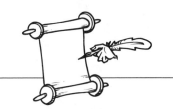

Wise Words

The method of reaching a conclusion by deducing general laws through observation is **deductive reasoning.** The method of reaching a conclusion by developing specific cases based on general laws is **inductive reasoning.**

East Meets West

An increasing number of Westerners are embracing Eastern traditions. Eastern cuisine and the martial arts (among other things) have joined the mainstream. Many of us are seeking feng shui advisors to help promote better health, wealth, and relationships. We're investigating Eastern philosophies and religions like Confucianism, Daoism, and Buddhism. We're consulting the *Yijing*. And we're trying acupuncture and acupressure, turning to natural herbs instead of using synthetic drugs. Many conventional medical centers have opened alternative healthcare facilities and include alternative mind-body therapies such as acupuncture, message, taiji, and supplemental herbal medication.

Yi Edicts

According to a 1997 survey conducted in the United States by the Harvard Medical School, "42 percent of respondents reported using at least one unconventional therapy in the past year. Based on these figures, it is estimated that 83 million Americans use alternative medicine." Moreover, the World Health Organization estimates that "4 billion people, or 80 percent of the world's population, use herbal medicine for some aspect of primary health care." Despite this, herbs are not endorsed by the U.S. Food and Drug Administration.

["Alternative Medicine," Microsoft Encarta Online Encyclopedia 2000.]

Yi Edicts

Acupuncture is a traditional Chinese medicine dating to around 200 B.C.E. It involves puncturing and stimulating specific points in the body to correct imbalances of qi that lead to disease. Besides using needles, acupuncturists also use heat (this treatment is called moxibustion), pressure (acupressure), or low levels of electromagnetic energy to stimulate acupuncture points.

Now, let's step back a bit for an assessment. Clearly, many people are ready and willing to accept alternative medicine, ideas, and concepts. There has been some positive response in the medical establishment (if limited). New Age and alternative therapies have become a lucrative industry. Why do we suppose this is happening? Let's consider a few possibilities.

The slow pace of testing and glacial speed with which new medication is made available not only frustrates but is of serious concern to suffering patients. Disturbing side effects and the often harsh quality of life extracted by standard treatments force many people to look elsewhere for help. The lack of cures for diseases such as cancer and AIDS leads many desperate sufferers to seek out other avenues of hope. Also, the continued interest in health in general, in physical fitness, and mental well-being has people welcoming natural remedies, organic food, and a calmer, more beneficial state of being. All this makes it hardly surprising that so many are reaching out for, or more to the point, looking back at ancient healing techniques. Of these, perhaps one of the more widespread and successful has been acupuncture. (Even some insurance companies include this treatment in their coverage plans!)

Making Sense of Qi

To fully understand the Chinese concept of qi, you must set aside your rational mind. Check your ego and must-know attitude at the door. Refrain from comparing qi to anything you know. Think the unthinkable.

Next, you will learn about another fundamental principle governing Chinese traditions. This is the principle of yin and yang.

The Least You Need to Know

➤ Qi is the underlying and unifying, nourishing and vital, physical and metaphysical life breath at the heart and development of all things.

➤ The first documentation of the word qi can be found in the *Shuoguazhuan (Explanation of the Trigrams)*, one of *the Ten Wings* attached to the *Zhouyi* during the Warring States Period (403–221 B.C.E.).

➤ Qi is not unique to the Chinese. It goes by many names and is known by cultures worldwide.

➤ Many Western physicians believe electromagnetic energy is the holistic and vital force governing the body and environment. This is actually misleading because qi underlies energy. Electromagnetism describes only one aspect of qi.

Chapter 9

Can You Spare Some Change? The Unchanging Truth About Yin and Yang

In This Chapter

➤ The origin of life? The big bang theory

➤ Wuji: the original source of all things

➤ Yin: the feminine principle expressed as the earth

➤ Yang: the masculine principle expressed as heaven

➤ Understanding the taiji

Like the concept of qi, the theory describing yin and yang was perhaps understood, but not fully developed at the time the *Zhouyi* was assembled at the end of the second millennium B.C.E. However, some 500 years later, when commentaries were added to the text, the concept of yin (representing the broken line) and yang (representing the solid line) was used to interpret the meaning of each hexagram and the interplay between them.

So, what is yin and yang? The Chinese believe they characterize the two most dynamic forces of the universe. They were born at the dawn of time, and their splitting apart from a unified state signified the birth of change. Their ceaseless movement drives nature forward through an eternal cycle of birth, growth, decay, and death.

In this chapter, you'll learn how the origin of these forces accords with modern science and ancient wisdom. But what do yin and yang mean? You'll learn that, too.

The Great Big Bang of Creation

The origin of life is an age-old question that has beguiled philosophers and scientists since the first appearance of civilization. How the universe originated, and who or what had a role in that origin is a mystery. In fact, the quest to understand life and humanity's role on earth has spawned myth, religious institutions, and endless scientific exploration and experimentation.

Western science offers the big bang theory. Roughly 15 billion years ago, the universe began with, well, a big bang! One millionth of a second after this dynamic explosion, the four fundamental forces of nature became distinct: gravity, electromagnetism, and the strong and weak nuclear forces. By the first second, the universe was filled with elementary particles. The most familiar of these are the negatively charged electrons, positively charged protons, and neutral neutrons. Together, these particles form the atom. Atoms combine to form molecules, the smallest unit of a substance that contains all the chemical properties of that substance.

By tracing the history of the universe to the "moment" before the big bang, cosmology theorists seek to find the Holy Grail of science, the primordial source. Known as a *singularity,* the primordial source is the state of unity when the totality of the universe existed within an atomic nucleus. To many physicists, the discovery of a singularity will lead to a single mathematical theory that will unite the physical world. Our question is, what would that equation mean? Where would we go from there?

Of course, theology has its viewpoint about the origins of life, actually many viewpoints. But, as fascinating as they are, delving into them here will not suit our purposes, so let's move on.

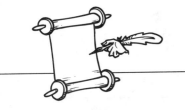

Wise Words

Singularity is the "moment" before creation when the entire universe was compressed into an atomic nucleus. It is the "moment" before time and space were made manifest. Singularity is the undivided whole, the state of unity.

Wise Words

Wuji is the wellspring out of which life emerges. It is the source of original qi, life's vital force.

Wuji: The Beginning of All Things

The ancient Chinese sages relied primarily on meditative knowledge to ascertain life's origin, choosing to eschew empirical data. Quite simply, these learned masters understood that the origin of the universe can be compared to your own birth. By tracing yourself to the confines of the womb, the ancients arrived at a similar conclusion to that of modern science. The mysterious source of life is an undivided whole.

The Daoists call the womb-like primordial source *wuji*. Meaning the beginning or the great void, wuji is the wellspring of life. It is the undifferentiated and purest source of all things. It is the fountainhead of original qi, life's vital force.

The Circle of Life

Wuji is depicted as a circle. While you may think the circle is empty, it is actually empty *and* full. It is filled with potential. Similar to an unfertilized egg, wuji is ready to give life. The moment sperm impregnates it, the egg is no longer a single entity, a unified state. It divides, forming two complimentary poles—the negatively charged yin and the positively charged yang. Yin and yang are the two dynamic forces of the universe, the two necessary components of change—the bedrock of the *Yijing*.

Master Class

The legend of the mythical figure Pan Gu and how he created the world dates to the Three Kingdoms period (C.E. 220–280). In the beginning there was an egg, where an enormous giant called Pan Gu slept. After 18,000 years Pan Gu awakened, wielding an axe to crack open the shell. The egg's light elements (symbolizing yang) rose to become Heaven; the heavy parts (symbolizing yin) descended to form the earth. With his feet firmly planted on the earth, Pan Gu's head supported Heaven. Each day as Pan Gu grew 10 feet taller, the sky rose 10 feet higher, and the earth became 10 feet thicker. This process continued for another 18,000 years. After Heaven and earth were sufficiently separated, Pan Gu died. His breath became the wind and clouds, his voice the clapping thunder. His eyes became the sun and moon. His body and limbs formed the mountains. His blood turned into the flowing rivers. His hair became the stars, and the fleas and lice on his body, humankind.

Yin: The Mother of Earth

Yin is nature's feminine principle. Expressed as the stable matter of earth, yin qi moves downward and inward. Yin is rich and dark. Womb and soil. Mother and earth, receptacles for new life amd new ideas—an idea embodied in Hexagram 2 (Kun, earth). When death occurs, Mother Earth accepts us back, recycling our spent remains into future growth. Passive in nature, yin is exhibited in the stillness of night. It is the restive shade, the tranquil, cool lake.

Wise Words

Yin is the feminine and passive principle of nature expressed as stillness, cold, and wetness. On the human level, yin represents sadness, fatigue, and greed. Also, yin is quiet meditation, intuitive wisdom, and creativity. Yin is the realm of the dead.

On the human level, yin is sadness, weakness, greed, and selfishness, traits associated with the dark side of our nature. Yin is our unconscious mind, where we shelter our innermost desires and secrets. Also, yin is right-brained and artistic. Meditating and practicing yoga are yin activities. So is reading and watching TV. Yin is our creativity and intuition. It is the maintenance and development of traditions, values, and relationships.

Some of yin's other qualities are illustrated in the following figure.

And, what does the white dot amid yin's blackness mean? It represents change. The white dot expresses the emerging presence of yang. It means nothing can be totally yin or yang. That would imply completion, perfection, balance, and nonmotion. For example, the shady (yin) side of a slope will eventually become sunny (yang). The blackest (yin) sky has the twinkling of white (yang) stars. Quiet, restful (yin) moments are followed by vigorous activity (yang). Get the idea?

Yin: nature's passive and feminine principle.

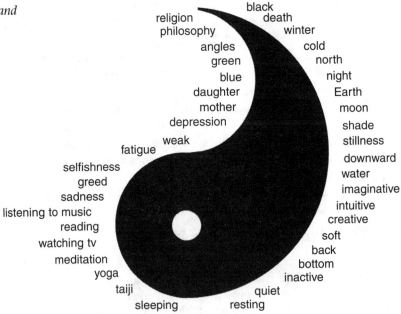

Yang: The Father of Heaven

Yang is nature's masculine principle expressed as the sky and Heaven. Accordingly, it makes sense that yang qi moves upward and outward. It's life's active force made manifest as bright sunlight, gusting wind, and summer's rising heat. Similarly, our goals, inspiration, and enlightenment are yang. They carry us forward by activating our minds. Also, yang is left-brained, detail-oriented, computational, and logical abstractions of mathematics and science. It's individualism and the acquiring of material possessions. Yang is our external expression of "heated arguments" and being "in love." In relation to the *Yijing*, yang's vitality and vigor are encapsulated in Hexagram 1 (Qian, Heaven).

Yang represents the father figure. Traditionally, the male is the disciplinarian, the firm authoritarian. He lays down the law. Meanwhile, his yin counterpart keeps the peace. Think of 1950s TV—Ozzie and Harriet Nelson are good examples.

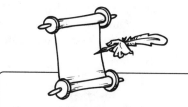

Wise Words

Yang is the masculine and active principle of nature expressed as hot summer days and gusting winds. On the human level, yang represents linear logic, aggression, being in love. Yang is the father figure, traditionally the disciplinarian and authoritarian.

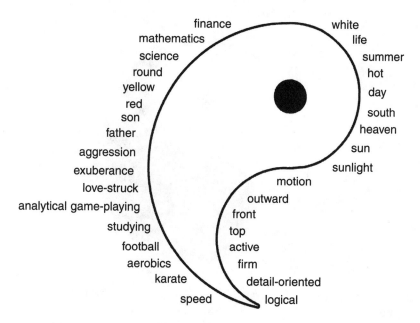

Yang: nature's active and masculine principle.

Of course, today this dynamic no longer applies. Amid yang's whiteness, yin's egg of change is multiplying. In other words, our fast-paced, technologically advanced, yang-oriented culture is succumbing to yin's influences. Traditional, restrictive sex

233

roles are relaxing. Fathers nurture and mothers no longer are homebound and silent. The individual and the family struggle for precedence. Secular beliefs no longer hold sway over the spiritual. Rational and separatist logic is questioned by holistic thinking. Our yang-dominated Western culture is evolving into yin. Similarly, our Eastern counterparts are undergoing a metamorphosis of their own. Their tradition-laden, insulated culture is under siege. What we Westerners call "development" is urging yang-based change into Eastern yin-dominated culture.

Yi Edicts

In mathematics, the number 1 (and odd numbers) is considered yang; the masculine 1 is straight and firm. The value of zero (and even numbers) is yin; the feminine 0 is round and soft like the womb.

The Great Ultimate Taiji

The *taiji* symbol exemplifies the process of universal evolution, the perpetual interplay between the dynamic forces of yin and yang. Born out of unity, yin and yang are infinitely linked. Like the positive and negative poles of a magnet and like the relationship between your mind and body, yin and yang are separate *and* united. They influence and empower each other, as well as sustain and enable each other. In yin's breadth, there is the seed of yang. In yang's expanse, there is the germ of yin. Together, they express the law of nature: the unending cycle of birth, growth, decay, and death. Nothing can escape this fate.

The taiji expresses the perpetual interplay between yin and yang.

Literally translated, the word ji means "central pillar," "basis," or the "basic reference." The word tai means "supreme" or the "greatest." Taken together, taiji means the "greatest pillar" or the "supreme basis." But wait! This describes wuji, you say. Actually, there is a difference. Wu means void, a vast boundless space. It is the state prior to the birth of life. Therefore, wuji is the ultimateless or the boundlessness out of which taiji is born.

Yin and Yang: Face and Vase

The ongoing exchange between yin and yang is evident in *Gestalt psychology.* Translated from German, Gestalt means "configuration." According to Gestalt therapists, we perceive or configure images as a well-organized whole rather than as an assemblage of separate parts. Take a look at the following images. What do you see? A vase or a face? Depending on your initial perception, shift your focus so that one image either recedes into the background or rises to the foreground. Known as a reversible figure, the image can be perceived in two different ways, each of which is accurate. The point is, face and vase and yin and yang empower each other.

The black and white dots of the taiji symbolize the shift between the emergent white foreground of yang and the retreating black background of yin. The idea of correlating the taiji to Gestalt psychology is borrowed and used with permission of Katya Walter in her inspiring book *Tao of Chaos: DNA & the I Ching: Unlocking the Code of the Universe* (Element Books, Ltd., 1994).

In the next chapter, you'll meet seventeenth-century philosopher and mathematician Gottfried Leibniz. He believed his binary notation (a mathematical system that uses only the numbers 0 and 1 to compute) proved the existence of God. Interestingly, his binary numeration conforms to the 64 hexagrams if 0 represents a broken yin line and 1 a solid yang line.

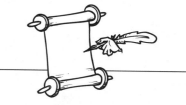

Wise Words

Taiji is the symbol representing the eternal interplay of yin and yang.

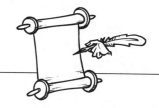

Wise Words

Gestalt psychology became popular in the early twentieth century. Translated from German, Gestalt means "configuration." Gestaltists believe we respond to a holistic experience. That perception *is* influenced by the configuration of parts.

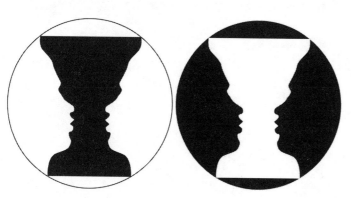

Yin and yang as Gestalt "figure and ground."

Notable Quotable

"The Ultimateless [wuji] and its parallel, the Supreme Ultimate [taiji]! When the Supreme Ultimate moves, it generates yang. When this movement peaks, it produces stillness. Stillness generates yin. Supreme stillness leads to movement. Thus, movement and stillness are the root of one another."

—Zhou Dunyi (C.E. 1017–1073), *Explanation of the Diagram of the Supreme Ultimate*

The Least You Need to Know

➤ Modern science holds that the totality of the universe was once compressed into an atomic nucleus. One second after the big bang explosion, protons (positive particles), electrons (negative particles), and neutrons (neutral particles) emerged.

➤ The ancient Chinese sages understood the entirety of the universe derives from wuji, out of which emerged the two dynamic forces of yin (negative) and yang (positive).

➤ Yin is nature's passive and feminine principle. Yin is the realm of the dead.

➤ Yang is nature's active and masculine principle. Yang is the realm of the living.

➤ The taiji symbolizes the eternal interplay of yin and yang.

Part 6

Modern Science to the Ancient Oracle

Here, we compare the Yijing with modern science of the twenty-first century. Whereas the ancient Chinese believed their ancestors provided the answers to their questions, modern physics, psychology, and chaos theory offer alternative explanations. What do these sciences have in common? The idea that everything and everyone affects and is affected by everything else. The idea that our thoughts and actions are connected to the whole of the universe. That life isn't chaotic, but ordered and purposeful. That we can access a sea of information and use it to improve our well-being. Ideas the Chinese have understood since ancient times.

We'll also talk about seventeenth-century mathematician and philosopher Gottfried Leibniz. When it was discovered that the progression of binary numbers from 1 to 63 perfectly correlated to a certain sequence of hexagrams, Leibniz set out to use this information to help convert the Chinese to Christianity. Certainly, this is an interesting piece of Yijing history!

Chapter 10

Gottfried Leibniz, Binary Numeration, and the *Yijing*

In This Chapter

➤ Who is Gottfried Leibniz?

➤ Understanding binary mathematics

➤ The theological implication of the binary system

➤ The correlation of the binary system to the 64 hexagrams of the *Yijing*

Unquestionably, German mathematician and philosopher Gottfried Leibniz was one of the seventeenth century's leading intellectuals. Although he is best known for inventing the mathematical method of calculus (for which he independently shares credit with Sir Isaac Newton) and for his radical philosophical concepts (like monads and pre-established harmony), Leibniz also made considerable contributions to a wide variety of other fields. These include, but are not limited to, theology, geology, physics, metaphysics, sinology, and politics. He was also an inventor, drafting plans for things like high-speed coaches that traveled along ball-bearing tracks, improved cookware, and shoes with springs that facilitated "fast getaways." Yet, despite his many accomplishments, Leibniz's primary goal was the conversion of all peoples to Christianity.

In this chapter, we'll focus on another of Leibniz's great interests: binary numeration, a mathematical system that uses only the numbers 0 and 1 to compute. Leibniz believed the system helped to prove God's creation of the world: Everything was created out of nothing (0) by God (1). What does this have to do with the *Yijing?* Joachim

Bouvet, a Jesuit missionary stationed in China, discovered by substituting 0 for a broken line and the number 1 for a solid line, the progression of binary numbers 0 to 63 perfectly correlated to the Fuxi (or Before Heaven) arrangement of hexagrams, a configuration that is similar in principle to the Xian Tian or Before Heaven sequence of trigrams you learned about in Chapter 5, "Once Upon a Time: The Mythical Origin of the *Yijing*." Would this discovery lead the Chinese to accept the Christian God? Or, was the discovery purely coincidental, the correlation meaningless? You shall see.

The Life of Leibniz

Gottfried Wilhelm von Leibniz (1646–1716) was born in Leipzig, Germany. According to John M. Mackie's book, *Life of William von Leibnitz* (Gould, Kendall, and Lincoln, 1845), something prophetic happened three days after Leibnitz's birth, which would set the tone of his life. At his baptism, the infant "opened his eyes and raised his head to receive the consecrated water bestowed" by the Lutheran clergyman. Leibniz's father, Friedrich Leibniz, a professor of philosophy at the University of Leipzig, recorded the astonishing event in his journal: "I prophetically look upon this occurrence as a sign of faith, and a most sure token, that my son will walk through life with eyes upturned to Heaven, burning with love of God, and abounding in wonderful works ...." Unfortunately, his father died when the youngster was six years old. However, his mother, Catharina Schumuck, would foster Gottfried's love of God, the power of which would play a significant role in his "wonderful works."

Yi Edicts

The expanse of Leibniz's knowledge was not fully realized until a 1903 discovery of some 15,000 letters and fragments of his works. This treasure-trove of information provided scholars a better glimpse into Leibniz's mind, allowing them to understand what he said of himself: "He who knows me by my published works alone does not know me at all."

At a young age, Leibniz possessed an insatiable desire for mental stimulation. He taught himself advanced Latin and Greek by the age of 12 "for I was burning to get sight of the ancients [philosophers] and the numerous Christian fathers." In 1661, at the age of 14, Leibniz entered the University of Leipzig where he earned degrees of Bachelor of Philosophy (1663) and Master of Philosophy (1664). Although mathematics was offered at Leipzig, he supplemented his knowledge at the University of Jena in eastern Germany. Studying under Erhard Weigel, Leibniz learned to develop mathematic proofs for nonmathematic subjects like philosophy, theology, and logic. In 1667, Leibniz earned a Doctorate of Law at the University of Altdorf in Nuremberg.

From 1676 until his death in 1716, Leibniz worked as councilor and librarian to Duke Johann Friedrich in Hanover. Although his responsibilities were rather mundane, his close ties with a powerful German court afforded him influence and contacts. In fact, during his lifetime, Leibniz corresponded with over 600 of Europe's intelligentsia as well as a large sampling of government officials and royals. While this steadfast endeavor may seem vainglorious, actually, his correspondents were flattered he favored them. Indeed, Leibniz had become the pride of Germany. But gaining fame, respect, and a menagerie of celebrated friends was not his primary goal. Instead, Leibniz aimed to win influential adherents who could realize his scheme—to find a truth that would reconcile the Catholics and Protestants and lead the Jews and Muslims to convert to Christianity.

Leibniz believed it possible to bring together religious opponents by focusing on each belief's similarities; by finding a common denominator. To Leibniz, his mathematical-cum-theological system of binary numeration provided a means.

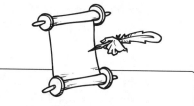

Wise Words

The **binary system,** or **base 2** numeration, uses only the digits 0 and 1 to compute. Leibniz believed the binary system had spiritual aspects relating to the creation of the universe from nothing (0) by the one (1) God.

Binary Mathematics 101

Before we can discuss binary's theological implications and its link to the *Yijing,* you must first understand its mathematical principles. The *binary system* uses only the digits 0 and 1 to compute. Referring to the following chart, you will see the number 1 is expressed as 01, the number 2 is expressed as 10, and three is 11. Because all possible permutations have been exhausted within the two place values, the number 4 carries over into the next position on the left. The process continues until all permutations (100, 101, 110, and 111) are met. The number 8 (1000) begins the next set of permutations and continues ad infinitum.

0 1 = 1	1 0 1 1 = 11
1 0 = 2	1 1 0 0 = 12
1 1 = 3	1 1 0 1 = 13
1 0 0 = 4	1 1 1 0 = 14
1 0 1 = 5	1 1 1 1 = 15
1 1 0 = 6	1 0 0 0 0 = 16
1 1 1 = 7	1 0 0 0 1 = 17
1 0 0 0 = 8	1 0 0 1 0 = 18
1 0 0 1 = 9	1 0 0 1 1 = 19
1 0 1 0 = 10	1 0 1 0 0 = 20

Binary numbers 1 through 20 and their decimal equivalents.

This method is also called *base 2* numeration because you count in powers or multiples of two. In case you're wondering, the universal standard is the base 10 system, which uses the numbers 0 through 9 (10 digits) to perform mathematical functions.

If you're computer-minded, you probably know that binary numbers are the fundamental principle behind computer science. Although the system has been used in digital computing since the early 1930s, Leibniz actually designed the first binary calculator in 1679.

In binary notation, the year 2001 becomes 11111010001. How does this figure? Look at the following illustration.

2001 =	0	1	1	1	1	1	0	1	0	0	0	1
	2^{11}	2^{10}	2^9	2^8	2^7	2^6	2^5	2^4	2^3	2^2	2^1	2^0
	2048	1024	512	256	128	64	32	16	8	4	2	1

Reading from right to left, notice that each place value progresses in powers of 2: 2^0 is $1 \times 1 = 1$; 2^1 is $1 \times 2 = 2$; 2^2 is $2 \times 2 = 4$; 2^3 is $4 \times 2 = 8$; 2^4 is $8 \times 2 = 16$; and so on to infinity. It can also be expressed this way: 2^3 is $2 \times 2 \times 2 = 8$; 2^5 is $2 \times 2 \times 2 \times 2 \times 2 = 32$; and 2^7 is $2 \times 2 \times 2 \times 2 \times 2 \times 2 \times 2 = 128$. So, $2001 = 2^{10}$ (1024) + 2^9 (512) + 2^8 (256) + 2^7 (128) + 2^6 (64) + 2^4 (16) + 2^0 (1).

Still need clarification? Okay, take a moment and find your pocket calculator. Pretend you're going shopping for enough numbers to make 2001. The number 1 means "yes, I'll take that number" and 0 means, "no I don't need that number." With your basket in your arm and moving left to right, you must pass on 2^{11} (2048) because you do not need this many numbers. Moving on, you add one 2^{10} (1024) to your basket. Now, you must accumulate 977 more numbers (2001 – 1024 = 977). Therefore, you take one 2^9 (977 – 512 = 465), one 2^8 (465 – 256 = 209), one 2^7 (209 – 128 = 81) and one 2^6 (81 – 64 = 17). You don't need 2^5 (32) because you only need 17 more numbers. Therefore, you select one 2^4 (17 – 16 = 1) and one 2^0 to complete your order.

Pop quiz! Leibniz was born in 1646. Compute his binary birth year in the space provided here. (The answer appears at the end of this chapter.)

1646 =												
	2^{11}	2^{10}	2^9	2^8	2^7	2^6	2^5	2^4	2^3	2^2	2^1	2^0
	2048	1024	512	256	128	64	32	16	8	4	2	1

Adding Binary Style

Feeling confident? Let's learn how to perform simple addition using binary numeration. Here are two examples. To facilitate easier understanding, follow these simple rules: $0 + 0 = 0$; $0 + 1 = 1$; $1 + 0 = 1$; and $1 + 1 = 0$, carry the 1. Regarding the latter, remember you're dealing with only the digits 0 and 1. Therefore, the number 2 (1 + 1) is undefined. This is similar to base 10 functions. For example, when you add 1 + 9 (visualize this vertically), technically the answer is 0 carry the 1 because the number 10 is undefined.

```
    1 0 | 2          1 0 1 | 5
 +  1 0 1 | 5       + 1 0 1 1 | 11
    1 1 1 | 7        1 0 0 0 0 | 16
```

Examples of binary addition.

Pretty easy, huh? Let's move on to multiplication.

Master Class

In 1974, a radio message was transmitted into space from the Arecibo radio telescope in Puerto Rico. The message consisted of 1,679 binary bits and contained basic information about the human race—the atomic numbers of hydrogen, carbon, nitrogen, oxygen, and phosphorus; the formula for DNA; an illustration of the DNA double helix; a rudimentary diagram of our solar system; a stick figure human being; the population of earth; and a drawing of the telescope. The signal was sent only once and was aimed at a group of 300,000 stars called the Great Cluster in Hercules. The message has progressed only about one thousandth of the distance (or 147 trillion miles) from its target 25,000 light years away. Ironically, the cluster at which it was directed will have moved by the time the signal arrives.

Multiplying the Binary Way

The following are two simple examples of multiplying using binary numbers. Many find this function easier to perform than adding. Here, 0 and 1 play their usual roles: $0 \times 0 = 1$, $0 \times 1 = 0$, $1 \times 0 = 0$, and $1 \times 1 = 1$.

```
    1 0 1 | 5           1 1 | 3
 x   1 1 | 3         x   1 1 | 3
    1 0 1 |             1 1 |
  1 0 1 0 |           1 1 0 |
  1 1 1 1 | 15       1 0 0 1 | 9
```

Examples of binary multiplication.

243

Yi Edicts

Many mistakenly credit Leibniz with inventing binary numeration. According to *History of Binary and Other Nondecimal Numeration* by Anton Glaser (Tomash Publishers, 1981), English mathematician and astronomer Thomas Hariot (1560–1621) and Bishop Juan Caramuel Y Lobkowitz (1606–1682), working independently of one another, developed the system before Leibniz. Leibniz presented the binary system in his 1703 publication called *Explication*, 33 years after Caramuel's findings in *Mathesis biceps*.

Examples of subtraction and division have not been included. Simply, they require advanced know-how and are beyond our scope here.

The Theology of Binary

Leibniz believed his binary-theological theory virtually proved the Christian doctrine of *creatio ex nihilo* (God's creation of the universe out of nothing) by illustrating the origin of all numbers through the use of 0 and 1. In other words, the universe (numbers) was created out of nothing (0) by the one (1) Christian God. Since numbers were common to all peoples, Leibniz saw this as an effective way to link people. He was convinced his philosophy provided a rational explanation for God's existence that did not rely upon the Christian incarnation, the union of God and humanity in Jesus Christ. However, this does not imply Leibniz ignored divine revelation. In fact, he believed faith in the Holy Scriptures was necessary to "awaken the inner light." Essentially, Leibniz thought his universal idea would unite all peoples and end religious discord, particularly among Christians.

Notable Quotable

"All creatures derive from God and from nothingness. Their self-being is of God, their non-being is of nothing. Numbers too show this in a wonderful way, and the essences of things are like numbers."

—Gottfried Leibniz, *On the True Theologia Mystica*, 1690

The Nature of Numbers

If this notion of mathematics-cum-theology seems far-fetched today, it was fully accepted by seventeenth-century scientists, philosophers, and mathematicians. Despite the fact the Bible offers few examples of God using numbers and mathematics to create the universe, it was understood God's wisdom was made manifest in the natural world, a totality that could be analyzed and interpreted mathematically. This notion has its roots in Pythagorean thought.

Born around 570 B.C.E., the ancient Greek philosopher, scientist, and mathematician Pythagoras of Samos believed numbers were a living reality, a principle of nature. Following this idea, the number 1 was not simply a quantitative integer, but a principle or essence underlying nature. The number 1 represented unity and harmony from which all things derive. Theon of Smyrna (born fourth century C.E.) explains the concept like this:

> "Unity is the principle of all things and the most dominant of all that is: All things emanate from it and it emanates from nothing. It is indivisible and it is everything in power. It is immutable and never departs from its own nature through multiplication ($1 \times 1 = 1$). Everything that is intelligible and not yet created exists in it; the nature of ideas, God himself, the soul, the beautiful and the good, and every intelligible essence, such as beauty itself, justice itself, equality itself, for we conceive each of these things as being one and as existing in itself."

(Excerpt taken from *The Pythagorean Sourcebook and Library* compiled and translated by Kenneth Guthrie [Phanes Press, 1987]. Used with permission.)

Most scholars generally agree Pythagoras received the notion of number theology during his 22 years of study among Egyptian and Babylonian priests. Also, apparently he learned about the essence of number while being initiated into the Orphic mysteries—a body of esoteric knowledge originating with the mythical Greek hero, Orpheus. Whatever the case may be, the Pythagorean interest in numbers influenced Christian, Jewish, and Islamic cultures. Intentionally or not, Leibniz drew upon these ancient beliefs.

Notable Quotable

" ... Numbers are the thoughts of God ... . The Divine Wisdom is reflected in the numbers impressed on all things ... the construction of the physical and moral world alike is based on eternal numbers."

—Saint Augustine (C.E. 354–430)

The 64 Hexagrams and the Binary System

From 1697 to 1702, Leibniz corresponded with Father Joachim Bouvet (d. 1732), a French Jesuit stationed in China. Selected by King Louis XIV of France for the mission, Bouvet was retained by emperor Kangxi as his mathematics instructor. In fact, the emperor was so impressed with Bouvet's knowledge, he granted him space within Beijing's (then Peking) Forbidden City compound for a church and a home.

In 1701, Bouvet received a table of Leibniz's binary numeration. Immediately, he recognized by substituting 0 for a broken line and the number 1 for a solid line, the progression of binary numbers 0 to 63 perfectly correlated to the Fuxi (or Before Heaven) arrangement of hexagrams, which is similar to the Before Heaven arrangement of trigrams symbolizing an ideal, harmonious, and perfect world. Upon making this discovery, Bouvet sent Leibniz two different designs of the 64 hexagrams. The first was the "circular and square" diagram. Although this arrangement is attributed to Fuxi (which Bouvet believed), it was actually composed by Neo-Confucian cosmologist Shao Yung about C.E. 1060. Because of space restrictions, we do not include the circular representation of hexagrams that surrounds the squared one (represented in the following table). A complete illustration can be found in Fritjof Captra's thought-provoking book, *The Tao of Physics* (Shambala, 1991).

The Fuxi (or Before Heaven) arrangement of hexagrams and its correlation to binary numbers 0 through 63.

246

The first number at the top of each hexagram denotes its decimal equivalent; the second number in parentheses is its hexagram number. For instance, the first hexagram in the table is Hexagram 2. In binary notation, the configuration of six broken lines equals a value of zero. The second one illustrated is Hexagram 23. Its binary value is one. Notice the binary numeration is a mirror image of how the notation is usually laid out. Here, the binary numbers are read left to right or top to bottom (100000). Normally, the notation reads right to left (000001).

The Design of Binary

The second arrangement Leibniz received from Bouvet is called "Fuxi's Hexagram Order" from a twelfth-century book, *Zhouyi Benji (The Zhouyi's Original Meaning)* by Neo-Confucian philosopher, Zhu Xi. Again, we have deliberately simplified the illustration to demonstrate its seeming conformity to the binary system.

Here, the binary numeration is placed in its familiar computational sequence. Notice the inherent "order and harmony" that so enthused Leibniz. In the first column of both diagrams, 0 (black yin) and 1 (white yang) are equally divided. Each again divides into two, the process continuing until 64 hexagrams are formed.

Was Fuxi Christian?

Based on the two tables of Fuxi's arrangement of hexagrams, Leibniz believed he uncovered proof that the Chinese were not "heathens." You see, at that time, two problems besieged China's missionaries. The first concerned whether the Chinese had a word comparable to the Christian "God." While many believed no word encapsulated the Christian deity, some Christian scholars, including Matteo Ricci, an Italian Jesuit and founder of the Catholic mission in China, were less rigid in their thinking. Ricci accepted two Chinese terms for God: Tian (Heaven) and Shang Di (Lord Above). Ricci preferred to translate God as Tian Zhu (Heavenly Ruler). (Note: Tian Zhu is not a Chinese term.)

The second problem concerned rites and ceremonies in honor of ancestors and Confucius. The question was, did the ceremonies have religious significance? While we won't let these questions detain us, a full accounting can be found in the book *Gottfried Wilhelm Leibniz: Writings on China,* by Daniel J. Cook and Henry Rosemont Jr. (Open Court, 1994).

Despite these debates, Leibniz maintained that the modern Chinese had strayed from the teachings of their ancient sage-kings; that, if the classical texts like the *Yijing* were scrutinized, you would find "pure Christianity." Basically, Leibniz was confident that if he could show his binary theology had been realized thousands of years earlier in China, then he could most certainly entice the Chinese to accept the Christian faith. Instead of quoting from the Holy Scriptures, he could show them their own facts—that they had lost or at least misunderstood the true meaning of Fuxi's works.

Left: Leibniz's binary system. Right: Zhu Xi's diagram.

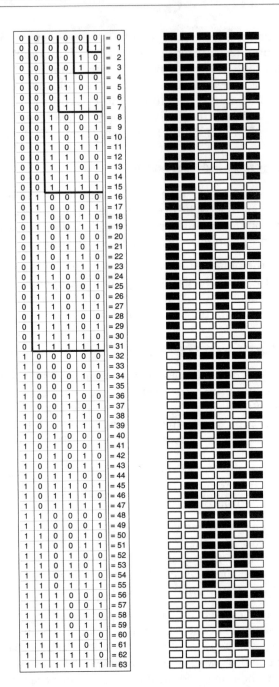

However, Leibniz's enterprise (and those of the like-minded missionaries) proved unsuccessful. In 1642, Pope Benedict XIV officially put an end to the controversies. He issued a mandate condemning the Chinese ceremonies and choosing the term Tian Zhu to designate the word God. In fact, missionaries in China were forced to take an oath not to even discuss Rome's decision. As a result, the active effort to convert the Chinese to Christianity failed.

Just a Coincidence

The question arises, is there any merit to Leibniz's claim that Fuxi understood binary theology? Or, is the correlation purely coincidental? We say the latter, for three chief reasons:

1. Fuxi was a mythical figure. If he did exist, he was probably a simple Paleolithic tribal chief who might have invented nets for fishing or tamed animals for agrarian/domestic use.

2. The solid and broken lines were not part of the original divinatory text, the *Zhouyi*.

3. Ancient Chinese mathematics was based on base 10 and base 12 numeration. In fact, at that time, they did not have a zero.

In the next chapter, you'll meet theoretical physicist David Bohm. You'll learn about his progressive ideas, which tell of a hidden primary reality he called the implicate order—the realm that provides the answers to your *Yijing* questions. Below are the answers for Leibniz's binary birth year.

$$1646 = \frac{0}{2^{11}} \quad \frac{1}{2^{10}} \quad \frac{1}{2^{9}} \quad \frac{0}{2^{8}} \quad \frac{0}{2^{7}} \quad \frac{1}{2^{6}} \quad \frac{1}{2^{5}} \quad \frac{0}{2^{4}} \quad \frac{1}{2^{3}} \quad \frac{1}{2^{2}} \quad \frac{1}{2^{1}}$$

| | 2048 | 1024 | 512 | 256 | 128 | 64 | 32 | 16 | 8 | 4 | 2 |

The Least You Need to Know

➤ German-born Gottfried Leibniz was one of the seventeenth century's leading intellectuals.

➤ Binary numeration uses only the numbers 0 and 1 to compute.

➤ Leibniz believed his binary numeration practically proved the Christian doctrine of *creatio ex nihilo* by illustrating that the universe (numbers) was created out of nothing (0) by the one (1) God.

➤ The Christian, Jewish, and Islamic interest in numbers derives from Pythagorean teachings.

➤ The similarity between the Leibniz binary system and the configuration of Fuxi's hexagram arrangement is coincidental.

Chapter 11

Science, Synchronicity, and the *Yijing:* Understanding a Holistic Universe

In This Chapter

➤ What is synchronicity?

➤ Understanding theoretical physicist David Bohm's holographic universe

➤ The implicate and explicate orders of reality

➤ The relationship between matter, consciousness, and synchronicity

➤ Synchronicity and the *Yijing*

A couple of months ago, I (Elizabeth Moran) received a gift from a friend. It was a dog-eared copy of the *I Ching or Book of Changes* (Princeton University Press, 1950), Richard Wilhelm's revered translation of the 64 hexagrams. On a whim, my friend bought the book for a buck because she felt that I "needed it." Curiously, the day before, I had been unable to locate my own copy of the same translation.

A couple of weeks later, my husband found my "lost" copy in the trunk of his car. While he proclaimed his discovery, a UPS truck pulled up bearing another translation I had purchased from Amazon.com. That same day I received an e-mail from my literary agent. An editor at Alpha (publisher of *The Complete Idiot's Guide* series) wanted to know if I would write *The Complete Idiot's Guide to the I Ching*.

These seemingly random coincidences are what noted psychologist Carl Jung called "synchronicity." It's what this chapter is all about. We'll focus on the groundbreaking work of theoretical physicist David Bohm. He believed in a unified cosmos. A cosmos in which everything is interconnected and interactive. A cosmos that is unpredictable and creative. Bohm postulated a hidden primary reality that provides information to the totality of humankind and our environment. As you'll soon learn, this fundamental reality makes acausal events like synchronicity possible. This notion is quite literally a quantum leap, from the absolute causal and predictable world of classical physics, the bedrock of scientific thought since the publication of Isaac Newton's *Principia* (1687).

It's pretty deep stuff but Bohm (along with many other respected scientists and psychologists) independently developed a new interpretative model of our physical and psychical connectivity with the universe. And what does all this have to do with the *Yijing*, an oracle used to determine a possible outcome to a specific question? Well, get comfortable, prop your feet up, and keep reading!

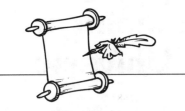

Wise Words

A word coined by Swiss psychologist Carl Jung (1875–1961), **synchronicity** is a phenomenon in which coincidences such as thoughts, ideas, objects, and/or events link together to form a theme that is significant to the observer.

Is It Synchronicity?

In a nutshell, the phenomenon of *synchronicity* can be described as a pattern of correlated coincidences that can take form as objects, thoughts, ideas, and events (or a combination) linked together in a common theme, meaning, and significance to the observer. Often, synchronicity is the eerie feeling that someone or something is operating "behind the scenes," guiding us along. Actually, that "someone" is what Westerners variously describe as a knowing, higher force, the sea of consciousness, or the almighty God. Many Easterners call this ultimate force the Dao.

Two of a Kind: Meaningless Happenstance …

There are two types of synchronicity. Perhaps the most common type is the meaningless occurrences of the trivial variety, uncanny coincidences that amuse more than awe. For instance, you're thinking about a friend when the telephone rings and, you guessed it, it's your friend. Or you share a common birth date with several friends and/or relatives. Or you got the job because you were in the right place at the right time. We've all encountered such curiosities. The question is, do they *mean* anything?

Austrian biologist Paul Kammerer (d. 1926) was a synchronicity fanatic. He enthusiastically spent his life observing, recording, and analyzing the reoccurrence of phenomena. The culmination of which was published in his 1919 book, *Das Gesetz der Serie (The Law of the Series)*. Although most of Kammerer's accounts were trivial oddities, he concluded there is an acausal principle of nature (random, without apparent cause) where likes attract to cause a series of coincidences. He called this principle "the law of the series." Not surprisingly, Kammerer was ridiculed for his progressive ideas, for challenging the orthodox mechanistic thought developed by Isaac Newton. In 1926, after years of humiliation, he committed suicide.

Master Class

Our distant relatives didn't question our inseparable link with the cosmos. In fact, they believed the cosmos was divine, that God or a higher order directly influenced their well-being. This idea began to change in the late seventeenth century with the publication of Isaac Newton's book, *Philosophiae Naturalis Principia Mathematica* (1687). Considered the beginning of classical or mechanical physics, the *Principia* explains how the universe is governed by a few simple rules described by mathematics. To Newton, the universe was entirely predictable and causal. Although deeply religious, Newton's rigid methods set the stage for a fundamental break between science and religion. His ideas became the foundation of scientific thought for 200 years. It was not until Einstein's theory of relativity and the formulation of quantum physics that Newton's scientific paradigm was challenged.

... and Meaningful Coincidence

The second type of synchronicity is the meaningful kind, invoking change. As we discussed in Chapter 1, "Ground Zero: Understanding the Basics About the *I Ching, Book of Changes*," change is the hallmark of the *Yijing*. Change moves us along. It helps us gain insight into who we are. In Carl Jung's enlightening book, *Synchronicity: An Acausal Connecting Principle* (Princeton University Press, 1973), he offers a terrific example of a meaningful coincidence involving a patient describing her dream about a scarab beetle:

> "While she was telling me this dream I sat with my back to the closed window. Suddenly I heard a noise behind me, like a gentle tapping. I turned round and saw a flying insect knocking against the windowpane from outside. I opened the window and caught the creature in the air as it flew in. It was the nearest analogy to a golden scarab that one finds in our latitudes, a scarabaeid beetle, the common rose-chafer."

The scarab beetle is a metaphor for rebirth and renewal. Jung's patient understood its significance, recognizing it as a sign of recovery. In short, this synchronistic event was

253

meaningful because it yielded change. The incident "spoke" to her directly. Before you read any further, take a trip down memory lane and jot down synchronicities that have touched your life. Ask yourself …

➤ Was the synchronistic series meaningless or meaningful?

➤ Did the series coincide with important or pivotal periods in your life?

➤ Did the series yield change?

By gaining an understanding of who you are, you will more fully benefit from the *Yijing's* power, as you shall soon learn.

In Sync with Nature

Synchronicity implies a holistic and unified universe. This is because *separate* events/objects/thoughts/ideas isolated in time and space combine to form a *whole* theme of meaning. Therefore, we can assume a purposeful relationship between acausal events. Synchronicity suggests that humankind and nature are in harmony—in sync. But what causes synchronicity? Well, in order to explain this, we must examine our current understanding of the physical world.

The World According to Bohm

Indisputably, David Bohm (1917–1992) was one of the most prominent and influential theoretical physicists of modern science. He was a pioneer, incorporating psychics, biology, psychology, linguists, philosophy, and religion into a new holistic world reality. He was a seeker of truth who challenged the prevailing laws of *quantum physics* (the study of subatomic particles) formulated mainly by Danish physicists Neils Bohr and Werner Heisenberg in the 1920s.

Master Class

The quantum theory in physics studies subatomic particles, the realm of the infinitesimal that is thought to be obscure and uncertain. This is because subatomic particles (like electrons) do not have defined locations and speeds. Due to this indeterministic nature, quantum physicists realized that isolation is an invalid method of observation. Considering the particle's whole environment is paramount to understanding how the world operates. Formulated in the 1920s, quantum physics was posited primarily by Neils Bohr and Werner Heisenberg.

In 1951, while teaching quantum theory at Princeton University, Bohm wrote a textbook. Entitled *Quantum Theory,* his book explained the ideas set forth by the founders of quantum mechanics. Upon completion of the book, which is now considered a classic, Bohm sent copies to Neils Bohr and Albert Einstein. Although Bohr did not respond, Einstein (who was also at Princeton at the time) did. In fact, the scientists struck up a fast friendship, enthusiastically exchanging ideas about the quantum world.

Einstein, like Bohm, did not subscribe to the accepted notion that subatomic particles were indeterministic. Rather, these particles were complex entities. Their movement was determined, motivated by a force providing "active information" to the whole of the environment. To explain his theory, Bohm gave the analogy of an airplane (electron) being guided by radio signals (active force). While the signals cannot provide the energy that drives the airplane, they can help the plane's pilot direct the movement produced by the plane's engines.

Bohm's theories about a holistic and connective universe were not based on pure speculation. While it's beyond our scope to discuss the body of his landmark work that supports his claims, we will focus on perhaps his most profound contribution, the holomovement and its two fundamental "aspects": the implicate and explicate orders. It is here that the cause of synchronicity will be explained. It is here that you'll begin to understand synchronicity's connection to the *Yijing*.

Wholeness and the Holomovement

Bohm firmly believed the cosmos is "an undivided and unbroken whole" that is in a constant state of flux and change. This idea bears a striking resemblance to the Eastern notion of yin and yang—that everyone and everything moves through a cycle of birth, life, decay, and death. Bohm called this unceasing flow of change the *holomovement. Holo* is the Greek word meaning whole, total, and complete. Bohm suggested that the cosmos acts like a massive flowing hologram, in which the whole (holo) message (gram) of reality is contained.

Merriam-Webster's New Collegiate Dictionary defines a *hologram* as a "three-dimensional image that is reproduced from a pattern of interference produced by a split coherent laser beam." How a hologram is created is not important. What is important is its intrinsic nature: Each part of the hologram contains all of the information about the whole image. For example, in a two-dimensional photograph, each part of the film corresponds to the same portion of the image. This is because the spatial dimensions are restricted to left and right, and up and down.

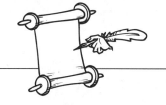

Wise Words

A **hologram** is a three-dimensional image in which each part of the image contains the entire picture. Hence, a hologram is a whole (holo) message (gram). The **holomovement** is the movement, change, and transformation of the hologram.

A hologram, however, has the added dimension of depth—forward and backward movement, or what Bohm called "enfolding" and "unfolding." On a cosmic level, Bohm believed that each part of the universe contains the whole of the cosmos enfolded or hidden within it. Confused? Keep reading for a better understanding of this complex subject.

The Implications of Bohm's Implicate Order

Bohm maintained that everyday reality is actually secondary to a primary hidden reality called the *implicate order*. To explain this concept, Bohm used the analogy of two glass cylinders, one inside the other, with the space between them filled with glycerin. Imagine placing a droplet of ink into the glycerin. Now, slowly rotate (clockwise or counterclockwise) the inner cylinder so that the droplet stretches out into a thread. Eventually, the thread will become so thin that it will disappear. You have just enfolded or diffused the ink drop into the glycerin so that its order has *seemingly* been caused to be random (its implicate order). But if you rotate the cylinder in the opposite direction, the thread reappears and soon becomes the ink drop again! Cool, huh?

Before connecting it to the phenomenon of synchronicity, let's carry this analogy to the next level. Imagine dropping and enfolding a series of ink drops into the glycerin such that the series forms a line of droplets. When the direction is reversed, the droplets are unfolded one at a time. However, if you spin the cylinder, the perception is one of a single ink drop moving along a path. The point here is that the sequence of enfolded droplets are actually separate and acausal events that emerge as a connective pattern. This describes synchronicity. Therefore, the notion of an implicate order presents the possibility that the universe possesses hidden and orderly realms beyond our current understanding.

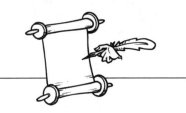

Wise Words

David Bohm's **implicate order** is a primary invisible reality whereby matter and consciousness emerge or unfold into the visible world around us. The implicate order suggests there is a hidden order to the universe, and therefore, gives meaning to acausal events like synchronicity.

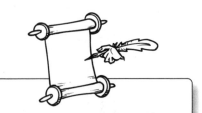

Wise Words

The **explicate order** represents the manifestations of objects, events, thoughts, and ideas that are unfolded from the much deeper implicate order of the undivided holomovement.

The Explanation of Bohm's Explicate Order

Simply, Bohm's *explicate order* is the unfolding of all separate objects, events, and thoughts derived from the much deeper implicate order of the undivided holomovement. In the ink drop experiment, the unfolding droplet represents the explicate order. In other words, the explicate order is reality as we know it.

A Quantum Potential of Possibilities

The active force organizing the implicate order is called the *quantum potential.* Returning to Bohm's analogy about the airplane that is guided by radio signals, the signals correspond to the quantum potential. Moreover, the quantum potential suggests the cosmos is full of, well, potential. Instead of space being a vast void of nothingness, it is full of information that is available and accessible by everyone and everything because of our connectiveness to it. The Daoists call this vast space wuji. Wuji is believed to be the wellspring of creation.

Although we won't delve into the subatomic physical proofs of the quantum potential, know that like the airplane analogy, it may cause electrons to "make choices" about its future. In the same way, our future is largely affected by the choices we make. The question is: Are these choices divinely inspired or are they the product of free will? Also, can an oracle, such as the *Yijing,* help us to make the correct choice? These age-old questions have been pondered for centuries.

The Source of All Things? The Superquantum Potential

Where does the quantum potential get its information? From the *superquantum potential* that organizes and directs the superimplicate order. Indeed, Bohm theorized that there exist infinite series of implicate orders that make up the superimplicate order, each one organizing the lower ones and influencing the higher realms. It is important to understand that each level is not separate and distinct. Rather, they are intertwining and interactive aspects of the holomovement. These higher realms are metaphysical, existing beyond time, space, and our own sensory perception. They are believed to be the source of true knowledge and wisdom.

The Holographic Brain

Bohm's concept of a holographic universe has much in common with how our brain functions. As you have learned, a hologram is comprised of

light whose waves are in perfect sync. This synchronizing of waves also occurs with deep meditation and prayer. The brain's theta waves (associated with the sleep or relaxed state) unite with or become in sync with the brain's alpha waves (associated with the active conscious state). In essence, practicing meditation, yoga, and taiji can enable you to become in perfect harmony with the cosmos. With balance comes meaningful insight into nature's truths. Into *your* truth!

Yet, there *is* evidence that supports a holographic brain. This has to do with memory storage. Referring to the analogy about a two-dimensional photograph, if a piece of film is damaged, the corresponding image is lost forever. However, if a holographic plate (brain) is damaged, the image (memory) only becomes blurred. A holographic brain suggests that memories are stored within and throughout the vast capacity of the brain. Until we fully understand the mechanics and function of our brain, we can only make educated guesses about how it acts upon our consciousness.

Yi Edicts

While Western scientists use logic and reason to increase knowledge about the world we live in, Eastern sages primarily use meditation, the intuitive art of going within your being to tap into universal truth and wisdom. This mastery of the inner realm is based on the belief that we (the microcosm) mirror the macrocosmic universe. In a meditative or balanced state, the conscious mind enfolds into the implicate order of true knowledge and unfolds its pearls of wisdom. In other words, you can become more enlightened by practicing meditation, yoga, or prayer.

Synchronicity and the *Yijing*

If you can accept Bohm's progressive ideas, then you can accept the notion that our thoughts, in some measure, can produce meaningful coincidences. Remember Carl Jung's patient who was recounting her dream about a scarab beetle only to have one manifest at that moment? Well, just like the separate ink drops in the glycerin experiment, the acausal events (the thought about the beetle and its physical manifestation) emerged as a pattern of meaning. The patient's thought enfolded into the realm of truth and unfolded as its explicate answer. She received a holo (whole) gram (message).

Notable Quotable

"The Chinese standpoint does not concern itself as to the attitude one takes toward the performance of the oracle. It is only we who are puzzled, because we trip time and again over our prejudice, viz., the notion of causality. The ancient wisdom of the East lays stress upon the fact that the intelligent individual realizes his own thoughts, but not in the least upon the way in which he does it. The less one thinks about the theory of the *I Ching,* the more soundly one sleeps."

—Carl Jung, 1949, in his foreword to *The I Ching or Book of Changes* (Princeton University Press, 1950)

Consulting the *Yijing* is like asking for an instant hologram. Carl Jung, in his foreword to the Richard Wilhelm translation, states it best: "In the *I Ching,* the only criterion of the validity of synchronicity is the observer's opinion that the text of the hexagram amounts to a true rendering of his psychic condition." Simply put, the hexagram's "answer" is in sync with your conscious needs, wants, and desires at the moment when you tossed the coins or stalks of yarrow. The answer is the instant unfolding of truth derived from the holistic and knowing universe.

Harkening back to the prophetic series of coincidences that spurred the production of this book (see the introduction for a reminder), I consulted the *Yijing* to determine if collaborating with Master Joseph Yu would be a harmonious or hazardous endeavor. I received Hexagram 8, an omen of good fortune and teamwork. This answer was in sync with my psychic condition of that moment. The answer validated my choice. To ask the same question a second time would have been foolhardy. Quoting Carl Jung: "The master speaks just once."

The ideas in this chapter were inspired in part by and used with permission of Allan Combs and Mark Holland in their thought-provoking book, *Synchronicity: Science, Myth, and the Trickster* (Marlowe & Company, 1996). In the next chapter, you'll learn about a new science called chaos theory. Simply, chaos theory and the *Yijing* share a hidden, ordered reality.

The Least You Need to Know

➤ Synchronicity is a phenomenon whereby coincidences such as ideas, physical objects, and/or events link together to form a theme significant in meaning to the observer.

➤ David Bohm was a theoretical physicist who postulated that the universe acts like a hologram—an image whose parts contain the entire image.

➤ The holographic universe has two aspects: the implicate and explicate order. The implicate order is a primary invisible reality where matter and consciousness emerge into the visible world, the explicate order.

➤ The quantum potential is the active force that drives the implicate order. It provides information to humankind and our environment.

➤ The *Yijing* provides a meaningful and instant synchronistic answer to a particular question.

Chapter 12

Chaos Theory and the *Yijing*

In This Chapter

➤ The definitions of chaos

➤ The butterfly effect and butterfly power

➤ Understanding the mysterious strange attractor

➤ How the *Yijing* is chaotic

Stepping into the twenty-first century, scientists and nonscientists surely look back at the last century and marvel at the monumental advancements made in just about every scientific discipline. Yet, three theories stand out: relativity (the equivalence of mass and energy), quantum mechanics (the study of subatomic particles), and chaos (the study of the inherent orderliness within the universe). While you are probably familiar with the first two theories, chaos theory may be new to you. This is because it *is* new, a concept "discovered" accidentally in the early 1960s by an American meteorologist named Edward Lorenz. In fact, many facets of chaos theory have yet to be understood. Nevertheless, chaos theory has attracted and been embraced by a variety of fields: physics, mathematics, computers, economics, psychology, and biology, just to name a few.

As you'll soon learn, chaos theory challenges us to ask questions about our perception of reality. More importantly, it asks us to think globally and holistically. You may be wondering what chaos theory and the *Yijing* have in common. At the core of both systems lie truth, harmony, and order. But, before we get into the striking similarities between the newest science and an ancient oracle, you must first understand what chaos theory is.

Chaos Defined

Webster's New Collegiate Dictionary offers two definitions of the word *chaos*. First, it's defined as "the confused, unorganized state of primordial matter before the creation of distinct forms." This definition accords with what might be its first textual reference, the eighth century B.C.E. poem by the Greek poet, Hesiod. Entitled *Theogony (Genealogy of the Gods),* the poem describes the creation of the universe out of chaos: "In the beginning there was chaos, nothing but void, formless matter, infinite space."

If *Webster's* first definition seems obscure, the second one provides the popular understanding. Defined as "a state of utter confusion," chaos infers individual turmoil and turbulence. It suggests disorder, crisis, and havoc. A common expression like "my life is chaotic" usually implies career- and/or relationship-related discord.

Wise Words

Webster's New Collegiate Dictionary offers two meanings of the word **chaos:** "the unorganized state of primordial matter before the creation of distinct forms" and "the state of utter confusion."

Notable Quotable

"Confusion is a word we have invented for an order which is not understood."

—American author Henry Miller (1891–1980)

But chaos isn't exclusive to individual confusion. A city, state, country, and even the world can seem chaotic at times. In these instances, chaos implies the systematic breakdown of communication, the violation and insurrection of authority. Often, chaotic behavior leads to riots, strikes, and anarchy. In short, chaos is messy. It is the antithesis of balance, harmony, and organization.

What Is Chaos Theory?

But there's also a third definition. To scientists, computer scientists, and mathematicians, the term chaos refers to the pattern and organization within *nonlinear* systems. Nonlinear systems are described as complex schemes whose rate of change is not constant. The weather; population growth; the stock market; changes in mindsets, fashions, and fads; traffic flow; and brain and heart activity are examples of complex nonlinear systems. In fact, you are a nonlinear system! Your physical and mental growth change at an irregular rate.

Chaos theory studies how these systems, once thought to be completely chaotic, unpredictable, and random, actually contain hidden ordered patterns. Yet, there's more to chaos theory than finding order amid apparent disorder. Here are a couple of its other defining features and how they relate to the human experience:

➤ A chaos system is very sensitive. A slight change, disturbance, or unaccounted variable can lead to an enormously different outcome. In human terms, a small change can alter your normal routine or the course of your life. A birth or death, the loss of a job, a job promotion, or a sudden insight, are examples of life-altering variables.

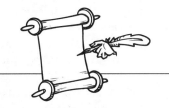

➤ A chaos system can evolve into a more complex state. In human terms, prayer and meditation can serve to help us rise to a higher level of clarity and maturity. As you'll soon learn, the *Yijing* is a tool that can assist *transcendence* to the next level of understanding, wisdom, and truth.

Don't fret if you don't understand chaos theory's components. As you progress through this chapter, they will become clearer. For now, know that chaos theory and the *Yijing* imply an underlying connectivity where order and disorder join to create a more complex state.

> ### Wise Words
>
> **Nonlinear** mathematics studies systems whose rate of change is not constant. It is the study of complex and unpredictable systems such as the weather, population growth, the stock market, and traffic flow. **Chaos theory** studies pattern and organization within nonlinear systems.

> ### Master Class
>
> In the Hindu–Buddhist tradition, the red dot of paint on a person's forehead (called the "bindi," "tilak," or "third eye") symbolizes **transcendence,** heightened awareness, and inner perception. It relates to the act of seeing intuitively; seeing "the big picture." The third eye corresponds to one of seven (in Buddhism, four) chakras, described as the energy centers in the body. In most Christian traditions, the smudge of ash placed on the forehead implies transcendence, the cycle of life, death, and rebirth in Jesus Christ. The smudge marks the first day of Lent, which represents Jesus' withdrawal into the wilderness for 40 days of repentance, reflection, and redirection. By observing Lent, followers seek to imitate Jesus' actions.

Chaos Theory's Unassuming Beginning

The notion of chaos theory began humbly in 1889 when Gösta Mittag-Leffler, a mathematics professor at the University of Stockholm, suggested a mathematics contest (open to anyone) to commemorate the 60th birthday of King Oscar II of Norway and Sweden. For the contest, four questions were posed. The most controversial concerned whether or not the solar system was stable. In other words, will the earth and the planets continue to infinitely orbit around the sun, keeping to their mandated patterns, or will some factor radically alter their paths and rearrange their order? (Much to the chagrin of modern scientists, the question remains one of the great unsolved mysteries of astrophysics.)

Jules Henri Poincaré, professor of mathematics at the celebrated University of Paris, won the prize for his solution attesting to the solar system's stability. His complex paper was published in Mittag-Leffler's journal, *Acta Mathemetica*. But, a short time later, a colleague of Mittag-Leffler's noticed an error in Poincaré's calculations. Instead of being disqualified, Poincaré was asked to rectify his theorem. After months of anguish and intense concentration, he concluded the problem could not be solved using prevailing *linear* mathematics, a system that could describe only the interaction of *two* celestial bodies. For example, celestial scientists could calculate how a single planet orbited around the sun, but could not calculate how the solar system operated as a whole. Also, physicists did not know how to include the influence of things like asteroids, comets, moons, and planetary rings. In fact, Isaac Newton (whose deterministic mathematical model of the natural world would rule for two centuries) believed divine intervention was sometimes necessary to maintain elliptical orbit.

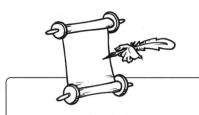

Wise Words

Attributed to the mechanical or Newtonian paradigm, **linear** mathematics describes the interaction of only two entities. The simple equations were thought to result in an accurate and predictable view of nature.

Determined to solve the "three-body" problem, Poincaré set about developing new mathematics that would describe an all-inclusive view of the universe. In his quest, he realized that the accumulation of small changes could produce colossal ones in the end. For example, take an asteroid orbiting the sun. Ordinarily, the gravitational pull of a planet on an asteroid has an insignificant effect. However, under the right conditions, the accumulation of minuscule fluctuations can cause the asteroid to career off its path and hurl into the farthest reaches of space!

In essence, Poincaré realized that a chaotic situation could be produced by minute disturbances that resonate and amplify throughout the solar system. Contrary to the accepted view, Poincaré understood the cosmos was holistic, that celestial bodies work in harmony with and not independently of each other. Unfortunately, his discovery went unnoticed.

A Butterfly Flapping Its Wings in Hong Kong Sets Off a Tornado in Texas

American meteorologist Edward Lorenz is considered to be the first true founder of chaos theory, although the term wasn't coined until years later. In 1960, he used a computer to forecast the weather by inputting data like temperature, air density and pressure, and wind speed and direction. Later, in order to verify his results and to save time and paper, Lorenz shortened the calculation to three (.506) decimal places instead of the original six (.506127). Although he understood that he entered a small change to the initial conditions, that he expected a proportionate difference in the end result. He was wrong. The weather projection was wildly different.

In weather forecasting, the phenomenon came to be known as the *butterfly effect*—the flutter (small changes) of a butterfly's wings in one part of the world could trigger disturbances that could multiply and result in a tornado (chaos) in another part of the world. Of course, this is an exaggeration, but Lorenz demonstrated that it's impossible to predict weather accurately beyond a few days. Now you can understand why TV weather meteorologists often present conflicting and/or altogether incorrect forecasts. Somewhere, an unsuspecting flutter sets forces in motion that can "rain on your parade."

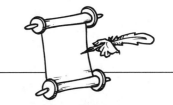

Wise Words

The **butterfly effect** relates to weather forecasting. It is the phenomenon whereby small changes lead to a chaotic and unpredictable outcome.

Yi Edicts

In 1975, mathematicians James Yorke and Tien-Yien Li coined the term chaos theory in an article called "Period Three Implies Chaos" for *American Mathematical Monthly.*

Butterfly Power

Butterfly power is part of human consciousness. If you ever doubted that one person could affect a positive impact on society, consider the following examples:

➤ From 1933 to 1945, Franklin D. Roosevelt, the 32nd President of the United States, led the country out of two great crises—the Great Depression and World War II. Called the New Deal, his peacetime domestic program introduced innovative reforms to reduce unemployment and restore economic security.

➤ In 1955, Rosa Parks helped to lessen racial discrimination by willfully disobeying a segregation law that required African Americans to relinquish their seats to white citizens on Alabama's municipal buses. Her courageous action rallied the support of both the black and white communities, who sought to end injustices based on skin color. In 1956, the U.S. Supreme Court ruled in favor of Parks, deeming segregation unconstitutional.

➤ In 1980, Candy Lightner in California and Cindi Lamb in Maryland founded MADD (Mothers Against Drunk Driving) as a consequence of their children being senselessly killed by drunk drivers. Since then, the grassroots organization has been instrumental in the enactment of laws raising the minimum drinking age and lowering the legal blood alcohol limit. Currently, there are two million members and supporters, with 600 chapters nationwide.

You, too, can spread your butterfly wings. Your thoughts and actions have an enormous impact on your family and society, even on your own well-being. But this news is not new. We all know that positive influences like honesty, kindness, and living the Golden Rule foster harmony. Conversely, negative influences such as gossip, prejudice, malice, and selfishness promote discord and ill will. So the next time someone is discourteous to you, think before you act. Return the unpleasant remark with a smile. Let your positive butterfly power radiate.

The Pretty Pattern of Chaos

Ironically, while the mathematical equations for Lorenz's weather model gave rise to chaotic and unpredictable behavior, his graphed equations exhibited an underlying order and symmetry. The following butterfly-shaped figure is called the Lorenz Attractor. It's the first 3-D image (2-D here) of chaos.

The Lorenz Attractor.

(The image was generated by and used with permission of Scott Ransom. The image was produced with Fractint 20.0.)

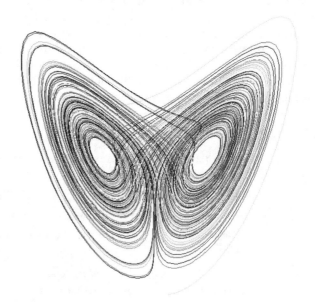

Now, you might be thinking, "Aha! The Lorenz Attractor is an abstract representation of a real-world phenomenon. So, too, are the configuration of six yin and yang lines comprising each hexagram of the *Yijing*." Well, not quite. As we discussed in Chapter 3, "Divination Chinese Style," the solid and broken lines were not part of the original divinatory text, the *Zhouyi*. Initially, they were sequences of numbers that linked a human question to a divine answer. So, the similarity between the Lorenz Attractor and the *Yijing* are the mathematics *within* each system. In other words, at the heart of the oracle, just as in the universe and human nature, are truth, balance, and order. The oft-used phrase, "The method [Lorenz Attractor] behind the madness [chaos]," should actually read, "The method *within* the madness." While "behind" implies the madness is caused by, even a result of, the method, "within" suggests the method is *part of the* madness—that the madness has an order which is the method. Hence, rendering the madness not madness at all, but a different way of being, with an order unto itself. Essentially, the Lorenz Attractor and the *Yijing* illustrate that "madness" or chaos is an illusion.

In 1963, Lorenz described his paradoxical findings in a paper called "Deterministic Nonperiodic Flow." However, because he wasn't a mathematician or a physicist, his work was basically ignored. Like Poincaré, Lorenz would have to wait to be discovered.

The Strangeness of Chaos

The Lorenz Attractor is an example of a *strange attractor*. Arguably, the strange attractor is the central premise around which chaos theory is based. Okay, but what's a strange attractor? Simply stated, it is the visual (and repeating) pattern of the behavior of a nonlinear (chaotic) system. "Strange" reflects the paradox of the system being chaotic yet ordered and patterned. "Attractor" is a little more difficult to define. According to Edward Lorenz in his book, *The Essence of Chaos* (University of Washington Press, 1993), an attractor is a "limit set ... consisting of every point that the orbit passes very close to, again and again." In other words, while experts understand that nonlinear systems are attracted to, or converge to, a set of points, they cannot explain why. Nor can they explain who or what is orchestrating chaos into a cohesive and ordered pattern.

Because of the attractor's mysterious nature, it has been suggested that chaos theory be called "divinamics." This word is taken from the ancient Roman concept *divinatio*, characterized by writer, orator, and statesman, Marcus Tullius Cicero (106–43 B.C.E.). Divinatio refers to mystical knowledge, prophetic insight, and supernatural foresight that are derived from a divine holistic order.

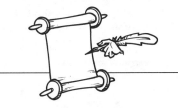

Wise Words

A **strange attractor** is the visual pattern of the behavior of a nonlinear system. Because non-linear systems are chaotic yet patterned, they are called "strange." The "attractor" organizes the pattern of the system.

Harkening back to Chapter 3, remember that the word divine means "of or relating to God or a god-like force."

Choosing the High or Low Road

The attractor helps the system to evolve. When a nonlinear system becomes agitated, the attractor collects the pathways causing the stress. A "phase transition" occurs. Either the system can choose to evolve or "self-organize" into the next level of complexity (or maturity on the human level), or it can collapse and self-destruct. The word "choose" may seem odd, but actually nonlinear systems somehow make choices about their next transition. The process of evolving into a more complex state is called *bifurcation*. To bifurcate means to split into two, to fork.

On the human plane, many would consider prayer and meditation to be strange attractors, for they inspire guidance from a higher power. If we choose to accept the guidance offered in holy books, listen to the "answer to our prayers," or acknowledge inner wisdom, we can transcend (bifurcate) to greater understanding and maturity.

Wise Words

Literally, **bifurcation** is the process of dividing into two parts. The term is derived from the Latin word, *bifurcus:* bi (two) + furca (fork). Bifurcation is the process of evolving into a more complex state.

We can let butterfly power carry us to new heights. We'll be on the high road to truth. Or, we can reject any kind of spiritual teachings or transcendental methods. We can choose the low road, allowing chaotic events to depress and weaken our spirit.

It seems many of us are choosing the higher path. Now more than ever, people are returning to places of worship. Spiritual and motivational speakers like Deepak Chopra, Tony Robbins, and Jack Canfield and Mark Victor Hansen (authors of the popular *Chicken Soup for the Soul* book series) are selling out seminars and speaking engagements, their books becoming instant bestsellers. Also, talk show diva Oprah Winfrey inspires the masses. In large part, she dedicates her life to enhancing the personal growth and development of others.

The Yijing Is Strange, Too

The *Yijing* is a strange attractor, too! It can be used as a tool to organize your own patterned chaos. When you consult the *Yijing*, you're divining guidance, knowledge, or illumination from a source greater than yourself. You learned in Chapter 2, "A Short History of the Ancient Chinese," that the ancient Chinese believed their ancestors counseled them. Yet, you may choose to believe that the collective consciousness, a holistic force (like David Bohm's implicate order, God, or even your own intuitive knowledge) provides the answer. The source is irrelevant. The answer to your inquiry is what is significant.

Those of you who have consulted the oracle can't deny how its answer is consistently meaningful, striking a deep chord of truth within your being. This suggests that the hexagram you receive is not random and unpredictable, but is drawn from the hidden order of your life. We seem to be given the hexagram we need at the moment of consultation. Stated another way, what we perceive as an unpredictable event is actually the limitations imposed by our sensory perception. Somehow, the *Yijing* attractor acts as a bridge between the Supreme Unknown and individual consciousness.

Closing In on Chaos

Space restricts us from exploring all aspects of chaos theory. However, we've provided ample resources in Appendix D, "Learning More About the *Yijing*, Ancient China, and Related Applications," and to assist your own investigation. Here, our goal is to illustrate, yet again, that the cosmos is holistic—that all of its parts dance to the tune of harmony and order. In fact, *Webster's New Collegiate Dictionary* defines the word *cosmos* as "an orderly, harmonious, systematic universe."

The ideas in this chapter were inspired in part by and used with permission of John Briggs and F. David Peat in their enlightening book, *Seven Life Lessons of Chaos: Spiritual Wisdom from the Science of Change* (HarperCollins, 1999), and by Judy Howard Petree in her brilliant Master's thesis correlating faith and prayer to chaos theory. Judy's work may be found at **www.wfu.edu/~petrejh4/ chaosind.htm.** Please look for her upcoming book titled *Faith as a Strange Attractor*.

The next chapter's all about understanding feng shui, the Chinese tradition of harnessing qi's positive aspects to increase the likelihood of better health, wealth, and relationships.

Yi Edicts

The word cosmos is derived from the Greek *kosmos*, meaning "adornment" and "ornament." Traditionally, Pythagoras, the sixth century B.C.E. mathematician and philosopher, is credited with relating cosmos to the universe. To him, the universe was beautiful, adorned with an order that inspires aesthetic appreciation.

The Least You Need to Know

➤ Nonlinear systems are complex and unpredictable systems such as the weather, population growth, the stock market, and traffic flow.

➤ Chaos theory studies pattern and organization within nonlinear systems.

➤ An American meteorologist, Edward Lorenz, is considered the first true founder of chaos theory.

➤ The strange attractor is the central premise on which chaos theory is based. The strange attractor organizes nonlinear systems.

➤ The *Yijing*, prayer, and meditation are considered strange attractors. They act as bridges between the Great Unknown and human consciousness.

Part 7

Understanding and Applying the Ancient Tradition of Feng Shui

Feng shui is the ancient Chinese art and science of improving your health, wealth, and relationships. In Chapter 13, "Increasing Your Health, Wealth, and Relationships with Feng Shui," you'll learn about the first school of feng shui, called Form School. Its theories focus on the qi riding the winds, carried down mountain ridges and waterways. Basically, the idea was to harness the positive aspects by situating a dwelling and a gravesite according to specific environmental factors. Also, you'll learn about Compass School. Primarily, this school focuses on how time (Heaven qi) and space (earth qi) affects the health and livelihood of a person.

Chapter 14, "Learning Yigua Feng Shui," offers you the beginning level of a system that uses the eight trigrams to determine your four favorable and four unfavorable directions. Also, you'll understand which rooms within your home bring good fortune, and which rooms may possibly bring misfortune. To be sure, you'll use this method to evaluate your own living space.

Chapter 13

Increasing Your Health, Wealth, and Relationships with Feng Shui

---

In This Chapter

➤ What is feng shui?

➤ Form School feng shui

➤ Assessing your living space and surrounding environment

➤ Compass School feng shui

The ancient Chinese practice of feng shui is the study of the environment, buildings, people, time, and how the qi of each interact. Taking these factors into consideration, feng shui seeks to harmonize our surroundings positively. With balance and harmony the probability of gaining a job, raise or promotion, getting married, stimulating better business, and warding off accidents and illness is greater.

In this chapter, you'll learn about the origin of feng shui. Also, you will understand how the search for auspicious qi gave rise to two schools of feng shui: Form School and Compass School.

In the Beginning ...

Finding a site on which to build a settlement and raise crops was a primary concern to any ancient civilization. Certainly, to the Neolithic Chinese who settled along the Yellow River some 5,000 years ago, locating the site that offered an abundance of sunshine and shade, protection from the cold winds of the north, and ample water to replenish their beings and nourish their crops were important considerations.

Yi Edicts

Sunshine and shade were the earliest meanings of yang (the active force) and yin (the passive force) respectively.

Wise Words

Literally, **feng shui** means "wind and water," two natural forces that direct qi to a settlement and burial site.

Yet, the two key factors that determined the auspiciousness of a site were the proximity of the mountains and waterways. Mountains were associated with the female and passive principle of nature. Like a caretaker, mountains were stable. They shielded and protected. They were dependable. On the other hand, water represented the male and nature's active force. Rivers, lakes, and the sea provided people with a means to transport goods, to trade, and therefore, to build wealth. Waterways were responsible for helping civilization to progress.

The criterion for locating a favorable site based on the balance between a host of natural factors illustrates the birth of feng shui, a tradition unique to the Chinese, but one that has grasped the interest of the modern world. The term *feng shui* comes from Guo Pu's (C.E. 276–324) *Zangshu (Book of Burial),* a text that many scholars believe explains the *Zangjing (Classic of Burial)* authored by Qing Wuzi of the late Han dynasty (C.E. 190–220). Setting aside its solemn origin, the *Zangshu* points out, "When qi rides the wind [feng], it is dispersed. When it encounters water [shui], it is retained. The ancients collected it and prevented it from dissipating. They directed its [qi's] course to secure its retention. Therefore, it [the method] is called *feng shui*." In other words, gentle winds carried qi, or "life's breath," down the hills and mountain slopes. Nourishing everything in its path, qi was retained and collected in water where it could help foster growth and prosperity.

Sunny Side Up, Please: Considering the Lay of the Land

The first reference to the practice of feng shui comes from the *Shijing (Book of Poetry)*, China's oldest anthology of rhymes dating to about 1100 to 600 B.C.E. In total, the *Shijing* contains 305 poems divided into folksongs (160), odes (105), and hymns (40). In particular, one poem prominently features Gong Liu, the Zhou people's high ancestor and great-grandson of Hou Ji (also known as Chief Millet, their agricultural deity). The poem recounts how Gong Liu led his people to a new land called Bin, located between Mount Qi and the west bank of the Yellow River. The following excerpt describes Gong Liu assessing the environment:

"... Honorable Gong Liu!
He measured the length and breadth of the land;

> He measured the shadows cast on the hills to deduce their height and to
>   determine the directions;
> He watched the sunshine and the shade;
> He studied the flowing streams …."

Gong Liu "measured" the landscape and how the water coursed through it. He "measured" the shadows cast by the hills to determine the four primary directions of north, south, east, and west. He searched for the ideal location where sun and shade were balanced. Ideally, he looked for a site on the southern slope of a mountain. Here, the dwelling would receive maximum sunshine and warmth during the winter. In the summer months, the dwelling would be shaded and cool. The mountain at its back served as a barrier, shielding the inhabitants from harsh winds and barbaric attacks coming from the north. Of course, a nearby source of water was mandatory. This was the criterion Gong Liu used to bring his people to Bin.

The Form School of Feng Shui

As civilization progressed, life became more complex, and feng shui became more specialized. As a result, two different schools of feng shui developed: Form School and Compass School. The first one we will discuss is called *Xingfa* or *Form School*. Also known as Luantau Pai (Mountain Head School), this method focused on the contour of the land, the shape of the mountains, and the curves of the waterways. The bible of this school and perhaps the earliest documentation of using geophysical features to locate an auspicious site is the *Zangshu (Book of Burial)*, the very book from where the term feng shui comes.

You might be curious about the book's title. As well as offering advice about locating the best site to build a home, the *Zangshu* (an article of fewer than 2,000 words) is primarily concerned with finding the best place to bury the dead. This is because the ancient (and many modern) Chinese believe their ancestors help them from Heaven. If you buried your relative in a favorable location, he or she would bestow good fortune on your family *and* your descendants. Therefore, it would behoove you to take great care in selecting a final resting place.

Wise Words

Xingfa (xing means "form" and fa means "method") or **Form School** is the oldest school of feng shui, formally dating to the late Han era's publication of the *Classic of Burial* written by Qing Wuzi.

The whole idea of Xingfa feng shui is to locate the long xue or dragon's lair, the point where qi converges on the terrain. This is accomplished by following the way qi travels down the mountain ranges (called the long mei or dragon veins), by studying how qi is carried by rivers (called shui long or water dragons), and by observing where it settles in ponds, lakes, and the sea. Indeed, recognizing the common point of intersection is a task reserved for the masters of this metaphysical and intuitive-based method.

Master Class

The Chinese went to great lengths to arrange their settlements according to the patterns of qi in the environment. If proper respect was not paid to the landscape, the results could be devastating. For instance, during the nineteenth and early twentieth centuries, the Chinese belief in feng shui forced many churches to remove their steeples because they cast ominous shadows. Also, the first railway from Shanghai to Wusong (nine miles away) was destroyed because the high speeds threatened the feng shui of peoples on both sides of the tracks. At one time, even the erection of telephone poles was vetoed. These modern examples make you wonder if feng shui was used as an excuse to resist innovation.

The Business of Burying

Needless to say, feng shui diviners were paid well to find the right place to bury the dead. In fact, it was not unusual for the diviner to be carried in a sedan chair to a prospective site. At the location in question, the diviner would thoroughly assess the environment, sometimes getting down on his hands and knees to inspect the quality of the soil, for example. Or, he could be seen rushing down a slope to evaluate the flow of qi. Based on many criteria, a site would be accepted or rejected.

Tales of feng shui diviners abound. In Stephan D.R. Feuchtwang's landmark Master's thesis, *An Anthropological Analysis of Chinese Geomancy* (1974), he offers a collection of stories. Here is a sampling:

➤ In Canton province, there's a hill that resembles a turtle, its head formed by stones protruding from the water. A feng shui master advised a rich client that the turtle would soon open its mouth, providing an auspicious place to bury his relative. From a boat, the two men cast the coffin into a whirlpool forming the creature's mouth. Later, the client felt he had been tricked. When he took the case to court, the diviner was ordered to return the coffin. The diviner then wielded a sword and severed the turtle's head, destroying its power. When the coffin surfaced, the diviner returned it to his client. Immediately, the rich man regretted his suspicions because he discovered his ancestor's bones were covered with golden scales. He learned not to doubt the feng shui master.

➤ At the death of their father, two sons each employed their own feng shui master to choose a gravesite benefiting himself only. On the day of the interment, the funeral procession came to a standstill when a choice had to be made between two paths, each leading to a different site. A raging argument ensued, lasting into the night. Each son then built a shelter for the coffin. But neither would accept the other's shelter. New ones were built, the process continuing until "there was a whole village of coffin shelters and both brothers had died." Finally, their widows agreed on a gravesite. As a result, their children prospered, gaining "civil degrees."

Yi Edicts

In 1949, when China became a communist nation, feng shui was outlawed. Most of the great masters fled to Hong Kong, where they are given much credit for transforming the metropolis into the financial hub of the East. Today, there are over 1,000 feng shui consultants and teachers in Hong Kong. An estimated 50 percent of its residents are believers.

While these stories may seem fantastic and ridiculous, the prerevolutionary Chinese took feng shui quite seriously. For instance, Si Zong (1611–1644), the last emperor of the Ming dynasty, worried that the northeastern Manchu barbarians would invade China. In an attempt to quell the barbarians' power, he ordered spies to sever the dragon vein running through the tribe's ancestral burial ground. However, his ploy did not work. The Ming dynasty was overthrown, and the emperor hanged himself in shame. Interestingly, the Manchu (who founded the Qing dynasty) emperors ordered that their predecessors' graves be protected and well taken care of.

Streets, Buildings, Fences, and Shrubbery: Urban Forms

Situating a township or dwelling where wind (feng) will not disperse qi and where water (shui) retains qi is the key to ensuring the probability of good fortune. But what if your home is not nestled amid mountain ranges and water? How does Form School theory apply to modern urban dwellers? The following will help you assess your surrounding environment:

Yi Edicts

If your home is not balanced by neighboring buildings, then trees, hedges, bushes, and even fences can serve as a substitute. For example, if your home backs onto a park or if it is situated on a corner, an appropriately sized hedge or fence can provide balance and protection.

Buildingscape: Symbolically, buildings can represent mountains. Ideally, you should choose a home that is balanced on both sides by structures comparable to yours. A corner house is unfavorable because one side's protection is separated by the street. It is unbalanced. Also, a corner house is subject to glaring headlights, traffic, and noise. While the back side of your home should also be supported, make sure the buildings there do not overwhelm or loom over it.

Topography: The most auspicious plane on which to live is either flat terrain or a sloping hill. Offering solid support and psychological security, these sites allow qi to meander in and around your dwelling. Conversely, those living on top of a hill or on a steep incline are subject to nature's forces (like landslides) and psychological vulnerability. Similar to a rushing river, life's vital force rushes by and is not given the opportunity to linger, permeate, and nourish. Often, individuals in these circumstances are prone to anxiety, insomnia, and financial difficulties.

Streetscape: The best way to evaluate the road(s) adjacent to your home is to imagine it is a watercourse. Following this idea, a gently rambling road becomes a meandering stream bringing you benevolent qi. A thoroughfare is similar to river rapids or an aqueduct that carries valuable qi away from the premises. Likewise, a home at a T- or Y-junction is unfavorable because you're the target of rushing torrents of qi surging up the paths. These patterns have been known to cause illness and misfortune. However, most people live along residential straight streets, a favorable configuration if noise and traffic are at a minimum.

Building Shape: The shape of your home impacts your well-being. Square or rectangular shapes (homes, room, and lots) are your best bet. Here, qi flows freely. It is uninhibited. Avoid homes with odd shapes (circular, angular), variegated roofs, or beamed ceilings. In these instances, qi acts like a ricocheting pinball creating a dizzying effect. Essentially, living amid a whirlwind of qi-inspired activity cannot lead to harmony, beneficial relationships, and prosperity.

Yi Edicts

The most important part of your home is its front door. Primarily, this is where qi enters. Make sure the door is proportionate to the size of an average person. If the entrance is too small, it hinders qi from entering. If it is too large, then qi's beneficial force can escape.

Neighboring Facilities: Before you offer your hard-earned cash as a down payment, don your favorite walking shoes and explore your neighborhood. Are there man-made factors that can pose possible health risks? For example, living in close proximity to high-tension power lines, factories, landfills, hospitals, police/fire stations, cemeteries, houses of worship, and airports is not favorable. These places are charged with the maladies of others and are best avoided. Also, while living next to schools may seem harmless, the imbalance of yang qi (youth) can cause insomnia and anxiety.

While these aspects are among those you should consider when evaluating your environment, a more detailed account can be found in *The Complete Idiot's Guide to Feng Shui* (Alpha Books, 1999). In it, you'll also learn how to arrange your living space to promote better health, wealth, and relationships.

The Compass School of Feng Shui

What is known in the West as the *Compass School* of feng shui does not have an equivalent name in Chinese. In China, the school that uses a compass and studies Heavenly (time) qi and earthly (space—the auspiciousness of each direction as well as geophysical features) qi is known as *Liqi Pai* (Patterns of Qi School). In the early 1980s when feng shui was introduced to the Western world, the term Compass School was invented. Today, it is an umbrella term covering the many methods of feng shui that study how time and space affect your well-being. The Xuan Kong (Flying Star) method is perhaps the best known, and certainly, the most sophisticated technique under the Compass School umbrella. Other methods include San He (Three Harmonies), Qi Men (Mystical Doors), and Yigua (Changing Trigrams). You'll learn about the latter in the next chapter.

The First Compass Method

The first method to come out of the Liqi Pai school was called Tuzhai Wuxing (Diagramatic Houses for the Five Families). Dating to the Spring and Autumn Period (722–481 B.C.E.), this method classified a person's home and family name under one of the *five phases* of qi: fire, earth, metal, water, and wood. While we won't concern ourselves with a detailed explanation, if the qi of the home was compatible with the qi of the family name, then the living environment would bring good fortune to the family. For example, if the house belonged to water qi and the family belonged to wood qi, the match was propitious because water produces (or helps foster the growth of) wood (plants). Conversely, if the family belonged to earth qi, the match could bring misfortune because wood depletes earth.

Because of its simplicity, Tuzhai Wuxing was short-lived. It was replaced with more complicated methods developed from the Hetu and Luoshu, the two

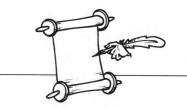

Wise Words

Compass School feng shui is a term invented by Westerners to represent what the Chinese call *Liqi Pai* (Patterns of Qi School). Compass school studies how time (Heavenly qi) and space (earthly qi) affect the well-being of an individual.

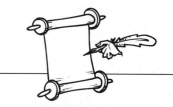

Wise Words

The **five phases** (in Chinese, wuxing) are five physical elements in nature that symbolize the movement of qi. They are: fire, earth, metal, water, and wood. The five phases are considered one of the fundamental principles of classical feng shui, Chinese medicine, and acupuncture.

cosmological maps from which the eight fundamental trigrams and hexagrams are derived. Please see Chapter 5, "Once Upon a Time: The Mythical Origin of the *Yijing*," for a refresher on these terms.

Kanyu See My Compass?

During the Warring States Period (403–221 B.C.E.) feng shui diviners formed the *Kanyu* school. According to the venerable dictionary called the *Shuowen Jiezi (Explanation of Words and Phrases)* written by Eastern Han dynasty (C.E. 25–220) scholar Xu Shen, the word kan (of kanyu) means "the way of Heaven." The word yu means "the way of earth." Together, kanyu means "the way of Heaven and earth." Diviners expert in the study of astronomy and geography as applied to site selection (and date selection) were aptly called *kanyujia* (jia means "expert").

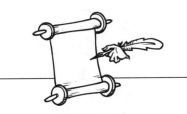

Wise Words

Kanyu (literally, "the way of Heaven and earth") was a school of feng shui that developed during the Eastern Han dynasty (C.E. 25–220). Diviners of this school were known as the **kanyujia**.

The tool of the trade for the feng shui diviner was the sinan, a two-part, south-pointing instrument consisting of a square base plate and a metal spoon made of magnetic lodestone. Inscribed onto the sinan were the 12 Heavenly stems (which records how qi changes over time), the 10 earthly branches (which records where qi is located on earth), and the 8 trigrams. The example provided in the following photograph dates to about C.E. 83.

The sinan was the precursor to the shipan and luopan compasses.

(Photograph courtesy of Val Biktashev.)

Over time, the sinan developed into the shipan compass. It consisted of a circular plate (representing Heaven) over a larger square base plate (representing earth). The sinan then evolved into the luopan compass used by feng shui practitioners today. Keeping to the design of its precursor, the south-pointing luopan has anywhere from 4 to 40 concentric information rings featuring things like the 8 main directions and the finer 24 distinctions; the 24 15-day periods of the solar year; the 28 constellations; the 8 trigrams; the 64 hexagrams; the 5 phases of qi; the 9 "stars" or numbers of the Luoshu; and the sexagenary (60) cycle of 12 stems and 10 branches. The following photograph is Joseph Yu's luopan compass.

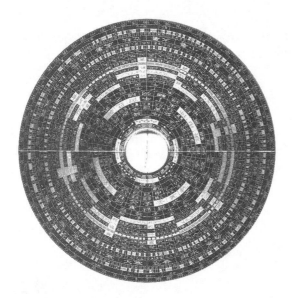

A modern luopan compass.

(Photograph courtesy of Joseph Yu.)

Regardless of which compass was being used, the feng shui master's objective was to create Heaven on earth by correlating the Heavenly (time) and earthly (space) qi forces. The dwelling or tomb that was situated according to the balance of these forces was considered auspicious. The occupants were blessed with good health, good wealth, and beneficial relationships.

Together Is Better

Today, Form School and Compass School have merged into one school of thought called classical or traditional feng shui. Like yin and yang, the two theories involve each other. Neglecting one aspect is like keeping one eye closed. For optimum sight, both eyes are necessary.

In the next chapter, we'll introduce you to the most popular method of feng shui, Yigua (Changing Trigrams) feng shui.

The Least You Need to Know

➤ Form School is the first and oldest school of feng shui, and studies how qi courses through the terrain and waterways.

➤ Feng shui means "wind and water."

➤ Compass School is a term invented by Westerners. It considers how time and space affect your prospects for greater health, wealth, and relationships.

➤ The tool of the trade for a feng shui practitioner is the compass.

➤ Today, Form School and Compass School have merged into one school of thought called classical or traditional feng shui.

Learning Yigua Feng Shui

In this chapter, you'll learn about the most popular method of classical feng shui. Known as Yigua (Changing Trigrams) and Bazhai (Eight House) in Chinese, the method is called the East/West System or Eight House by Westerners. But whatever it's called, the technique's purpose is to determine your four auspicious and four inauspicious directions as well as the four good and four bad directions (areas) within your home. With this information, you'll be able to orient your rooms (among other things) accordingly so as to take full advantage of positive qi.

The Legend of Yigua Feng Shui

Yigua methodology is purported to have originated with Yi Xing (C.E. 673–727), a Zen Buddhist monk, famous astronomer, metaphysicist, and royal advisor to the Tang dynasty. According to legend, ambassadors from neighboring barbarian countries (Korea, Vietnam, and Japan) requested emperor Xuan Zong (C.E. 685–762) to grant them feng shui texts to help their countries prosper. To the emperor, however, prosperity meant power. Sharing power could potentially threaten his empire. Based on this supposition, he commanded Yi Xing to write a false feng shui classic to give as gifts to the ambassadors. Yi Xing, being a kind and virtuous monk, instead used his wisdom and vast knowledge to create Yigua—a simple method, easy to use.

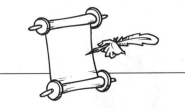

Wise Words

Yigua (literally, Changing Trigrams) feng shui is a technique of determining a person's four auspicious and four inauspicious directions. Also, it is used to determine a dwelling's four favorable and four unfavorable directions (or areas within the home). According to tradition, the methodology originated with Yi Xing (C.E. 673–727), a Zen Buddhist monk.

Simply stated, Yigua feng shui believes each of the eight compass directions holds a different type of qi that is either favorable (promoting fortune) or unfavorable (causing misfortune) to a person's natal qi, which is represented by his or her personal trigram and is determined by the birth year. Also, the qi associated with the eight cardinal directions influences the propitiousness of your home, which is also assigned to a trigram. Specifically, this means each trigram (Zhen, Xun, Kan, Li, Qian, Kun, Gen, and Dui) correlates to four auspicious and four inauspicious directions. If the qi of the house is compatible with the qi of the person, then the occupant will benefit by the supporting nature of the home. In essence, the person's qi will "go with the flow," move in sync with his or her home's qi. However, if the qi of the home and the qi of the person are incompatible, then the occupant will not feel fully comfortable in his or her living space. It's out of sync with the movement of his or her home's qi. The person's qi is "going against the grain."

Determining Your Chinese Solar Birth Year

The first requirement for conducting a Yigua reading is to determine your personal trigram (Zhen, Xun, Kan, Li, Qian, Kun, Gen, Dui). To accomplish this, you need your year of birth and gender. However, before you proceed, understand feng shui uses the Chinese solar calendar, which variously marks February 4 or 5 as the first day of the year. Therefore, if you were born between January 1 and February 3, you must use the year *prior* to your actual birth year. For example, let's take a woman born on January 18, 1963. She would use the year 1962 to calculate her personal trigram.

If you were born on February 4 or 5, you must consult the following table to determine your Chinese birth year. In this circumstance, the time you were born is an important factor. For example, let's say you were born at 8:00 P.M. on February 4, 1930. You would use 1929 as your year of birth because 1930 didn't begin until 8:52 P.M. If you were born at 11:00 P.M. on February 4, 1930, then you would stay with 1930.

Now that you know your Chinese birth year, consult the following chart to determine your personal trigram. For example, if you are a male born in 1930, you belong to the Dui trigram. If you are a female born in 1930, your trigram is Gen.

Table 1

Solar Year Date	Time Year Began	Solar Year Date	Time Year Began	Solar Year Date	Time Year Began	Solar Year Date	Time Year Began
1924 Feb 5	9:50 a.m.	1946 Feb 4	6:05 p.m.	1968 Feb 5	2:08 a.m.	1990 Feb 4	10:15 a.m.
1925 Feb 4	3:37 p.m.	1947 Feb 4	11:55 p.m.	1969 Feb 4	7:59 a.m.	1991 Feb 4	4:08 p.m.
1926 Feb 4	9:39 a.m.	1948 Feb 5	5:43 a.m.	1970 Feb 4	1:46 p.m.	1992 Feb 4	9:48 p.m.
1927 Feb 5	3:31 a.m.	1949 Feb 4	11:23 a.m.	1971 Feb 4	7:26 p.m.	1993 Feb 4	3:38 a.m.
1928 Feb 5	9:17 a.m.	1950 Feb 4	5:21 p.m.	1972 Feb 5	1:20 a.m.	1994 Feb 4	9:31 a.m.
1929 Feb 4	3:09 p.m.	1951 Feb 4	11:14 p.m.	1973 Feb 4	7:04 a.m.	1995 Feb 4	3:14 p.m.
1930 Feb 4	8:52 p.m.	1952 Feb 5	4:54 a.m.	1974 Feb 4	1:00 p.m.	1996 Feb 4	9:08 p.m.
1931 Feb 5	2:41 a.m.	1953 Feb 4	10:46 a.m.	1975 Feb 4	6:59 p.m.	1997 Feb 4	3:04 a.m.
1932 Feb 5	8:30 a.m.	1954 Feb 4	4:31 p.m.	1976 Feb 5	12:40 a.m.	1998 Feb 4	8:53 a.m.
1933 Feb 4	2:10 p.m.	1955 Feb 4	10:18 p.m.	1977 Feb 4	6:34 a.m.	1999 Feb 4	2:42 p.m.
1934 Feb 4	8:04 p.m.	1956 Feb 5	4:13 a.m.	1978 Feb 4	12:27 p.m.	2000 Feb 4	8:32 p.m.
1935 Feb 5	1:49 a.m.	1957 Feb 4	9:55 a.m.	1979 Feb 4	6:13 p.m.	2001 Feb 4	2:20 a.m.
1936 Feb 5	7:30 a.m.	1958 Feb 4	3:50 p.m.	1980 Feb 5	12:10 a.m.	2002 Feb 4	8:08 a.m.
1937 Feb 4	1:26 p.m.	1959 Feb 4	9:43 p.m.	1981 Feb 4	5:56 a.m.	2003 Feb 4	1:57 p.m.
1938 Feb 4	7:15 p.m.	1960 Feb 5	3:23 a.m.	1982 Feb 4	11:46 a.m.	2004 Feb 4	7:46 p.m.
1939 Feb 5	1:11 a.m.	1961 Feb 4	9:23 a.m.	1983 Feb 4	5:40 p.m.	2005 Feb 4	1:34 a.m.
1940 Feb 5	7:08 a.m.	1962 Feb 4	3:18 p.m.	1984 Feb 4	11:19 p.m.	2006 Feb 4	7:25 a.m.
1941 Feb 4	12:50 p.m.	1963 Feb 4	9:08 p.m.	1985 Feb 4	5:12 a.m.	2007 Feb 4	1:14 p.m.
1942 Feb 4	6:49 p.m.	1964 Feb 5	3:05 a.m.	1986 Feb 4	11:09 a.m.	2008 Feb 4	7:03 p.m.
1943 Feb 5	12:41 a.m.	1965 Feb 4	8:46 a.m.	1987 Feb 4	4:52 p.m.	2009 Feb 4	12:52 a.m.
1944 Feb 5	6:23 a.m.	1966 Feb 4	2:38 p.m.	1988 Feb 4	10:43 p.m.	2010 Feb 4	6:42 a.m.
1945 Feb 4	12:20 p.m.	1967 Feb 4	8:31 p.m.	1989 Feb 4	4:27 a.m.	2011 Feb 4	12:32 p.m.

Chinese solar years.

*Personal trigram quick
reference chart.*

Table 2

YEAR	MALE	FEMALE	YEAR	MALE	FEMALE
1924	Xun	Kun	1968	Kun	Kan
1925	Zhen	Zhen	1969	Xun	Kun
1926	Kun	Xun	1970	Zhen	Zhen
1927	Kan	Gen	1971	Kun	Xun
1928	Li	Qian	1972	Kan	Gen
1929	Gen	Dui	1973	Li	Qian
1930	Dui	Gen	1974	Gen	Dui
1931	Qian	Li	1975	Dui	Gen
1932	Kun	Kan	1976	Qian	Li
1933	Xun	Kun	1977	Kun	Kan
1934	Zhen	Zhen	1978	Xun	Kun
1935	Kun	Xun	1979	Zhen	Zhen
1936	Kan	Gen	1980	Kun	Xun
1937	Li	Qian	1981	Kan	Gen
1938	Gen	Dui	1982	Li	Qian
1939	Dui	Gen	1983	Gen	Dui
1940	Qian	Li	1984	Dui	Gen
1941	Kun	Kan	1985	Qian	Li
1942	Xun	Kun	1986	Kun	Kan
1943	Zhen	Zhen	1987	Xun	Kun
1944	Kun	Xun	1988	Zhen	Zhen
1945	Kan	Gen	1989	Kun	Xun
1946	Li	Qian	1990	Kan	Gen
1947	Gen	Dui	1991	Li	Qian
1948	Dui	Gen	1992	Gen	Dui
1949	Qian	Li	1993	Dui	Gen
1950	Kun	Kan	1994	Qian	Li
1951	Xun	Kun	1995	Kun	Kan
1952	Zhen	Zhen	1996	Xun	Kun
1953	Kun	Xun	1997	Zhen	Zhen
1954	Kan	Gen	1998	Kun	Xun
1955	Li	Qian	1999	Kan	Gen
1956	Gen	Dui	2000	Li	Qian
1957	Dui	Gen	2001	Gen	Dui
1958	Qian	Li	2002	Dui	Gen
1959	Kun	Kan	2003	Qian	Li
1960	Xun	Kun	2004	Kun	Kan
1961	Zhen	Zhen	2005	Xun	Kun
1962	Kun	Xun	2006	Zhen	Zhen
1963	Kan	Gen	2007	Kun	Xun
1964	Li	Qian	2008	Kan	Gen
1965	Gen	Dui	2009	Li	Qian
1966	Dui	Gen	2010	Gen	Dui
1967	Qian	Li	2011	Dui	Gen

If you were born between January 1 and February 3, use the year prior to
your actual birth year. If you were born on February 4 or 5, consult Table 1
to determine your Chinese solar birth year.

Now, let's learn how to determine your home's trigram.

Every Home Has a Trigram

To determine to which trigram your house belongs, imagine it is sitting with its back against a certain direction. This direction corresponds with a trigram. Refer to Table 3 that follows to determine your home's trigram.

Table 3

Trigram to house correspondence chart.

QIAN	DUI	LI	ZHEN	XUN	KAN	GEN	KUN
SITS: NW	W	S	E	SE	N	NE	SW

For example, take a house sitting west. It belongs to the Dui trigram. A house sitting south belongs to the Li trigram and a house sitting southwest belongs to the Kun trigram. It is important to understand that by sitting we mean the *back* side of the house. Often this corresponds to the back yard or an alley. The sitting side is significant because its qi supports the house.

Before we proceed, take this time to determine your home's trigram.

Changing Trigrams

In order to ascertain which directions are favorable to you and which directions are favorable to your home's qi, you begin with the trigram in question. As an example, let's say your personal trigram is Zhen. Referring to Table 4, begin with number 1 and read left to right across the chart. Zhen will transform into each of the remaining seven trigrams to produce the associated directions favorable and unfavorable to Zhen. Note: The names Sheng Qi (Life Qi), Yan Nian (Prolonged Years), Tian Yi (Heavenly Doctor), Fu Wei (Stooping Position), Huo Hai (Misfortune), Liu Sha (Six Devils), Wu Gui (Five Ghosts), and Jue Ming (Ultimate End of Life) are used to describe the nature of qi associated with a certain direction of the house. Collectively, they are called the Eight Wandering Stars.

1. Zhen's top yin line changes into yang. This new configuration produces the Li trigram. Li is associated with the south. For Zhen, south corresponds to the star called Sheng Qi, the most fortunate level of auspice bringing prosperity, respectability, good health, and beneficial relationships.

2. All of Zhen's lines transform to produce the Xun trigram. Xun is associated with the southeast. For Zhen, southeast corresponds to the star called Yan Nian, the second most fortunate level of auspice bringing longevity and beneficial relationships.

3. Zhen's middle (yin) and bottom (yang) lines change. This new configuration produces the Kan trigram, associated with the north. For Zhen, north corresponds to the star called Tian Yi, the third most fortunate level of auspice bringing good physical and mental health and harmonious relationships.

Master Class

Sinologists (people who study Chinese history, literature, language, and culture) and masters of feng shui disagree about the order of Yan Nian and Tian Yi. Despite the dispute, both parties agree the order is insignificant as long as the changing trigram formula remains the same: When all lines change, this corresponds to Yan Nian; when the middle and bottom lines change, this corresponds to Tian Yi.

4. Here, no lines change. Hence, the trigram remains the same. Since Zhen is associated with the east, this direction corresponds to the star called Fu Wei, the fourth most fortunate level of auspice bringing emotional and physical stability, and peace.

5. Zhen's bottom yang line changes into yin to produce the Kun trigram. Kun is associated with the southwest. For Zhen, the southwest corresponds to the star called Huo Hai, the fourth most harmful level of auspice bringing accidents, arguments, and injury.

6. Zhen's top and bottom lines change into the Gen trigram. Gen is associated with the northeast. For Zhen, the northeast corresponds to the star called Liu Sha, the third most harmful level of auspice bringing possible malicious encounters and failed relationships.

7. Zhen's top and middle lines change producing the Qian trigram. Qian is associated with the northwest. For Zhen, the northwest corresponds to the star called Wu Gui, the second most harmful level of auspice bringing possible fires, accidents, and disaster.

8. Zhen's middle yin lines change to yang producing the Dui trigram. Dui is associated with the west. For Zhen, the west corresponds to the star called Jue Ming, the first most harmful level of auspice associated with the loss of life, devastating disease, and unproductive careers.

Because of space restrictions, we cannot provide a chart similar to Zhen's for the remaining seven trigrams. On your own, use the same "changing trigram formula" to determine the fortunate and harmful directions appropriate to your trigram and the trigram corresponding to your home.

Table 4

ZHEN

Trigram	Changing Trigram Formula	Trigram	Direction		Wandering Star Auspice
1 Zhen	Top Line Changes	Li	S	D	**Sheng Qi** Prosperity & Respectability
2 Zhen	All Lines Change	Xun	SE	O	**Yan Nian** Longevity & Beneficial Relationships
3 Zhen	Middle Line Bottom Line Change	Kan	N	O	**Tian Yi** Good Health & Harmonious Relationships
4 Zhen	No Lines Change	Zhen	E	G	**Fu Wei** Peace & Stability
5 Zhen	Bottom Line Changes	Kun	SW		**Huo Hai** Accidents, Arguments & Injury
6 Zhen	Top Line Bottom Line Change	Gen	NE	D A	**Liu Sha** Malicious Encounters & Failed Relationships
7 Zhen	Top Line Middle Line Change	Qian	NW	B	**Wu Gui** Litigation, Accidents & Injury
8 Zhen	Middle Line Changes	Dui	W		**Jue Ming** Disease, Misfortune, & Unproductive Careers

The Zhen trigram's four favorable and four unfavorable directions.

I Can Feel the Good Qi!

Now that you understand which directions can promote good health, wealth, and beneficial relationships, you can effectively evaluate your living space. Orient your bedroom, home office, den, and any other room that is frequently used in one of the four areas where positive qi resides. Relegate rooms like the laundry room and guest bedroom to inauspicious areas so as to avoid harmful qi's force.

Room for Improvement

The most important part of your home is the main entrance. Qi enters a house through the front door in the same way that food enters the body through the mouth. If your door is located in the direction corresponding to Sheng Qi, then it ushers in qi with plenteous opportunities. Sheng Qi gives you the impetus to succeed

Yi Edicts

The qi that rides the wind (feng) and enters through the door indicates the overall potential for the house. If a door admits unfavorable qi, do not use it. Use another door located in a favorable direction. Also, close windows that are in bad areas, keeping them open in good areas.

and prosper. If your door is located in Yan Nian, then the probability for maintaining good health and enjoying good business, social, and romantic relationships increases. If your door corresponds to Tian Yi qi, expect the likelihood of increased strength, vitality, and sound relationships. If your door corresponds to Fu Wei, then your home will be a peaceful, harmonious place.

Conversely, if your door is situated in Huo Hai, arguments could plague the occupants. However, if you're a lawyer, this location is advantageous. Huo Hai qi would promote a litigator's debating skills. If your door is situated in Liu Sha, be mindful of affairs and other unfortunate events that could cause a relationship to fail. If your door is situated in Wu Gui, beware of accidents and lawsuits. Again, lawyers and doctors would benefit by this qi. Finally, if your door is situated in Jue Ming, be prepared for the worst! This is the most inauspicious direction, bringing serious illness, death, unproductive careers, and financial misfortune.

Master Class

Sleep with the crown of your head pointed toward one of your four favorable directions. However, be mindful of the layout of your room. The top of your bed should be positioned against a wall and not at an angle. You should not sleep below a window or with your feet pointed toward a door. Also, be mindful of qi highways obstructing a sound night's sleep. If your bed is placed between a door and window (or window and window), keep one closed to prevent the gush of qi rushing past your being.

Charted Qi

If you're short on time and long on curiosity, Table 5 represents a condensed and simplified version of Table 4. Referring to Table 5, locate your personal trigram at the top of the chart and run your finger down the column. Remember, numbers 1 through 4 represent your favorable directions; numbers 5 through 8, the unfavorable directions. Next, locate your home's trigram and determine its favorable and unfavorable directions (areas).

Table 5 WANDERING STAR AUSPICE		EAST GROUP				WEST GROUP			
		Zhen	Xun	Kan	Li	Qian	Kun	Gen	Dui
		D I R E C T I O N S							
Great Prosperity & Respectability	1	S	N	SE	E	W	NE	SW	NW
Longevity & Beneficial Relationships	2	SE	E	S	N	SW	NW	W	NE
Good Health & Harmonious Relationships	3	N	S	E	SE	NE	W	NW	SW
Peace & Stability	4	E	SE	N	S	NW	SW	NE	W
Accidents, Arguments & Injury	5	SW	NW	W	NE	SE	E	S	N
Possible Malicious Encounters & Failed Relationships	6	NE	W	NW	SW	N	S	E	SE
Possible Accidents, Lawsuits & Injury	7	NW	SW	NE	W	E	SE	N	S
Possible Disease, Misfortune & Unproductive Careers	8	W	NE	SW	NW	S	N	SE	E

The eight trigrams and their corresponding good and bad directions.

For example, the four auspicious directions associated with a Zhen person are south, southeast, north, and east. A Zhen person's four inauspicious directions are southwest, northeast, northwest, and west. The same scenario applies if your home belongs to the Zhen trigram.

East Meets West

Upon closer examination of Table 5, you'll notice that half of the trigrams each share the same four auspicious and inauspicious directions. Specifically, the directions favorable to the trigrams Zhen, Xun, Kan, and Li are north, south, east, and southeast. Conversely, west, northwest, southwest, and northeast represent their unfavorable directions. These trigrams belong to the East Group, so called because of the distinction of favorable eastern compass directions. The West Group trigrams are composed of Qian, Kun, Gen, and Dui. Their favorable directions correlate to the west, northwest, southwest, and northeast. Unfavorable to them are the eastern directions of north, south, east, and southeast.

What's the significance of the East and West Groups? Well, as we discussed earlier in this chapter, a person is inherently compatible with his or her home if he or she belongs to the same East or West Group as the home does. In other words, a Zhen person would feel comfortable in a Xun, Kan, Li, or Zhen house. A Zhen person would not feel fully comfortable in a Qian, Kun, Gen, or Dui home, trigrams belonging to the West Group. What happens when an individual and a home belong to opposing groups? While it is beyond the scope of this chapter to discuss how to remedy this situation, pay attention to how qi flows through your home. Clearing clutter, keeping the home clean, and positioning furniture correctly will help bolster a positive experience within the home. For more helpful tips, please consult *The Complete Idiot's Guide to Feng Shui* (Alpha Books, 1999).

Master Class

Instead of asking someone "What's your sign?" be bold and ask for his or her birth date. This information will lead you to find the person's personal trigram. In turn, knowing someone's trigram will help you to determine if you're inherently compatible with the person in question. Generally, people belonging to the same East or West Group are compatible. Those of opposing groups are not. The compatibility or incompatibility of natal qi may, in part, account for harmony or conflict at work or within the family.

All in the Family

You might be wondering about the significance of the changing trigram formula. For instance, why does the first change (changing the top line of the trigram) correlate with Sheng Qi and not, say, Jue Ming, the most inauspicious type of qi? The answer lies in the relationship between the trigrams. Referring to the figure (the bagua tree) that follows (for a reminder about what this is, please see Chapter 5, "Once Upon a Time: The Mythical Origin of the *Yijing*"), let's take a deeper look into the changing trigram formula as it relates only to a trigram's four auspicious directions. To be consistent, we will use the Zhen trigram as an example.

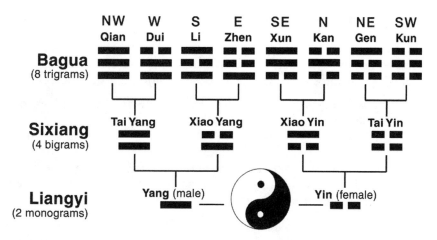

The levels of fortune and misfortune related to each trigram can be traced to its relationship to each of the other seven trigrams.

1. *Top line changes:* Zhen ⚏ changes into Li ☲. Zhen and Li share the same bigram, Xiao Yang. They're two peas in a pod. Kindred spirits. It makes sense then that Li and its associative direction, south, bring the greatest fortune to Zhen.

2. *All lines change:* Zhen ⚏ changes into Xun ☴. Zhen and Xun belong to the same Xiao family of bigrams—Xiao Yang and Xiao Yin. Notice that the bigrams are polar opposites, a factor that denotes harmony and balance. While Zhen and Xun's bigram (or qi) bases are harmonious, so, too, are the top lines. Zhen's yin ▬▬ ▬▬ line is balanced by Xun's yang ▬▬▬▬ line. As a matter of interest, Zhen (thunder) and Xun (wind) are opposite each other in the Xian Tian (Before Heaven) bagua. All things considered, Xun is Zhen's second best friend.

3. *Middle and bottom lines change:* Zhen ⚏ changes into Kan ☵, which is derived from the same bigram as Xun (Zhen's second best friend). Yet, while Zhen and Kan's bigram bases are opposite, and thus harmonious, their top lines are both yin. In essence, two out of three lines are compatible. Therefore, Kan offers the third most fortunate level of auspice.

4. *No lines change:* Here, Zhen remains unchanged. Like a lion resting in his den, Fu Wei qi brings safety and stability.

As you have just discovered, auspicious pairs come either from the same bigram (Zhen-Li and Zhen-Zhen) or from opposing bigrams (Zhen-Xun and Zhen-Kan). The trigrams that are not compatible with Zhen's qi come from different bigram families. In Zhen's case, its parent bigram belongs to the Xiao family. It is incompatible with the Tai family. Thus, the imbalance of yin and yang made manifest by the lines gives rise to conflicting, inharmonious, and damaging qi.

Yigua 501

Basically, the Yigua technique seeks to establish a metaphysical connection between time (determined by your birth year) and space (the eight cardinal directions) to bring you increased prosperity, good health, and harmonious relationships.

Unfortunately, we have only scratched the surface, offering you the most rudimentary understanding of this interesting method. Like the *Yijing,* Yigua feng shui has mathematical undertones that are quite profound. Specifically, you can mathematically determine a trigram's good and bad directions by merging the Luoshu (Magic Square) numbers with the Xian Tian (Before Heaven) trigram sequence. This is then correlated with the Hou Tian (After Heaven) bagua. The result is what is known as the Xian Tian number sequence, a diagram that mathematically yields the same rank of auspice as the changing trigram formula we discussed in this chapter.

We hope you have enjoyed *The Complete Idiot's Guide to the* I Ching. Certainly, you will agree the oracle is a complex artifact that requires years of study. Here, we've provided a solid foundation, a springboard for more advanced knowledge. Be sure to check out the following appendixes; they'll help to advance your learning.

The Least You Need to Know

➤ Yigua methodology is purported to have originated with Yi Xing (C.E. 673–727), a Zen Buddhist monk, famous astronomer, metaphysicist, and royal advisor to the Tang dynasty.

➤ The purpose of Yigua feng shui is to determine your four favorable and four unfavorable directions as well as the four good and four bad directions (areas) within your home.

➤ Your personal trigram is determined by your birth year.

➤ Your home's trigram is determined by the direction it "sits" against.

➤ A trigram's good and bad directions are related to its relationship to each of the other seven trigrams.

Glossary

acupuncture   A traditional Chinese medicine dating to around 200 B.C.E. It involves stimulating specific points in the body to correct imbalances of qi that lead to disease. Besides using needles, acupuncturists also use heat (moxibustion), pressure (acupressure), or low levels of electromagnetic energy to stimulate acupuncture points.

bagua   The eight fundamental trigrams of the *Yijing* that represent all possible cosmic and human conditions.

bifurcation   The process of dividing into two parts. The term is derived from the Latin word, *bifurcus: bi* (two) + *furca* (fork). Bifurcation is the process of evolving into a more complex state.

binary numeration   Also called base 2, binary numeration uses only the digits 0 and 1 to compute. Seventeenth-century mathematician and philosopher Gottfried Leibniz believed the binary system had spiritual aspects relating to the creation of the universe from nothing (0) by the one (1) God.

bindi   The red dot of paint on a person's forehead. Also called the tilak or third eye, the bindi symbolizes transcendence, heightened awareness, and prophetic insight. It relates to the act of seeing intuitively; seeing "the big picture."

bu   Meaning crack-making, the Chinese character bu ⼘ is derived from the shape of the crack formed on the bone or shell after it has been heated. While this character was once pronounced puk after the sound of the bone cracking, it is now pronounced "boo."

butterfly effect   Relates to weather forecasting. It is the phenomenon whereby small changes lead to a chaotic and unpredictable outcome.

chaos   According to *Webster's New Collegiate Dictionary,* the word chaos has two meanings: "the unorganized state of primordial matter before the creation of distinct forms" and "the state of utter confusion."

chaos theory   It studies pattern and organization within nonlinear systems (a system whose rate of change is not constant).

charge   A charge represents a pair of antithetical (positive and negative) statements or questions. These paired charges were engraved on opposite sides of a turtle's shell.

Compass School   A term invented by Westerners to represent what the Chinese call Liqi Pai (Patterns of Qi School). Compass School studies how time (Heaven qi) and space (earth qi) affects the well-being of an individual and his or her dwelling.

Dazhuan Literally, the *Great Commentary,* the *Dazhuan* is also called the *Xicizhuan (Appended Words)*. Considered the most important of the seven commentaries attached to the *Zhouyi,* the *Dazhuan* offers a metaphysical analysis of change. It is divided into upper and lower sections called the *Xici Shangzhuan* and *Xici Xiazhuan.*

deductive reasoning The method of reaching a conclusion by deducing general laws through observation.

divination The practice of foretelling human events with the aid of the divine. The word divination is taken from the Latin word *divinus,* which means "of or relating to God or a god-like force."

dragon's lair Known as long xue in Chinese, the dragon's lair is the place on the terrain where qi converges.

explicate order Postulated by theoretical physicist David Bohm (1917–1992), the explicate order represents the manifestations of objects, events, and thoughts that are unfolded from the much deeper implicate order of the undivided holomovement. The explicate order represents everyday reality.

feng shui A Chinese practice that seeks to harmonize your environment positively to promote the likelihood of better health, wealth, and relationships. Literally, feng shui means "wind and water," two natural forces that direct qi to a settlement or burial place.

Fibonacci sequence A sequence of numbers named after a thirteenth-century mathematician, Leonardo of Pisa, also known as Fibonacci. Each number in the series is the sum of the two previous numbers. The Fibonacci sequence is made manifest in human proportions, art and architecture, music and poetry, and science and technology. The sequence exemplifies how we conform to mathematical principles found in the universe.

five phases Wuxing in Chinese, the five phases are five physical elements in nature that symbolize the movement of qi. They are: fire, earth, metal, water, and wood. The five phases is considered one of the fundamental principles of classical feng shui, Chinese medicine, and acupuncture.

Form School Called Xingfa (xing means "form" and fa means "method") in Chinese, Form School is the oldest school of feng shui, formally dating to the late Han era's publication of the *Classic of Burial* written by Qing Wuzi.

Gestalt psychology A method that became popular in the early twentieth century. Translated from German, Gestalt means "configuration." Gestaltists believe we respond to a holistic experience. That perception is influenced by the configuration of parts.

Golden Ratio Related to the Fibonacci sequence. By dividing each number in the sequence by the number that precedes it, the result produces a ratio that stabilizes at 1.61834. The Golden Ratio was understood by many ancient cultures who believed that everything in nature could be expressed mathematically.

gua This Chinese word means trigram (three-lined gua) or hexagram (six-lined gua).

guaci The term in Chinese describing the hexagram statement or prediction.

Guicangyi Literally, *Restored to the Earth,* the *Guicangyi* is a system of yarrow stalk divination said to be created by the celebrated (and perhaps mythical) king, Huang Di.

Hetu Also known as the River Map, the Hetu is said to be a gift from Heaven to Fuxi. It is a pattern of black (yin) and white (yang) dots found on a fantastic dragon-horse coming out of the Yellow River. The Hetu symbolizes a perfect, balanced, and motionless world.

hexagram   A six-lined symbol composed of a combination of solid and broken lines. In total, 64 hexagrams comprise the *Yijing*.

hologram   A three-dimensional image in which each part of the image contains the entire picture. A hologram is a whole (holo) message (gram).

holomovement   The movement, change, and transformation of the hologram.

Hou Tian   Also called the After Heaven bagua, the Hou Tian is related to the Luoshu (Magic Square). The Hou Tian sequence of trigrams denotes motion, change, and transformation.

implicate order   Postulated by theoretical physicist David Bohm (1917–1992), the implicate order is a primary invisible reality where matter and consciousness emerge or unfold into the visible world around us. The implicate order suggests there is a hidden order to the universe.

inductive reasoning   The method of reaching a conclusion by developing specific cases based on general laws.

Kanyu   Literally, "the way of Heaven and earth," Kanyu was a school of feng shui that developed during the Eastern Han dynasty (C.E. 25–220). Diviners of this school were known as the kanyujia.

liangyi   The two monograms of yin and yang. The liangyi produces the four bigrams, the sixiang.

Lianshanyi   Literally, *Linking Mountains,* the *Lianshanyi* is a system of yarrow stalk divination purportedly created by the legendary (and perhaps mythical) sage-king, Shennong.

linear mathematics   Attributed to the mechanical or Newtonian paradigm, linear mathematics describes the interaction of only two entities. The simple equations were thought to result in an accurate and predictable view of nature.

Longshan culture   Dating to 3,000 B.C.E., this ancient Chinese culture is named for a major archeological find in Shandong province in the early 1930s. The Longshan are also known as the Black Pottery culture.

Lower Classic   Known as the Xia Jing in Chinese, the Lower Classic is comprised of Hexagrams 31 through 64. These hexagrams delve into the ruling philosophy of the Zhou and are summarized by Hexagram 2.

luopan   A compass used by feng shui practitioners today. The luopan has anywhere from 4 to 40 concentric information rings featuring things such as the 8 main directions and the finer 24 distinctions; the 24 15-day periods of the solar year; the 28 constellations; the 8 trigrams; the 64 hexagrams; the 5 phases of qi; the 9 "stars" or numbers of the Luoshu; and the sexagenary (60) cycle of 12 stems and 10 branches.

Luoshu   Also known as the Luo River Writing, the Luoshu is a pattern of black (yin) and white (yang) dots purportedly found on a turtle shell. When the dots are transcribed into numbers, they yield a diagram called the Magic Square of Three.

Magic Square of Three   Related to the Luoshu. It is considered magical because 3 cells add up to 15 along any horizontal, vertical, or diagonal line.

mandate of Heaven   A proclamation mandated by the assemblage of Zhou ancestors in Heaven. For example, Heaven mandated the conquest of the Shang by the Zhou.

milfoil plant   Also known as the yarrow plant, its stalks are used as divination casting tools. The milfoil's proper name is *Achillea millefolium.* A member of the sunflower family,

Achillea refers to the Greek hero Achilles, who understood the medicinal properties of the plant. The species name millefolium or "thousand leafed" refers to the plant's numerous dissections of leaves, which are clustered at the base of the stalk.

Neolithic   Also called the New Stone Age, the Neolithic era represents the final stage of human development beginning some 10,000 years ago. It is characterized by the use of polished stone tools, crop cultivation, and permanent settlements.

nonlinear mathematics   This studies systems whose rate of change is not constant. It is the study of complex and unpredictable systems such as the weather; population growth; the stock market; heart and brain activity; the waves breaking on the shore; traffic flow; and changes in mindsets, fashions, and fads.

Paleolithic   Also called the Old Stone Age, the Paleolithic era refers to the first stage of human development, the hunting and gathering period that began about two million years ago and ended about 15,000 years ago.

Pinyin   Officially called Hanyu Pinyin Wenzi, Pinyin is a system of spelling phonetically Chinese words using the Latin alphabet. It was developed by the Chinese and has been recognized as the international standard since 1979.

plastromancy   The practice of heating and interpreting the cracks formed on the plastron or bottom shell of turtles.

qi   The underlying and unifying, nourishing and vital, physical and metaphysical life force at the center of all things.

quantum mechanics   A theory in physics that describes the subatomic particles comprising matter and how they interact with each other and with energy.

quantum potential   Postulated by theoretical physicist David Bohm (1917–1992), the quantum potential represents the active principle of the implicate order. It provides information to the totality of humankind and our environment.

romanize   To romanize Chinese means to use the Roman (Latin) alphabet to spell its sounds. English, Spanish, German, French, and Italian (among others) use the Latin alphabet.

scapulimancy   The practice of heating and interpreting the cracks formed on the scapula or shoulder bones of mammals.

Shang Di   Meaning Lord Above, Shang Di was the principle deity of the Shang. The shang of Shang Di should not be confused with the shang of the Shang dynasty. Although spelled the same, the two words are written with different characters and are pronounced differently.

shipan   A compass comprised of a circular disc (symbolizing Heaven) over a square base plate (representing earth).

Shuoguazhuan   Literally, *Explanation of the Trigrams,* the *Shuoguazhuan* is one of the seven essays attached to the *Zhouyi*. It outlines the eight natural phenomena that are assigned to the eight trigrams, a three-term sequence of yin and yang lines. Besides being correlated with a meteorological aspect, each trigram is matched with a host of other things like a familial relation, direction, season, and animal.

sinan   A south-pointing compass consisting of a magnetized spoon and a square base plate.

singularity   The "moment" before creation when the entire universe was confined within an atomic nucleus. It is the "moment" before time and space were made manifest. Singularity is the undivided whole, the state of unity.

sixiang   The four bigrams (two-tiered symbols composed of solid and broken lines) called the tai yin, xiao yin, tai yang, and xiao yang. The four bigrams produce the eight trigrams, the bagua.

sortilege   Divination by drawing lots. The ancient Chinese used the stalk of the milfoil or yarrow plant in a procedure that randomly formed the six-lined hexagram graph.

strange attractor   The visual (and repeating) pattern of the behavior of a nonlinear system. Because nonlinear systems are chaotic yet ordered and patterned, they are called "strange." The "attractor" organizes the pattern of the system.

synchronicity   A word coined by Swiss psychologist Carl Jung (1875–1961), synchronicity is a phenomenon in which coincidences such as thoughts, ideas, objects, and/or events link together to form a theme that is significant to the observer.

taiji   The symbol representing the eternal interplay of yin and yang. The word tai means "supreme" or the "greatest" and ji means "central piller" or "basic." Taken together, taiji means "greatest pillar" or "supreme basis."

Ten Wings   Known as the *Zhuan* in Chinese, the *Ten Wings* is a collection of essays of unknown authorship appended to the *Zhouyi* centuries after King Wen and the Duke of Zhou composed it. In total, there are seven essays (in 10 parts).

tianzi   Meaning "Sons of Heaven," it is what the Zhou kings called themselves. The conquest of Shang was sanctioned by Tian (Heaven), the pantheon of Zhou ancestors.

trigram   A three-tiered symbol composed of a configuration of solid (yang) and broken (yin) lines. Each trigram represents an aspect of nature, familial relation, direction, and season, among other things. Collectively, the eight fundamental trigrams are called the bagua.

Tuanzhuan   Literally, *Commentary on the Hexagrams,* the *Tuanzhuan* is one of the seven essays appended to the *Zhouyi.* It deals with the auspice of the hexagrams, which can be determined by the proportion and arrangement of the yin (broken) and yang (solid) lines within the hexagram and their relationship to the line text. The *Tuanzhuan* uses Confucian thought to explain each hexagram. It is divided into upper and lower sections.

Upper Classic   Known as the Shang Jing in Chinese, the Upper Classic is comprised of Hexagrams 3 through 30 (which are summarized by Hexagram 1). These hexagrams describe the revolution against the Shang, the establishment of the Zhou dynasty, the conquest of the 99 rebel tribes still loyal to the Shang, and the suppression of Wu Geng's (the Shang king's son) attempted coup d'état. The historical tale ends with the succession of Cheng Wang, the young Zhou king who ascended the throne after his father's (King Wu) untimely death.

Wade-Giles   A system of spelling Chinese sounds using the Latin alphabet. Developed by British sinologists Sir Thomas Francis Wade (1818–1895) and Herbert Allen Giles (1845–1935), the Wade-Giles system is still used today in many Western publications. In 1979, however, the Chinese spelling system, Pinyin, officially replaced the cumbersome Wade-Giles method.

Wenyanzhuan   Literally, *Elaboration on Qian and Kun,* the *Wenyanzhuan* is one of the seven commentaries appended to the *Zhouyi.* It gives a detailed explanation of the meaning and significance of Hexagrams 1 (Heaven) and 2 (earth), which summarize Hexagrams 3 through 30 and 31 through 64 respectively.

wuji   The wellspring out of which life emerges. It is the source of original qi, life's vital force.

Xian Tian   Also known as the Before Heaven bagua, the Xian Tian represents a world in perfect balance. A world that is motionless and static. A world where change is nonexistent.

Xiangzhuan   Literally, *Commentary on the Images,* the *Xiangzhuan* is one of the seven essays attached to the *Zhouyi.* It divides each hexagram into the *Daxiang (Big Image)* and *Xiaoxiang (Small Image).* While the *Daxiang* describes the image inherent in the hexagram, the *Xiaoxiang* describes the image inherent in each of the six yao (broken or unbroken lines). Also, the *Xiangzhuan* commentary divides the hexagram into its trigram parts. The idea is to understand the hexagram by examining the nature of each trigram. The *Xiangzhuan* is divided into upper and lower parts.

Xuguazhuan   Literally, *Sequence of the Hexagrams*, the *Xuguazhuan* is one of the seven commentaries appended to the *Zhouyi.* It attempts to explain the sequence of hexagrams, interpreting the order in terms of the waxing and waning cycles of nature and human nature.

yang   The masculine and active principle of nature expressed as hot summer days and gusting winds. On the human level, yang represents linear logic, aggression, being in love. Yang is the father figure, traditionally the disciplinarian and authoritarian.

Yangshao culture   Also called the Painted Pottery culture, this period in China coincides with the Neolithic era. Dating to before 5000 B.C.E., the Yangshao culture gets its name from the abundant archeological finds made in 1920 near Yangshao village in Henan province.

yao   This Chinese word refers to one of the six lines comprising each hexagram.

yaoci   The term in Chinese meaning "line text." In total, each hexagram has six line texts. The exceptions are Hexagram 1 and 2; they each have an additional line text. The yaoci offers more information and advice about your concern, problem, or dilemma.

yarrow stalk   The stalk of a yarrow (or milfoil) plant used to divine the *Yijing.* Although 50 stalks are called for, only 49 are needed to cast the oracle.

Yigua   Literally, "changing trigrams." Yigua feng shui is a technique of determining a person's four auspicious and four inauspicious directions. It is also used to determine the good and bad directions (or areas) within your home. According to tradition, the methodology originated with Yi Xing (C.E. 673–727), a Zen Buddhist monk.

Yijing   Literally, "jing" means book, and more specifically, canon. "Yi" means to change. Together, *Yijing* means the *Book of Changes.* The Zhou ruler King Wen and his son the Duke of Zhou assembled it sometime at the end of the second millennium B.C.E. The *Yijing* is a book of divination. It models the cycles of life, specifically the decay and death of the Shang dynasty and the rise and growth of the Zhou dynasty. By projecting our situation into the model, we can seek an intelligent solution.

yin   The feminine and passive principle of nature expressed as stillness, cold, and wetness. On the human level, yin represents sadness, fatigue, and greed. Also, yin is quiet meditation, intuitive wisdom, and creativity. Yin is the realm of the dead.

Zaguazhuan   Literally, *Parity of the Hexagrams,* the *Zaguazhaun* is one of the seven commentaries attached to the *Zhouyi.* It describes the relationship between the hexagram pairs.

Zhouyi   Literally, the *Changes of Zhou,* the *Zhouyi* is a system of yarrow stalk divination created by King Wen and his son the Duke of Zhou. In the Han dynasty, the *Zhouyi* was renamed the *Yijing* when commentaries were appended to the divinatory text.

Zhuan   Known as the *Ten Wings* in English, the *Zhuan* is a collection of essays of unknown authorship attached to the *Zhouyi* centuries after King Wen and the Duke of Zhou composed it. In total, there are seven essays (in 10 parts).

History of the Far East

Chinese Periods and Dynasties

The following dates are taken from the *Xinhua Zidian (New Chinese Word Dictionary)*, the standard Pinyin Chinese–Chinese dictionary published in 1971 in Beijing. The dates reflecting China's legendary and prehistoric periods, and the dynastic dates of the Shang and early Zhou, are speculative and subject to dispute.

Chinese Dynasties and Periods

Dynasty	Period
Legendary Period	
Three Emperors	2852–2597 B.C.E.
Fuxi	2852–2737 B.C.E.
Shennong	2737–2697 B.C.E.
Huang Di	2697–2597 B.C.E.
Shao Hao	2597–2513 B.C.E.
Zhuan Xu	2513–2435 B.C.E.
Five Rulers	2435–2197 B.C.E.
Di Ku	2435–2365 B.C.E.
Di Zhi	2365–2356 B.C.E.
Yao	2356–2255 B.C.E.
Shun	2255–2205 B.C.E.
Yu	2205–2197 B.C.E.
Prehistoric Period	
Yangshao culture	c. 5000 B.C.E.
Longshan culture	c. 2500 B.C.E.
Xia dynasty	c. 2100–c. 1600 B.C.E.

Dynasty	Period
Historical Period	
Shang dynasty	c. 1600–1045 B.C.E.
Zhou dynasty	1045–221 B.C.E.
Western Zhou	1045–771 B.C.E.
Eastern Zhou	770–256 B.C.E.
Spring and Autumn Period	722–481 B.C.E.
Warring States Period	403–221 B.C.E.
Qin dynasty	221–206 B.C.E.
Han dynasty	206 B.C.E.–C.E. 220
Western Han	206 B.C.E.–C.E. 24
Eastern Han	C.E. 25–220
Three Kingdoms	220–280
Wei	220–265
Shu Han	221–263
Wu	222–280
Jin dynasty	265–420
Western Jin	265–316
Eastern Jin	317–420
Southern and Northern dynasties	420–589
Southern	420–589
Northern	386–581
Sui dynasty	581–618
Tang dynasty	618–907
Five dynasties and Ten Kingdoms	907–960
Song dynasty	960–1279
Northern Song	960–1127
Southern Song	1127–1279
Liao dynasty (Khitan Tartars)	916–1125
Jin dynasty (Jurchen Tartars)	1115–1234
Yuan dynasty (Mongol)	1271–1368
Ming dynasty	1368–1644
Qing dynasty (Manchu)	1644–1911
Republic of China	1912–1949
People's Republic of China	1949–present

The Shang and Zhou Family Trees

For your convenience, here are simplified family trees for the Shang and Zhou royals whom we discuss in preceding chapters and in the hexagram translation and interpretation. Reign dates are not included because they are problematic and subject to dispute.

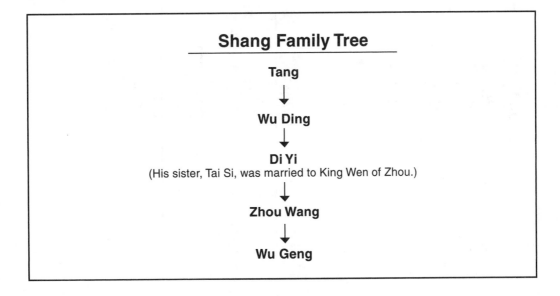

Shang Family Tree

Tang

↓

Wu Ding

↓

Di Yi
(His sister, Tai Si, was married to King Wen of Zhou.)

↓

Zhou Wang

↓

Wu Geng

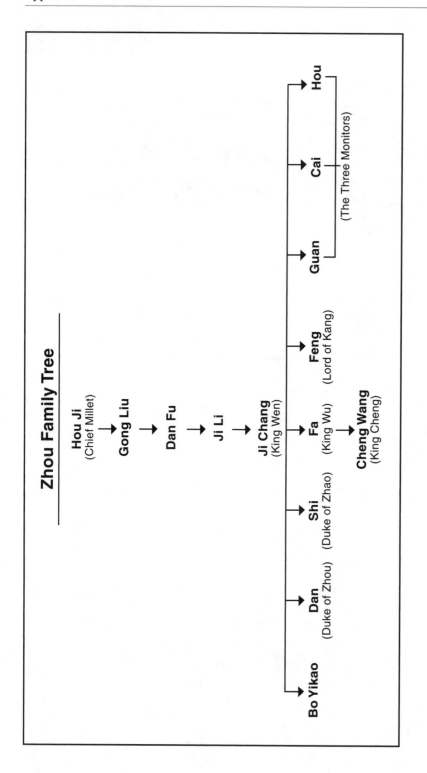

Zhou Family Tree

Hou Ji
(Chief Millet)

→ **Gong Liu**

→ **Dan Fu**

→ **Ji Li**

→ **Ji Chang**
(King Wen)

→ **Bo Yikao**

→ **Dan**
(Duke of Zhou)

→ **Shi**
(Duke of Zhao)

→ **Fa**
(King Wu)

→ **Cheng Wang**
(King Cheng)

→ **Feng**
(Lord of Kang)

→ **Guan**

→ **Cai**

→ **Hou**

(The Three Monitors)

Learning More About the *Yijing,* Ancient China, and Related Applications

Books and Magazine Articles

An Anthropological Analysis of Chinese Geomancy, by Stephan D.R. Feuchtwang. Vitagna, 1974.

"Astronomical Dates in Shang and Western Zhou," by David W. Pankenier. *Early China,* Vol. 7, 1981–1982.

Before Confucius: Studies in the Creation of the Chinese Classics, by Edward L. Shaughnessy. The State University of New York Press, 1997.

Before Writing: From Counting to Cuneiform, Vol. 1, by Denise Schmandt-Besserat. The University of Texas Press, 1992.

Blueprint for Immortality: The Electric Patterns of Life, by Harold Saxton Burr. The C.W. Daniel Company, Ltd., 1972.

The Body Electric: Electromagnetism and the Foundation of Life, by Robert O. Becker, M.D., and Gary Selden. Quill, 1985.

A Brief History of Chinese Civilization, by Conrad Schirokauer. Harcourt Brace and Company, 1991.

The Cambridge History of Ancient China from the Origins of Civilization to 221 B.C.E., edited by Michael Loewe and Edward L. Shaughnessy. Cambridge University Press, 1999.

"Chinese Oracle Bones," by Hung-hsiang Chou. *Scientific American,* April, 1979.

The Complete Idiot's Guide to Feng Shui, by Elizabeth Moran and Val Biktashev. Alpha Books, 1999.

Confucianism, Buddhism, Daoism, Christianity, and Chinese Culture, by Tang Yi-Jie. The University of Peking and The Council for Research in Values and Philosophy, Cultural Heritage and Contemporary Life, Series III, Asia, Volume 3, 1991.

Discourse on Metaphysics and the Monadology, by Gottfried Wilhelm Leibniz (translated by George R. Montgomery). Prometheus Books, 1992.

DNA and the I Ching: The Tao of Life, by Johnson F. Yan. North Atlantic Books, 1991.

Does God Play Dice? The Mathematics of Chaos, by Ian Stewart. Bladwell Publishing, 1990.

Earth Ascending: An Illustrated Treatise on the Law Governing Whole Systems, by Jose Arguelles. Bear and Company, 1984.

Encounters with Qi: Exploring Chinese Medicine, by David Eisenberg, M.D., with Thomas Lee Wright. W.W. Norton and Company, 1985.

The Essence of Chaos, by Edward N. Lorenz. University of Washington Press, 1993.

Explanation of Words and Phrases, by Xu Shin. Written during the Eastern Han dynasty (C.E. 25–220). The version used was further annotated by Duan Yucai (1735–1815).

Fascinating Fibonacci: Mystery and Magic in Numbers, by Trudi Hammel Garland. Dale Seymour Publications, 1987.

Fortune-tellers and Philosophers: Divination in Traditional Chinese Society, by Richard J. Smith. Westview Press, Inc., 1991.

God and The New Physics, by Paul Davies. Touchstone, 1983.

Gottfried Wilhelm Leibniz: Writings on China, translated with an introduction, notes, and commentaries by Daniel J. Cook and Henry Rosemont Jr. Open Court Publishing Company, 1994.

Heaven, Earth, and Man in the Book of Changes: Seven Eranos Lectures, by Hellmut Wilhelm. University of Washington Press, 1977.

History of Binary and Other Nondecimal Numeration, by Anton Glaser. Tomash Publishers, 1981.

The Hypothesis of a New Science of Life: Morphic Resonance, by Rupert Sheldrake. Inner Traditions International, Ltd., 1981.

The I Ching and the Genetic Code: The Hidden Key to Life, by Dr. Martin Schonberger. Aurora Press, Inc., 1992.

I Ching: Book of Changes, translated by James Legge (edited by Ch'u Chai and Winberg Chai). University Books, 1964.

The I Ching or Book of Changes, by Richard Wilhelm (translated by Cary F. Baynes). Princeton University Press, 1950.

Innumeracy: Mathematical Illiteracy and Its Consequences, by John Allen Paulos. Vintage Books, 1988.

"An Interpretation of the Divinatory Inscriptions of Early Chou Bronzes," by Chang Cheng-Lang (Zheng Zhenglang). *Early China,* Vol. 6, 1980–1981.

The Invisible Landscape: Mind Hallucinogens and the I Ching, by Terence McKenna and Dennis McKenna. HarperCollins, 1993.

Jesus Christ Sun of God: Ancient Cosmology and Early Christian Symbolism, by David Fideler. Quest Books, The Theosophical Publishing House, 1993.

Leibniz and the Kabbalah, by Allison Coudert. Kluwer Academic Publishers, 1995.

Leibniz, Mysticism and Religion, edited by Allison Coudert, Richard H. Popkin, and Gordon M. Weiner. Kluwer Academic Publishers, 1998.

Life by the Numbers, by Keith Devlin. John Wiley and Sons, Inc., 1998.

Life of Godfrey William von Leibnitz, by John M. Mackie. Gould, Kendall, and Lincoln, 1845.

More Joy of Mathematics: Exploring Mathematics All Around You, by Theoni Pappas. Wide World Publishing/Tetra, 1991.

The Mystery of Numbers, by Annemarie Schimmel. Oxford University Press, 1993.

Newton's Clock: Chaos in the Solar System, by Ivars Peterson. W.H. Freeman and Company, 1993.

On Dialogue, by David Bohm. Routledge, 1996.

On Synchronicity: An Acausal Connecting Principle, by Carl Jung. In *Collected Works,* Vol. 8, Princeton University Press, 1981.

The Origin of the Zhouyi (in Chinese), by Liu Zheng. Chinese Environmental Science Publications, 1993.

The Presence of the Past: Morphic Resonance and the Habits of Nature, by Rupert Sheldrake. Inner Traditions International, Ltd., 1995.

The Pythagorean Sourcebook and Library, compiled and translated by Kenneth Sylvan Guthrie. Phanes Press, 1988.

"Qi Through the Centuries and Around the World," by Dr. John Baker. *Qi: The Journal of Traditional Eastern Health and Fitness,* Vol. 1, No. 4, Winter 1991.

Science and Civilisation in China (6 volumes), by Joseph Needham. Cambridge University Press, 1956.

Seven Life Lessons of Chaos: Spiritual Wisdom from the Science of Change, by John Briggs and F. David Peat. HarperCollins, 1999.

A Short History of Chinese Philosophy: A Systematic Account of Chinese Thought from Its Origins to the Present Day, by Fung Yu-Lan. The Free Press, 1948.

"Some Hexagrams Found on Yin Shang Scapulae" (in Chinese), by Zheng Zhenglang. *Journal of Archeology*, Vol. 4, 1980.

"Some Observations About Milfoil Divination Based on Shang and Zhou Bagua Numerical Symbols," by Zhang Yachu and Liu Yu. *Early China,* Vol. 7, 1981–1982.

Sources of Shang History: the Oracle-Bone Inscriptions of Bronze Age China, by David N. Keightley. University of California Press, 1978.

Synchronicity: C.G. Jung, Psychoanalysis, and Religion, by M.D. Faber. Praeger, 1998.

Synchronicity: Science, Myth, and the Trickster, by Allan Combs and Mark Holland. Marlowe and Company, 1996.

Tao of Chaos: DNA and the I Ching: Unlocking the Code of the Universe, by Katya Walter. Element Books, Ltd., 1994.

The Tao of Physics, by Fritjof Capra. Shambala, 1991.

Understanding the I Ching: The Wilhelm Lectures on the Book of Changes, by Richard and Hellmut Wilhelm. Princeton University Press, 1995.

The Universal History of Numbers: From Prehistory to the Invention of the Computer, by Georges Ifrah. John Wiley and Sons, Inc., 2000.

Wholeness and the Implicate Order, by David Bohm. Routledge, 1996.

"Worshipped and Cursed: Turtles in Chinese Culture," by Cheng Yuan-ching (translated by Jonathan Barnard). Sinorama Magazine, 1999.

Zuozhuan, by Zuo Qiuming. Written during the Spring and Autumn Period (770–476 B.C.E.)

Web Sites

American Healing Arts, Inc.
www.aafengshui.com
Developed by Elizabeth Moran and Val Biktashev, authors of *The Complete Idiot's Guide to Feng Shui,* this outstanding Web site offers valuable information about the fundamentals of classical feng shui and the *Yijing.*

Feng Shui Information Resource Index
www.geocities.com/Athens/Delphi/9911
Created by Bill Clement, this site has been designed to promote quality information about traditional forms of feng shui, Chinese astrologies, and martial arts. Also, it features book selections, Web links, and guest articles. The site is contnually evolving with new information.

Feng Shui Research Center
www.astro-fengshui.com
Assembled by Master Joseph Yu, this exceptional Web site educates the reader about traditional feng shui, Chinese astrologies, and the *Yijing.* In addition to offering correspondence courses, Joseph conducts seminars worldwide.

Feng Shui Ultimate Resource
www.qi-whiz.com
Don't miss Cate Bramble's articulate articles, book recommendations, and descriptions of authentic and faux schools of feng shui.

Science, Religion, and Chaos Theory
www.wfu.edu/~petrejh4/chaosind.htm
Compiled by Judy Howard Petree, this outstanding Web site correlates chaos theory to faith and prayer. Please look for her upcoming book, *Faith as a Strange Attractor.*

Shavano Institute
www.shavano.org
This nonprofit organization has a plethora of information about the lifework of David Bohm. The numerous articles were written by Will Keepin, Ph.D.

Contact the Authors

Elizabeth Moran
American Healing Arts, Incorporated
269 South Beverly Drive, PMB 280
Beverly Hills, California 90212, USA
Telephone: 323-852-1381
Fax: 323-852-1341
E-mail: GlobalFengShui@aol.com
Web site: www.aafengshui.com

Master Joseph Yu
Feng Shui Research Center
175 West Beaver Creek Road, Unit 5
Richmond Hill, Ontario L4B 3M1, Canada
Telephone/Fax: 905-881-8878
E-mail: Josephyu@astro-fengshui.com
Web site: www.astro-fengshui.com

Common Questions and Practical Answers About Divining the *Yijing*

Q: Can I ask the *Yijing* the same question twice?

A: You cannot ask the *Yijing* the same question twice in the same divination session. However, you can ask a question in two different ways. For example, you can ask: "What will be the outcome if I move to Chicago this year?" and "What will be the outcome if I stay in Los Angeles and do not move?"

Q: How long do I have to wait before asking the *Yijing* the same question again?

A: You should not ask the *Yijing* the same question again until the changes made manifest in the line text(s) have become evident. Generally, unless your original question involves a time frame longer than three months, you can ask the oracle again in three months' time.

Q: Can I ask the *Yijing* different questions, but pertaining to the same subject?

A: While you can pose different questions to the *Yijing* regarding the same subject, you cannot keep asking the oracle questions until you get a desired answer! This is disrespectful. For example, say you're considering asking Jean to marry you. It is appropriate to ask the *Yijing*, "What will be the result if I ask Jean to marry me this Saturday?" and "What will be the result if I never ask Jean to marry me?" It is not appropriate to ask additional questions like, "What will be the result if I ask Jean to marry me before church on Sunday?" "What will be the result if I ask Jean to marry me on Friday during dinner?" Continual questioning on the same subject will often result in Hexagram 4 (signifying ignorance), connoting foolishness and immaturity.

Q: Is the coin-toss or yarrow stalk method more accurate?

A: The two different methods each yield accurate results. However, they yield different probabilities for the four types of lines drawn. In the coin-toss method, there are eight possible ways to arrive at 6, 7, 8, or 9. You have a 37.5 percent or 3/8 chance of drawing young yang (7); a 37.5 percent or 3/8 chance of drawing young yin (8); a 12.5 percent or 1/8 chance of drawing old yin (6); and a 12.5 percent or 1/8 chance of drawing old yang (9). For the yarrow stalk method, there are 16 possible ways to arrive at 6, 7, 8, or 9. You have a 44 percent or 7/16 chance of drawing young yin (8); a 31 percent or 5/16 chance of drawing young yang (7); a 19 percent or 3/16 chance of drawing old yang (9); and a 6 percent or 1/16 chance of drawing old yin (6). In other words, the changing (or old) yin lines are the hardest to draw.

Q: Can I ask the *Yijing* a question and use both the yarrow stalk and coin-toss methods?

A: No. You must choose either the coin-toss or the yarrow stalk method. While the three-coin method takes about 15 minutes to perform, the more time-consuming yarrow stalk procedure can take one hour.

Q: Does the type of coin or stalk I use make a difference?

A: The coins must be of the same denomination: three pennies, nickels, dimes, or quarters. Likewise, the stalks must be of the same type, not an assemblage of drinking straws, sticks, and skewers. Also, you must keep your divination tools clean. Store them in a decorative container or display them in a beautiful vase or bowl.

Q: Can I ask questions that do not pertain to me?

A: Yes. In Chapter 7, "How to Interpret Your *Yijing* Reading," Master Joseph Yu asks the *Yijing* about the outcome of the 2000 presidential race. However, because you are not involved in the question at hand, it is often difficult to interpret the answer. This is because when the question pertains to your dilemma, concern, or problem, you can intuit the answer. In other words, the text speaks to you directly. You do not have this innate connection with regard to other people. Nevertheless, if a diary is maintained about the subject in question, you will be able to interpret the insights offered by the oracle. Practice makes perfect!

Q: What kinds of questions can I ask the *Yijing*?

A: The *Yijing* can be used only in matters of importance; that is, matters where a direction is needed. Usually, the questions revolve around situations that can impact or alter the course of your life. Changing jobs and careers; moving; proposing marriage; establishing a new relationship or enterprise; hiring or firing a person; purchasing a home, car, or stock; and litigation are just a few examples. The *Yijing* is not used to decide insignificant matters or daily trivialities.

Q: What is the proper way to phrase a question?

A: It is important to understand that you consult the *Yijing* to gain knowledge about how to properly handle your situation. You do not consult the *Yijing* to receive a direct yes or no answer. Therefore, instead of asking yes or no questions—ones beginning with "is," "will," or "should"—ask "what," "why," or "how" questions that inspire a feeling and invoke an innate meaning. Also, your question must be clear and precise. For example, do not ask, "Should I collaborate with Mary?" Ask, "What will be the result if I collaborate with Mary on this book project?"

Q: What advice can you offer about divining the *Yijing*?

A: Respect the oracle. Form your questions carefully. Act with integrity. When you meditate on your question, it is important that you do not attach what you hope the answer will be. Your mind must be open, empty, and accepting.

Q: Do I have to accept the *Yijing's* advice?

A: Sometimes the best course of action is to not act on the *Yijing's* advice. First, read the present hexagram statement. Then, read the changing line text(s) (if any) and the future hexagram statement. If you act on the advice offered by the line text(s), the result of your action is made manifest in the future hexagram statement. If the future hexagram statement is not favorable, then take care not to arrive at the projected outcome.

Index

317